MALCOLM COWLEY

A CHECKLIST OF HIS WRITINGS, 1916-1973
by Diane U. Eisenberg
with an Introduction by Malcolm Cowley

Southern Illinois University Press
Carbondale and Edwardsville

Feffer & Simons, Inc.
London and Amsterdam

Library of Congress Cataloging in Publication Data

Eisenberg, Diane U.

   Malcolm Cowley, a checklist of his writings,
   1916-1973.

   Includes index.
   1. Cowley, Malcolm, 1898-   --Bibliography.
I. Title.
Z8196.8.E58 [PS3505.0956] 016.0704'092'4 75-8953
ISBN 0-8093-0748-0

CONTENTS

PREFACE   vi

INTRODUCTION BY MALCOLM COWLEY   xi

PART 1: BOOKS

A. BOOKS BY MALCOLM COWLEY   1

B. BOOKS EDITED AND WITH INTRODUCTIONS BY
   MALCOLM COWLEY   7

C. INTRODUCTIONS TO BOOKS BY OTHERS   14

D. CONTRIBUTIONS TO BOOKS EDITED BY OTHERS   16

E. BOOKS TRANSLATED   22

PART 2: CONTRIBUTIONS TO PERIODICALS

F. BOOK REVIEWS   24

G. ESSAYS AND ARTICLES   99

H. SHORT FICTION   162

I. PROSE TRANSLATED   162

J. INTERVIEWS; QUESTIONNAIRES; SYMPOSIA   164

K. LETTERS   167

PART 3: POETRY

L. COLLECTIONS   171

M. INDIVIDUAL POEMS   172

N. POEMS TRANSLATED   192

PART 4: WRITINGS ABOUT MALCOLM COWLEY

O. PRAISE AND DISPRAISE: A BRIEF SELECTION   194

   INDEX   199

PREFACE

Malcolm Cowley, critic, poet, and literary histo-
rian born in 1898, has been a central figure in the
American literary scene for more than fifty years.
His judgments on books and authors, which astutely
blend aesthetic insights with social consciousness,
have exerted a significant influence on American
letters; and the influence has been wider because
his "pieces," as he calls them, are minor works of
art in themselves, beautifully structured and written with clarity, modesty, and logic. "I am a re-
visionist by trade," he says of himself in conversation; "I hate to write and love to revise." Even
his short pieces receive inordinate care. He says
in the epilogue to Think Back on Us, "The relatively
short book review was my art form for many years;
it became my blank-verse meditation, my sonnet sequence, my letter to distant friends, my private
journal. . . . Perhaps, by making things harder
for myself, I also made them harder for other reviewers and thereby contributed a little toward
raising the standards of the profession."[1]

1. Think Back on Us: The Literary Record (Carbondale: Southern Illinois University Press,
   1967), pp. 385,391.

He did raise those standards, one feels after
reading over the reviews; and he showed a gift for
choosing and presenting the durable works and the
significant situations of his time. The same gift
is evident in his reevaluative essays on earlier
American writers. In several instances those essays helped to find a new audience for authors
whose work had fallen into neglect.

When his literary contributions are traced
through something like 1200 items published in more
than seventy periodicals, they reveal the very wide
range of his interests. Alfred Kazin, reporting
Cowley's impact on the young writers of the 1930s,
has written:

> Cowley was an expressive poet, and he had
> such a gift of clear style, he had such dis-
> tinguished literary standards and associa-
> tions, he had translated so many books from
> the French, he had known so many writers and
> worked on so many magazines, that I felt in
> reading him that I had been led up to the
> most immense spread of literary tidbits.[2]

Tidbits, perhaps, but also bread and beef and
fixin's enough to cover a banquet table. Essen-
tially it is the "immense spread" of Cowley's interests, his keen involvement with so many aspects
of literature and the literary life, which demands
that bibliographical attention be paid to his
writings. Cowley has been a man of letters working
in a variety of modes: he writes books and book
reviews, poetry, essays (often in the form of introductions to books by others), memoirs, short
fiction, and he has translated a number of dis-

2. Alfred Kazin, Starting Out in the Thirties
(Boston: Little, Brown, 1962), p. 17.

tinguished works. His writing has appeared in a
striking diversity of publications. Thus, when his
life's work, his oeuvre, is presented chronologi-
cally, in checklist form, what emerges is an historical record of the writing profession in America
during the past fifty years. ("No glitter, no jack-
pots," Cowley says; "just one man's struggle through
changing times with the laborious, lovely, but un-
profitable trade of putting words into patterns
that he hopes will be permanent.")

This checklist tries to include everything by
Malcolm Cowley, prose and poetry, that appeared in
print from 1916 through the publication of his most
recent book, A Second Flowering (1973). One field
not fully covered, however, is that of selections
from his work reprinted in anthologies intended
primarily for classroom use. I have listed some of
these, but Cowley urged me not to cover the field
comprehensively. "There are so many of those classroom selections," he said, "in books that appear
to be carefully edited, but they have nothing much
to do with my original work. It would be nearly
impossible to track them all down. I didn't start
to save the books until a few years ago and,
look,"--he pointed behind him--"those two shelves
are full already."

Two other shelves are filled with translations
of his work, and these are listed here under the
separate English titles of "Books by Malcolm Cowley."

Letters from Cowley printed in magazines or in
books by others (e.g., Harold Loeb, The Way It Was)
are included in a separate section. As for the unpublished correspondence, the bulk of it is at The

Newberry Library, Chicago, which also holds his
literary papers; it will eventually have everything now in Cowley's possession. Correspondence
with Hart Crane and William Faulkner is in the
Beinecke Library at Yale. American Literary Manuscripts gives a list of other libraries with
smaller collections.

Among Cowley's papers at Newberry is a brown
folder of clippings from newspapers and magazines,
chiefly of the years 1919-21. Not all the clippings
could be identified (except as being of his authorship), since their running heads had been cut off.
At Cowley's home are several publications of Peabody
High School, Pittsburgh, with contributions of his
from 1914-15, and a copy of Aesthete 1925 containing
pieces by Cowley and others under the pseudonym of
Walter S. Hankel; Cowley could not remember which
of these were his. I am not aware of other omissions,
though surely there must be things I overlooked.
Information about them would be gratefully accepted
if addressed to me in care of The Newberry Library.

I am most grateful to The Newberry Library, and
especially to James M. Wells, Richard Colles Johnson,
Sandra Herzog, and Wendy Towner for their successful
efforts toward publication of this checklist. I am
also indebted to Dr. Jackson Bryer, of the English
Department at the University of Maryland, for his
good advice and continuous encouragement, and to
Dr. Myron Lounsbury of the American Studies Department, also at Maryland, for confirming my choice
of Malcolm Cowley as a bibliographical subject.
Thanks are due to Belle Rosenbaum for giving me
access to the indices of the New York Herald

<u>Tribune</u> <u>Books</u>. Librarians with whom I corresponded were extremely cooperative. I especially appreciate the assistance of Lloyd Pauls at the Library of Congress and Carol Parke at the Yale University Library.

Malcolm Cowley has helped me throughout the project, patiently answering my questions in letters that anticipated the task of the bibliographer by their scrupulous accuracy. He and Mrs. Cowley graciously made available those books and periodicals which could be found only at their home. The prime reward of my endeavor has been the privilege of sharing time with the Cowleys.

October 31, 1974   Diane U. Eisenberg

INTRODUCTION

. . . and I Worked at the Writer's Trade[1]

I got started in the writer's trade strictly from
hunger, as people used to say in excusing their de-
linquencies. In the early spring of 1919 I was out
of the Army, I was twenty years old, I was hungry,
and I was living in sin without paying the rent.
One of the persons I went to see was a former boy
friend of my girl friend; Clarence Britten was his
name, and he was literary editor of the Dial, then
a political fortnightly that had moved from Chicago
to New York under the somewhat reluctant patronage
of an eccentric millionaire. Britten looked at me
appraisingly, asked after Peggy, made one or two of
his abrupt gestures, then pushed half a dozen novels
across the desk. "Try reviewing these," he said,
"but don't give them more than a hundred words a-
piece." If and when the reviews were published, they
would each bring me a dollar.

Six times one dollar seemed to me a happy pros-
pect for the following month, when the little checks

1. This Introduction is a somewhat revised version of a talk given by Mr. Cowley to the Newberry Library Associates on March 23, 1971.
It was occasioned by the celebration of the
Library's acquisition of a further section of
the Malcolm Cowley Papers and the opening of
an exhibition selected from them.

would come in, but meanwhile there was the problem
of buying food for dinner that evening. I wrote in
Exile's Return, with you's standing for I's,

> . . . So you would carry the books to a bench
> in Union Square and page through them hastily,
> making notes--in two or three hours you would be
> finished with the whole armful and then you would
> take them to a secondhand bookstore on Fourth
> Avenue, where the proprietor paid a flat rate of
> thirty-five cents for each review copy; you
> thought it was more than the novels were worth.
> With exactly $2.10 in your pocket you would buy
> bread and butter and lamb chops and Bull Durham
> for cigarettes and order a bag of coal; then at
> home you would broil the lamb chops over the
> grate because the landlady had neglected to pay
> her gas bill, just as you had neglected to pay
> the rent. You were all good friends and she would
> be invited to share the feast. Next morning you
> would write the reviews, then start on the search
> for a few dollars more.

The search led me to other editorial offices, for
I was now definitely apprenticed to the trade of
putting words on paper. Reading Diane Eisenberg's
checklist of my published writings, the result of
more patient researches among back files than most
of the writings deserve, I find that each of the
early items helps to evoke a way of life now van-
ished together with most of the magazines that made
it barely possible. Mrs. Eisenberg does not list
those brief reviews in the fortnightly Dial--for
how could she identify the deservedly anonymous?--
but one of her entries for the summer of the same
year records my first signed appearance in a magazine that paid for contributions:

    F5   "Through Yellow Glasses." New Republic
              XIX (July 23, 1919): 401.
              Victorious, by Reginald Wright
              Kauffman.

As I read those cabbalistic words, I can see
myself walking in cracked shoes under the Ninth
Avenue elevated. It is a spring afternoon and the
sun is projecting a pattern of crossties on the
pavement. Under my arm I carry a square brown note-
book in which the first dozen pages are filled
with clippings of my published work: not only those
unsigned reviews in the Dial but earlier ones in
the Harvard Advocate and a long poem that has just
appeared in the Little Review. I am hurrying to
the offices of the New Republic, where Francis
Hackett, the literary editor, has agreed over the
telephone to give me a few moments.

Hackett, a big, red-faced Irishman looking like
Jupiter in pince-nez glasses, is seated behind a
scarred enormous desk that will be my desk ten
years later, though the possibility does not then
enter my mind. He glances at my little collection
of press clippings, reads the reviews from the
Dial, then calls to his assistant. "Miss Updike,"
he says, "perhaps you can find a book for this
young man." Taking off his pince-nez, he gives me
an Olympian smile of dismissal. Miss Updike looks
at my cracked shoes, then picks out a novel by
Reginald Wright Kauffman that she thinks might be
worth five hundred words--or ten dollars, I calcu-
late, at the New Republic rate of two cents a word.
She gives me the book as if she were pouring a
saucer of milk for a starved kitten.

End of the memory, and almost the end of my first
attempt to keep two persons alive by free-lance book
reviewing. It had provided at best one meal a day,
and the meals were usually deficient in proteins

and carbohydrates. There was always that exasperat-
ing delay between writing a review and getting
paid for it. I was crossing Sheridan Square one
morning after no breakfast when the sidewalk sud-
denly came up and hit me in the face. I didn't lose
consciousness for more than a moment. Less fright-
ened than surprised, I picked myself up and floated
into a lunchroom to spend my last dime for a stale
bun and a cup of coffee. As I sat at the counter
feeling not at all hungry and more than usually
clear-headed, I surrendered my pride in living on
the underside of society and in being a free arti-
san trading words for bread. I told myself that a
job would have to be found, and not long afterward
I found it, too, by answering want ads and accepting
a very low salary. At least there would be enough
to keep the two of us fed.

In the fall I went back to college, where I had
a scholarship of sorts and could apply for loans
from the dean's office. I planned to earn a degree
by taking six courses in one semester, a heavier
load than any Harvard student is now permitted to
stagger under. To make things more difficult, I
was married by then, and my wife was in frail ·
health. Nevertheless, in the intervals between
studying and nursing, I managed to do some writing
for publication, as I am reminded by other items
in Mrs. Eisenberg's checklist. Mary Updike, God
bless her, remembered the starved kitten and sent
me at least two packages of books for review. I
must have been the only undergraduate at Harvard
or elsewhere who was a fairly regular contributor
to the New Republic.

Still another entry for the same period records
the beginning of what was to be a long and close
collaboration:

> F9   "The Woman of Thornden." Dial LXVIII
> (February 1920): 259-62.
> A Challenge to Sirius and The Four
> Roads, by Sheila Kaye-Smith.

Clarence Britten, out of kindness to me or to Peggy,
I don't know which, had decided that I ought to do
a signed piece for the Dial. As an occasion for it,
he sent me two novels by Sheila Kaye-Smith, an
English novelist then held in some estimation. The
review was accepted while I was back at college,
but weeks passed and it did not appear. Meanwhile
Britten had lost his job. The Dial had been sold
by its eccentric angel and purchased by two other
millionaires, Scofield Thayer and Sibley Watson,
both of them fresh out of Harvard. They planned to
transform the fortnightly Dial into the most distinguished monthly magazine of the arts that had
appeared in this country. For the purchase price
of I don't know how much, they had acquired the
name, a modest list of subscribers, and a barrel,
so called--it was really a small box--full of
accepted but unpublished manuscripts. Having read
their way through the barrel, they decided that
nothing in it was worthy to appear in a magazine
of high literary standards--nothing, that is, except my piece on Sheila Kaye-Smith, which would
then serve as the only link between the old and the
new. It appeared in the second issue of the monthly
Dial, just as I was packing to leave Harvard with
my precariously earned degree.

Leave I must, but I had no destination except,

vaguely, New York. Two days before we planned to
go, if I could pay for the railroad tickets, there
were footsteps on the stairs and a knock at the
door of my attic room. A young man, a stranger,
gave me an envelope and said, "Mr. Copeland told
me not to wait for an answer." Inside the envelope
was a ten-dollar bill folded in a note from Charles
Townsend Copeland--"Copey," as everyone called him--
my favorite English instructor. "I thought you could
use this," Copey had written in his angular hand.
The ten dollars paid our fares to Grand Central,
in those days of cheaper transportation, with enough
left over for a taxi to the house in Greenwich
Village where our former landlady had offered to
put us up for a few days. We rode there holding
hands, through streets still heaped with grimy
snow from a storm two weeks before.

Our prospects were bleak as the Manhattan streets,
but we felt more cheerful now that Peggy had partly
recovered her health. She began to circulate once
more among her Village friends, and one of them
found us three rooms on the top floor of a tenement,
reached by climbing five flights of stairs that
smelled of Italian cooking. A check arriving in the
nick of time--but every check did that--paid the
first month's rent of sixteen dollars. Our bed was
borrowed, our chairs were begged, and my writing
table was bought for next to nothing at a Salvation
Army store. Soon I was writing every day--poems
mostly, but also any sort of prose for which a
market could be found at a penny a word; only the
New Republic and the monthly Dial were more generous.
Mrs. Eisenberg's checklist testifies to many after-

noons spent tramping from one editorial office to
another.

As I look back on those years, it seems to me
that I must have had a rather special cast of mind.
I wanted to be a writer, but not a celebrated
writer appearing in glossy magazines. I wanted to
live obscurely, limit my needs, and preserve my
freedom to write something perfect, at some moment
in the future. While waiting for that moment I was
willing to do hackwork, a meager source of income,
as I had learned, but one that I judged to be re-
spectable, if the work was honestly performed. Always I tried to make it better work than I was paid
for doing, with the result that my little commissioned pieces had qualities not to be found in my
life at the time: punctuality, for example, and
neatness and logic. Editors liked them because they
could be sent to the printer without revision.

Editors are sometimes excessively kind to very
young writers, especially if these are talkative or
show any sign of promise. With special gratitude
I remember Henry Seidel Canby and his assistant
Amy Loveman. I first dropped in on them when Dr.
Canby was starting a new weekly supplement, the
Literary Review of the New York Evening Post; work-
men were still installing partitions in what were
to be their offices. Miss Loveman listened through
the din of hammers while I gave her a lecture on
contemporary French poetry. Once or twice she
smiled maternally, and she let me carry away two
books for unsigned reviews. Later that spring Dr.
Canby invited me into his by then completed sanctum;
we talked about trout fishing and he reproved me for

using worms. Then he suggested that I take, each
week, half a dozen books that the Literary Review
was planning to discard. I should page through them
and, if I found that one or two deserved attention,
I should write the reviews. For this I was to be
paid ten dollars a week. I accepted the arrangement,
which made me, at the time, the only salaried book
reviewer in New York.

Of course I was writing for other journals as well,
and, in one way or another, I managed to get along.
When checks were slow in arriving, I played penny
ante on Saturday nights and could count on winning
ten dollars if the game lasted till morning. For two
weeks I was a stagehand at the Provincetown Players
and earned twenty dollars a week. Why, I was prosper-
ous, and independent too, and when I was offered a
regular job by Sweet's Architectural Catalogue I came
near turning it down. But I finally accepted it, and
held it for a year, until I was offered a fellowship
to a French university by the American Field Service,
with which I had served during the war. Peggy and I
got ready to go abroad.

As I look back at this account of a literary apprenticeship, it seems to me that I have very often
mentioned small sums of money. There is a good reason
for that, considering that money is the central problem of a young writer's life, or of his staying alive.
True as the statement is today, it was even more true
in the 1920s, when there were fewer sources of literary livelihood. Universities didn't then invite young
novelists or critics to join their English staffs or
young poets to give paid readings. There were very
few literary prizes; there were no subsidies by foun-

dations. Fellowships to foreign universities, like
the one I had lately been awarded, were scarce and
meager and hard to come by. The result was that more
dependence had to be placed on small sums paid by
magazines for contributions. The smaller one's gross
income, the more important each little payment became
and the more pride one took in earning it.

The poverty of young American writers was the central reason for their exodus to Europe during the
1920s. Of course there were other reasons too, nota-
bly the Prohibition Amendment and the triumph of business over art in American society, from which young
writers felt no less alienated than their successors
fifty years later; but there was also the real attrac-
tion of cheaper living in Europe. Take my own exper-
ience in the years 1921 to 1923. The fellowship I had
been awarded was for twelve thousand francs, or one
thousand dollars at what was then the rate of exchange. It was renewed for the following year, and I
also earned a little money by writing for American
periodicals, but not more than five hundred dollars
for each of the years. On this total of three thousand dollars, I paid for our passage to France, lived
there in rather more comfort than at home, traveled a
little, and had just enough money left for our passage to New York. As regards the writing I did for
American periodicals, there are several examples in
Mrs. Eisenberg's checklist, but I shall mention only
one:

G9   "Henri Barbusse." Bookman LVI
        (October 1922): 180-82.
        Barbusse became famous overnight
        with Under Fire, a literarily and
        politically provocative novel.

The story of that article begins like many other
stories, at a sidewalk table outside the Café du Dôme.
There one summer afternoon I found Ivan Opffer, a
feckless Dane I had known in the Village. Ivan told
me that the Bookman had commissioned him to draw portraits of the best-known French authors. "Why don't
you come along and do an article to go with the next
picture?" he said. His next scheduled visit was to
Henri Barbusse, author of a famous anti-war novel,
Le Feu. We found that the roads around his little
country house were patrolled by gendarmes in pairs,
on bicycles; one pair stopped us and asked to see our
passports. "That's how things are in France," Barbusse
said as he offered each of us a long, emaciated hand:
he had the visionary look of a John Baptist. I asked
him questions and took notes in two languages, while
Ivan made hasty sketches on big sheets of drawing
paper. Ivan was wonderful at catching facial expressions, but he never would learn to draw hands. My little profile in words was of course written on spec,
but it resulted in a commission to do six others, all
with Ivan's handless figures as illustrations. Lec-
tured at by one author after another, I learned something about French literary politics and was modestly
paid for writing what amounted to classroom reports
on my studies.

I also contributed to magazines published in Europe, sometimes rather obscure ones, as Mrs. Eisenberg's checklist shows. Here is one item that recalls
a story:

M73   "Madrigals." Mécano (Leiden), numbers
         4 and 5 (1923), n.p.
         Three short, rather scabrous poems
         printed in a Dutch Dadaist magazine

          edited by Theo van Doesburg.
          Never reprinted.

   Again the story starts at the Dôme, where, one
spring afternoon, I found my good friend Tristan
Tzara, the founder of Dada. A Rumanian living in
Switzerland, he had been brought to Paris in 1919
by Louis Aragon, also my friend, and André Breton.
Now he was having trouble with the French Dadaists,
originally his disciples, but he was still held in
reverence by Dadaist groups springing up in Germany,
Belgium, and Holland. That afternoon Tzara was sit-
ting with an eager, rather innocent--so it seemed
to me--Dutch Dadaist named Theo van Doesburg; later
he was to become internationally known, for I forget
what. Tzara introduced me as a poète Dada americain.
Van Doesburg asked whether I wouldn't contribute to
a little magazine he was publishing in Leiden. Why,
yes, gladly, I said, thinking of some scabrous songs
I had written for my own entertainment. It would be
amusing to print them in a Dutch Dadaist paper when
they couldn't appear, at the time, anywhere in the
English-speaking world:

          masochistic Mazie
          very nearly crazy
          almost
                    very nearly
                              quite
          insane
          scratched her pretty asshole
          over broken glass
                              coal
          cinders
                    Joy
                         Sex
                              Pain
          WASn't she insane?

That was the first of the "Madrigals." There was

another about sadic Sam from Alabam, there were two
lines about fetishistic Fanny, who married Jack the
Ripper, and they were duly printed in joint numbers
4 and 5 of Mécano. A year later Hemingway published
other scabrous lyrics in a German semi-Dadaist
magazine called Der Querschnitt, one which had the
greater distinction of paying its contributors.

In the late spring of 1923, money was short and
we started to think about going back to New York.
I felt that there ought to be something tangible
and ponderable as a memento of those two years in
Europe. An essay on Racine, just finished, was a
brief work in which I took pride. From our rooms
above the former blacksmith shop in Giverny, a
Norman village, I carried the essay to a printer in
Paris and received his estimate: for two hundred
copies of a stapled pamphlet he would charge me
less than thirty-five dollars at the current rate
of exchange. That brings me to the very first item
in Mrs. Eisenberg's checklist:

A1   Racine. Paris: Privately printed,
            1923. 22 pp.
            Of the 200 original copies only 15
            are known to survive.

Let me explain why the pamphlet is so rare. The
two hundred copies, dedicated to Copey "in default
of a better gift," I said, went back with me to
New York, and there I started mailing them out to
friends. There, too, I made the humiliating discovery that I hadn't two hundred friends or bowing
acquaintances who might be interested in Racine; at
most I could stretch the list to forty or fifty
names. The remaining copies of the pamphlet lay
piled in various closets for several years, until I

got tired of carrying them from one habitation to
another; then I dropped them into a wastebasket,
except for a dozen or more copies that I saved. In
1960 or thereabouts I looked at the catalogue of a
rare-book dealer and found that one copy of the
pamphlet, "slightly foxed," was being offered for
thirty-five dollars, or a little more than I had
paid for the whole edition. The price ten years
later had risen to seventy-five dollars. By that
time, however, I had only two copies left and
couldn't be tempted to sell them.

When I got back to New York in August 1923, I had
only five dollars in my pocket, but this time my
prospects were somewhat brighter than they had been
in 1920. I paid a visit to my former boss at Sweet's
Architectural Catalogue and was promptly hired back
at a better salary. For a long time I was kept too
busy to write anything for publication except a few
reviews for the Dial for Dr. Canby. But I dreamed of
moving to the country and living once again as a
free-lance writer, and already I was taking steps
in that direction. First, I began to look for other
periodical outlets, then I rented a little house on
Staten Island that had a vegetable garden, then I
bought a very old Model T Ford, and then, as a
decisive step, I resigned from Sweet's to see
whether I could live for a year by writing. When the
year ended in the spring of 1926, I helped to load
our three sticks of furniture and our four boxes of
books on a wheezing Model T truck, and we set out
for Sherman, Connecticut. Friends of mine--Hart
Crane, Allen Tate, Slater Brown, Matthew Josephson--
lived in the neighborhood, and they had found us an

old farmhouse with exterior nonplumbing that rented
for ten dollars a month.

I note some further entries that explain how we
kept ourselves going.

> G21   "Do Artists Make Good Husbands?"
>   _Charm_ II (August 1924): 28-29, 83,
>   91.
>   "Contrary to popular fiction stories,
>   an artist's marriage is usually suc-
>   cessful."

Bamberger's department store, in Newark, was
starting a rather elaborate magazine for distribu-
tion to its customers. The first editor was Bessie
Breuer, a friend of Peggy's; later she became a
novelist, sound and perceptive but not widely per-
ceived. Bessie tried to help us by dreaming up
articles for me to write--outlandish articles, so it
seemed to this serious literary person, but still I
accepted the challenge, much as if I had been an
engineer asked to design an outlandish bridge. When
Bessie was succeeded by another able editor, Lucie
Taussig, I began suggesting my own subjects, often
drawn for New Jersey history. I also wrote a monthly
book page for _Charm_ and presented the literary scene
in terms that I hoped would interest New Jersey
housewives.

> F51   "Mr. Moore's Golden Treasury." _New
>   York Herald Tribune Books_, August 2,
>   1925, p. 5.
>   _An Anthology of Pure Poetry_, edited
>   with an introduction by George Moore.

That must have been the first review I wrote for
Irita Van Doren. I don't remember whether I asked
her for the book or whether she suggested my reviewing it after her friend Harrison Smith had written a front-page article about my first translation

from the French, <u>On</u> <u>Board</u> <u>the</u> <u>Morning</u> <u>Star</u>, a cycle
of pirate stories by Pierre MacOrlan; in either case
I was soon contributing regularly to Mrs. Van Doren's
book section. Among the kind-hearted editors I have
known, she was by far the kindest. She had taken
over <u>Herald</u> <u>Tribune</u> <u>Books</u> after the sudden death of
Stuart Pratt Sherman, its first editor, and she made
a success of her editorship from the beginning.
Young ambitious people wanted to write for her. On
Wednesday afternoons, I think it was, when she held
a sort of open house for reviewers and would-be
reviewers, they used to gather in her waiting room
from their garrets and cellars. That year it always
rained on Wednesday afternoons, or so it seems to
me now. The picture that stays in my mind is of one
young woman--I never learned her name--sitting with
wet shoes and a dripping skirt, her lank hair
framing an eager face, as she waited for a word or
still better a book from Mrs. Van Doren.

Irita was an Alabama woman with a soft voice and
an enchanting smile, but she could be firm at
moments; she could even be ruthless when that was
the kindest thing to be. Once she accepted a
reviewer, she kept him on her staff year after year--
sometimes too long--and looked for interesting books
for him to write about. It was partly owing to her
loyal friendship that I was able to carry out my
project of living deep in the country with nothing
to sell but words.

We didn't live well. There was always something
to eat in the house, but sometimes there wasn't very
much, and on those days I would wait for the mail-
man in hope of his bringing me a nick-of-the-time

check. If the check arrived, I would drive over back
roads to New Milford, Connecticut, and deposit it in
what passed for my bank account. I didn't dare to
cash the check in New Milford, since the account was
seldom large enough to cover it. Instead I would
drive sixteen miles to Pawling, New York, buy grocer-
ies, and pay for them with a check of my own. It
would have to pass through the New York clearing
house and the Boston clearing house before it
reached New Milford, a process that would take three
or four days. By that time my deposit would have
been collected and credited to my account, and the
check written in Pawling would be honored. It sounds
complicated, but it was all part of the writer's
trade, just as much as the proper use of semicolons.

There is one more of Mrs. Eisenberg's entries to
mention, the one that records publication of my first
book and hence the end of an apprenticeship. Once
again it recalls a story.

L2   Blue Juniata. New York: Jonathan Cape
      and Harrison Smith, 1929. 115 pp.
      56 poems in five parts: 1. Blue Juniata;
      2. The Adolescent; 3. Valuta; 4. The
      City of Anger; 5. Old Melodies: Love
      and Death.
I have told the story elsewhere[2], but truly it
belongs here, with other memories of an apprenticeship that was drawing to its close. Hart Crane is the
hero of it. The story begins in the summer of 1928,
when Hart came back to the rooms he rented in Addie
Turner's house, five miles from Patterson, New York,
after a disastrous winter in California. I had moved

2. In my contribution to Robber Rocks: Letters
   and Memories of Hart Crane, by Susan Jenkins
   Brown (Middletown, Conn.: Wesleyan University
   Press, 1969).

across the state line that spring, after contracting
to buy, if I could make the payments, sixty acres of
abandoned farmland and a hungry-looking house half a
mile from Mrs. Turner's. We saw Hart almost daily
that summer. Like everyone else we noticed that his
bristly hair was turning gray and that his face was
redder and puffier. Those were signs of a physio-
logical change, from being a "heavy social drinker,"
as we had always known him, to being a "problem
drinker," the first stage of true alcoholism. He
was paying more and more visits to Wiley Varian,
the cashiered army officer who ran a speak-easy on
Birch Hill. "Sometimes Hart gave a party," and then,
says Nathan Asch, who was living in the same big
house that summer, "we, the writers rejected by New
York booming with the market of the twenties, con-
soled ourselves with the gaiety we could engender
ourselves. We drank the liquor from either Varian's
or one of the other bootleggers, and then we shouted
and then we danced. . . . We did not speak to each
other, but rather each of us howled out, and we did
not dance with our wives or even with each other,
but whirled around Hart's room, faster and faster,
as if we were truly possessed." Yes, we did it on
only one occasion; I think it was on his birthday,
July 21. Hart wasn't much of a party giver.

Instead he was a party goer. He distinguished
himself, though I don't remember how, at the Fourth
of July party given by Slater and Sue Brown, and
he came back from New York for the party on Labor
Day. Everybody speaks of that summer in terms
of parties. What I remember with more pleasure are
the long, intensely quiet mornings, the games of

croquet at the Browns', where we gathered on Sunday
afternoons, the weekday afternoons spent fishing by
myself or walking in the woods with Hart, and the
talks about poets and poetry. Hart had a purely un-
selfish project that summer; he was going to prod me
into collecting a book of poems. "I have it at least
in mind," he wrote to Isidor and Helen Schneider in
July, "to try my best to get his poems accepted by
some publisher or other before a twelvemonth. He'll
never do much about it himself, as you know, and his
collection is really needed on the shelves these
days.

   Hart was right in thinking that I would have been
slow to do anything about it myself. I had sixty-odd
poems, all printed in magazine publication--but I
felt no urgent desire to make a book of them. Al-
though the book would come in time, I rather pre-
ferred to be unknown for the moment, except to magazine readers, and therefore unclassified, free to
move in any direction. But Hart kept prodding me.
Early in July he made me assemble a sheaf of poems;
then we pored over them, rejecting some by mutual
consent and discussing which of the others belonged
together, in exactly what order. Hart believed that
emotions, and the poems that expressed them, should
follow one another in the right sequence. He thought
naturally in terms of structure and of "the book,"
which, he insisted, should be more than a random
selection of poems by one author. In the poems themselves he did not change a word--not even later,
when he retyped the whole manuscript--since both of
us felt that a poet should speak in his own voice.

   When he left for New York early in August, there

was a book of sorts and one that might have been
printed, but I still had only a vague notion of
showing it to a publisher. Hart's notion was more
definite. On October 24 he asked me--it wasn't the
first time, since some of his letters have been
lost--"to bring in all the mss material of your
poems which I was in the process of editing last
summer. I'll soon have plenty of time to give the
matter, and I have a suspicion that something will
come of it now." On November 20 he announced in a
drunken early-morning letter that the poems had
arrived the day before. "I'll be careful with the
mss," he said, "and your book'll be out within 7
months," that is, within the "twelvemonth" he had
mentioned in his letter to the Schneiders. On December 1, a week before sailing for Europe, he wrote,
"It has been a pleasure for me to spend part of the
last two days in typing the mss of your book.
. . . I now have the two copies, one to turn over
to the 'secret' arbiter here and one to take with
me to England." He had omitted one poem that both
of us had questions about and had changed the
position in the manuscript of three others. "Really
the book as we now have it," he said, "has astonish-
ing structural sequence," thus ending the sentence
with two of his favorite words. The original manuscript was being returned to me by registered mail.

A few weeks later, when Hart was in London or
Paris, I heard from the "secret arbiter." He turned
out to be Gorham Munson, then an editor at the
George H. Doran Company (which later merged with
Doubleday). Munson and I had been on opposite sides
of the quarrels in 1923 that preceded the deaths of

Broom and Secession; of course that was why Hart
hadn't mentioned his name. Now Munson laid the
quarrels aside. In the name of his company he offered me a contract for the book--it had by then
acquired a title, Blue Juniata--together with a
modest advance against royalties. Hart's project
was bearing fruit, and in less than the twelvemonth
he had specified.

At this point, however, the project was interrupted by the stiff-necked character of the author.
Grateful as I was to Hart, I had a Pennsylvania
Dutch side that hated to be--as my forebears would
have said--"beholden" to anyone for the structure
and publication of my first book. I thanked Munson
for the offer and said I would think about it. Then
I showed the original manuscript to Harrison Smith,
a friend of mine (as of Hart's and the Van Dorens')
who had started a publishing house in partnership
with Jonathan Cape of London. Hal, as everyone
called him, promptly accepted it and gave me a
slightly larger advance than Doran had offered.

I took the manuscript home--we were spending the
winter in a cramped apartment on Avenue B, south of
the present East Village--and set to work on it.
First I gave the poems a completely different sequence, not emotional or dialectical, as Hart had
suggested (and as he himself had followed in White
Buildings), but autobiographical. The new framework
made it possible to use a few of the poems that Hart
and I had earlier decided to omit; they were callow,
as we agreed, but callowness was part of the story
I was telling. Then I divided the book into five
sections and furnished notes, in prose, to introduce

three of these. I revised most of the poems once
again, a task that continued through the winter
(though it was interrupted when I had to do translations to pay the rent). Meanwhile Hart had carried
his copy of the earlier manuscript to Paris and was
trying to persuade his rich friend Harry Crosby to
publish it at the Black Sun Press. I learn from
John Unterecker's biography of Hart that he was on
the point of succeeding when I wrote him late in
January that the book was coming out in New York.

By the middle of June, Blue Juniata was in type
and I sent an extra set of galleys to Hart. I was
a little afraid that his vanity would be wounded by
my failure to accept his suggestions, but I need not
have been, for Hart had almost no vanity of the
sort. He was not interested in whether the book em-
bodied his ideas, but only in whether it was put
together effectively. "Since reading the proofs,"
he wrote me on July 3, 1929, "I'm certain that the
book is even better . . . a much more solidified
unit than it was before. I haven't had the original
mss with me for comparison, but wherever I have
noted changes they seem to be for the better.
Really, Malcolm--if you will excuse me for the
egoism--I'm just a little proud of the out come of
my agitations last summer." It had been exactly a
twelvemonth since he started them.

So I end with this message of gratitude to a
dead friend. As I piece together the story, I think
again how different Hart was, on that wide and
amiable side of him, from the drunken rioter he is
often pictured as being. All this took place in the
time of his noisiest riots, and yet he devoted sober

weeks to editing and typing and peddling someone
else's manuscript. He was absolutely lacking in professional jealousy--except toward T.S. Eliot, and
that was a compliment to Eliot; otherwise Hart was
jealous only of the great dead. The little victories gained by his friends delighted him more than
his own victories. "You're a lucky boy!" he wrote
me after reading some favorable reviews of Blue
Juniata. "I'm very glad about it all"--and he truly
was. He was the first person to whom I sent an in-
scribed copy of the book. "If it's bad," I wrote on
the flyleaf, "the sin be on your head." He carried
the book with him when he went to Mexico. My first
wife was there too, getting a divorce, and finally
they sailed for New York together. Peggy retrieved
the book from his stateroom on the Orizaba the day
after he died.

November 2, 1974   Malcolm Cowley

PART 1. BOOKS

A.   BOOKS BY MALCOLM COWLEY

A1   <u>Racine</u>. Paris: Privately printed, 1923. 22 pp.
     Of the 200 original copies only 15 are known
     to survive (see Introduction). Later ap-
     peared in the <u>Freeman</u> (see G15, G16).
A2   <u>Blue</u> <u>Juniata</u> (see L2).
A3   <u>Exile's</u> <u>Return</u>: <u>A</u> <u>Narrative</u> <u>of</u> <u>Ideas</u>. New York:
     W.W. Norton, 1934. 308 pp.
     Most of <u>Exile's</u> <u>Return</u> first appeared as
     pieces for the <u>New</u> <u>Republic</u> (see G68, G73-74,
     G76-78, G84-85, G87, G90-92, G95).
A3a Revised edition: <u>Exile's</u> <u>Return</u>: <u>A</u> <u>Literary</u>
     <u>Odyssey</u> <u>of</u> <u>the</u> <u>Nineteen</u> <u>Twenties</u>. New York:
     The Viking Press, 1951. 322 pp.
     Contains newly added prologue, epilogue (see
     G228), appendix, and material on Ezra Pound
     (see G227), F. Scott Fitzgerald, and Hart
     Crane (see G144). Omits former prologue, a
     section called "The Other Side of the Tracks,"
     and former epilogue (later reprinted in
     <u>Think</u> <u>Back</u> <u>on</u> <u>Us</u>; see A10). Most chapters
     have been revised (see prologue for MC's
     explanation of revisions).

Reprinted sections: "Travellers' Cheque" in
<u>Discovery</u> <u>of</u> <u>Europe</u>, edited by Philip Rahv
(Boston: Houghton Mifflin Co., 1947),
pp. 529-38 (includes "Valuta," "Transatlantic
Review," and "Paris Express"); "Big Town High
School" in <u>Art</u> <u>of</u> <u>the</u> <u>Essay</u>, edited by Leslie
A Fiedler (New York: Crowell, 1958), pp. 56-
62; "Ambulance Service," "Valuta," and "Epi-
logue: New Year's Eve" in <u>Fitzgerald</u> <u>and</u> <u>the</u>
<u>Jazz</u> <u>Age</u>, edited by Malcolm and Robert Cowley
(New York: Charles Scribner's Sons, 1966),
pp. 27-32, 95-96, 175-77 (see B15); "War in
Bohemia" in <u>A</u> <u>Preface</u> <u>to</u> <u>Our</u> <u>Times</u>, edited by
William E. Buckler (New York: American Book
Co., 1968), pp. 313-22; "Echoes of a Suicide"
in <u>American</u> <u>Literature</u>: <u>The</u> <u>Makers</u> <u>and</u> <u>the</u>
<u>Making</u>, edited by Cleanth Brooks, R.W.B.
Lewis, and Robert Penn Warren (New York:
St. Martin's Press, 1973) II: 2788-97.

A3b   Croatian edition: <u>Izgubljena</u> <u>generacija</u>,
translated by Klara Dušanović. Zagreb:
Novinarsko izdavačko poduzeče, 1958. 319 pp.

A3c   Japanese edition: <u>Bômei-sha</u> <u>kaeru</u>, translated
by Kenzaburô Ohashi and Yoshio Shirakawa.
Tokyo: Nan'un-dô, 1959. 216 pp.

A3d   English edition: <u>Exile's</u> <u>Return</u>. London: The
Bodley Head, 1961. 322 pp.

A3e   Italian edition: <u>Il</u> <u>ritorno</u> <u>degli</u> <u>esuli</u>,
translated by Bruno Oddera. Milan: Rizzoli
Editore, 1963. 312 pp.

A4   (With others) <u>After</u> <u>the</u> <u>Genteel</u> <u>Tradition</u>:
<u>American</u> <u>Writers</u> <u>since</u> <u>1910</u>. New York: W.W.
Norton, 1937. 270 pp.

"A writer-by-writer study of the post-1910
rebel generation."
Contains "Foreword: The Revolt against Gentility," pp. 9-25 (see G111); "Dos Passos:
Poet against the World," pp. 168-85 (see
F151, G112); "Postscript: Twenty Years of
American Literature," pp. 213-34 (see G117);
and "A Literary Calendar: 1911-1930," pp.
235-50 (see G116).

A4a   Revised edition: After the Genteel Tradition:
American Writers 1910-1930. Carbondale:
Southern Illinois University Press, 1964.
Adds "Edwin Arlington Robinson," pp. 28-36
(see F471).

A5   The Dry Season (see L3).

A6   The Literary Situation. New York: The Viking
Press, 1954. 259 pp.
"An informal history of our literary times."
Most of The Literary Situation appeared ori-
ginally as magazine pieces (see G206, G210-11,
G218, G230, G235-36, G238-39, G241-42, G244-
45, G247-53, G255, G257).
Reprinted excerpt: "War Novels: After Two
Wars" in Modern American Fiction: Essays in
Criticism, edited by A. Walton Litz (New
York: Oxford University Press, 1963), pp.
296-314; in The National Temper: Readings in
American History, edited by Lawrence W.
Levine and Robert Middlekauff (New York:
Harcourt, Brace and World, Inc., 1968), pp.
329-46; and in The Military Novel (Madison,
Wisconsin: U.S.A.F. Institute, 1964), pp.
152-70.

A6a   German edition: <u>Literatur</u> <u>in</u> <u>Amerika</u>, trans-
        lated by Eckart Kroneberg. Freiburg-im-
        Breisgau: Walter, 1963. 291 pp.

A6b   Swiss edition: <u>Literatur</u> <u>in</u> <u>Amerika</u>, trans-
        lated by Eckart Kroneberg. Olten: Walter,
        1963. 291 pp.

A6c   Polish edition: <u>O</u> <u>sytuacji</u> <u>w</u> <u>literaturze</u>,
        translated by Ewa Krasnowolska. Warsaw:
        Panstwowy Instytut Wydawniczy, 1969. 374 pp.

A7   (With Daniel P. Mannix) <u>Black</u> <u>Cargoes</u>: <u>A</u> <u>His-</u>
        <u>tory</u> <u>of</u> <u>the</u> <u>Atlantic</u> <u>Slave</u> <u>Trade</u>. New York:
        The Viking Press, 1962. xiv, 306 pp.
        MC says in his Introduction, "I must accept
        most of the responsibility for the chapters on
        'The Middle Passage,' 'The Yankee Slavers,'
        and 'The Dream of a Slave Empire.'"
        Chapter 5, "The Middle Passage," printed in
        <u>American</u> <u>Heritage</u> XIII (February 1962):
        22-25 (see G291).

A7a   Danish edition: <u>Den</u> <u>Atlantiske</u> <u>slave</u> <u>handels</u>
        <u>historie</u>, translated by Lise Hurwitz. Copen-
        hagen: Neils Bings Forlag, 1962. 301 pp.

A7b   English edition: <u>Black</u> <u>Cargoes</u>. London:
        Longmans, 1963. xiv, 306 pp.

A7c   Italian edition: <u>Carico</u> <u>nero</u>, translated by
        Elsa Pelitti. Milan: Longanesi, 1964. 450 pp.

A7d   Spanish edition: <u>Historia</u> <u>de</u> <u>la</u> <u>trata</u> <u>de</u>
        <u>negros</u>, translated by Eduardo Bolivar Rodrí-
        guez. Madrid: Alianza Editorial, 1968. 283 pp.

A7e   Romanian edition: <u>Corăbiile</u> <u>negre</u>: <u>O</u> <u>istorie</u>
        <u>a</u> <u>Negotului</u> <u>cu</u> <u>sclavi</u> <u>din</u> <u>Atlantic</u>, <u>1518-</u>
        <u>1865</u>, translated by Marcela Bantea. Bucharest:
        Editura stiintificǎ, 1968. 376 pp.

A8   Van Wyck Brooks. n.p., 1963. 10 pp.
      A memoir by MC. Also includes a eulogy by
      the Reverend Roland D. Oaks, Vicar of St.
      Mark's Church, Bridgewater, Connecticut,
      May 7, 1963.

A9   The Faulkner-Cowley File: Letters and Memories,
      1944-1962. New York: The Viking Press, 1966.
      184 pp.

A9a   English edition: The Faulkner-Cowley File:
      Letters and Memories, 1944-1962. London:
      Chatto & Windus, 1967. 184 pp.

A9b   Japanese edition: Faulkner to watashi:
      shokan to tsuioku, 1944-1962, translated by
      Kenzaburô Ôhashi and Harakawa Kyôichi.
      Tokyo: Tôyama-Bô, 1968. 321 pp.

A9c   French edition: William Faulkner, correspon-
      dence et souvenirs de 1944 à 1962, trans-
      lated by René Hilléret. Paris: Gallimard,
      1970. 215 pp.

A10   Think Back on Us . . . A Contemporary
      Chronicle of the 1930s, edited by Henry Dan
      Piper. Carbondale: Southern Illinois
      University Press, 1967. 400 pp.
      Selected articles, mostly from the New
      Republic, with a new epilogue, "Adventures
      of a Book Reviewer" (see A3a, D4, F141,
      F149-52, F155, F160, F162, F164, F167-68,
      F170, F176, F180, F182, F184, F186, F188,
      F191, F193-94, F197-99, F201-2, F205, F217,
      F221, F226-28, F231-33, F235, F237, F240,
      F243-45, F247-48, F250, F252, F257, F270-71,
      F273, F283-84, F297, F304-5, F308, F312-14,
      F320, F324, F334-35, F344, G63, G70, G80,

G83, G89, G95, G97, G99, G100-2, G104, G106-
7, G109, G112, G114, G123, G125, G128, G133-
34, G136-37, G139-40, G145, K6, K9).

All   Blue Juniata: Collected Poems (see L4).

A12   A Many-Windowed House: Collected Essays on
         American Writers and American Writing, edited
         with an introduction by Henry Dan Piper.
         Carbondale: Southern Illinois University Press
         1970. 261 pp.

         (See B7, B13, C2, C14, D10, D17, F426, F437,
         G178-79, G188, G194-95, G202-5, G207-8,
         G212-13, G217, G267, G282, G285-86, G288,
         G294, G298, G328).

A12a   Mexican edition: Facetas de la Crítica: en-
         sayos sobre literatura y escritores norte-
         americanos, translated by Agustín Bárcena.
         Mexico City: Editorial Pax-Mexico, 1972.
         xxiii, 318 pp.

A13   A Second Flowering: Works and Days of the Lost
         Generation. New York: The Viking Press, 1973.
         276 pp.

         Contains chapters on Fitzgerald, Hemingway
         in Paris, Dos Passos, Cummings, Wilder,
         Faulkner, Wolfe, Hart Crane, and Hemingway's
         last years, besides an introductory chapter,
         "The Other War," and a concluding chapter of
         summary and evaluation. Almost all the
         material had appeared in magazines (see
         listings in the Index for the authors dis-
         cussed), but was rearranged and rewritten fo
         the book.

A13a   English edition: London: André Deutsch, 1973
         276 pp. Bound from sheets of the first

American printing.

B.   BOOKS EDITED AND WITH INTRODUCTIONS BY
      MALCOLM COWLEY

B1   Adventures of an African Slaver, Being the
      True Account of the Life of Theodore Canot
      [Théophile Conneau] . . . as Told in the Year
      1854 to Brantz Mayer. New York: Albert and
      Charles Boni, 1928. xxi, 376 pp.

B1a   English edition: Adventures of an African
        Slaver. London: G. Routledge & Sons, 1928.
        xxi, 376 pp.

B1b   Japanese edition: Dorei shônin bôkenki,
        translated by Ôba Masafumi. Tokyo: Tôgensha,
        1965. 243 pp.

B2   Books That Changed Our Minds, edited by Malcolm
      Cowley and Bernard Smith. New York: Doubleday,
      Doran, 1939. viii, 285 pp.

        Twelve essays on thinkers, scientists, and
        writers of the nineteenth and twentieth
        centuries. "A Foreword on the Books That
        Changed Our Minds," pp. 3-23 (see G130,
        G132), and "An Afterword on the Modern Mind,"
        pp. 239-61 (see G138, G138a), by MC.

B3   The Portable Hemingway. New York: The Viking
      Press, 1944. xxiv, 642 pp.

        Introduction appeared in part in the New
        Republic (see G177) and in part in the
        Saturday Review of Literature (see G180).
        Introduction reprinted in Writers of Today,
        vol. 2, edited by Denys Val Baker (London:

Sidgwick and Jackson, 1948), pp. 3-18.
Introduction abridged in Hemingway: A Col-
lection of Critical Essays, edited by Robert
P. Weeks (Englewood Cliffs, New Jersey:
Prentice-Hall, 1962), pp. 40-51; The Personal
Voice: A Contemporary Prose Reader, edited
by Albert J. Guerard, Maclin B. Guerard,
John Hawkes, and Claire Rosenfield (Phila-
delphia: Lippincott, 1964), pp. 444-45; and
Reading for Rhetoric, edited by Caroline
Shrodes, Clifford Josephson, and James R.
Wilson (New York: Macmillan Co., 1967),
pp. 157-74. (For partial reprintings of
Introduction, see G177 and G180).

B4   Aragon, Poet of the French Resistance, edited
by Hannah Josephson and Malcolm Cowley. New
York: Duell, Sloan and Pearce, 1945. xii,
167 pp.

Selections from Louis Aragon's wartime
poetry, stories, and articles, which were
printed and circulated by the underground
movement. MC edited the poetry; Mrs. Josephson edited the prose.
Contains translations by MC: "Twenty Years
After," pp. 19-20 (see N3); "I Wait for Her
Letter at Sunset," p. 21 (with Rolfe Humphries; see N8); "the Time of Crossword
Puzzles," pp. 22-23 (see N4); "Little Suite
for Loudspeaker, II," pp. 24-25 (with Rolfe
Humphries; see N9); "The Waltz of the Twenty-
Year-Olds," pp. 26-27 (with Rolfe Humphries;
see N2); "The Interrupted Poem," pp. 32-33
(with Rolfe Humphries; see N5); "Tapestry of

the Great Fear," p. 35 (see N10); "Richard
II Forty," pp. 39-40 (with Rolfe Humphries;
see N6); "Elsa, I Love You," pp. 42-43 (with
Rolfe Humphries; see N7); "Nights," pp. 44-
48 (with Rolfe Humphries; see N11); "Tears
Are Alike," p. 51 (with Rolfe Humphries; see
N12); "Christmas Roses," pp. 70-71 (with
Helen Burlin; see N13); and "The Martyrs, by
Their Witness," pp. 136-44 (see I7).
Introduction appeared partly in the Saturday
Review of Literature (see G190) and partly
in the New Republic (see G187).

B4a   English edition: Aragon, Poet of Resurgent
France, edited by Hannah Josephson and
Malcolm Cowley. London: The Pilot Press, 1946.
ix, 182 pp.

B5   The Portable Faulkner. New York: The Viking
Press, 1946. vi, 756 pp.
The introduction was excerpted from a longer
manuscript which was not published complete
until 1952 (see D12).
Introduction evaluated by MC in Critic (see
G321), and the evaluation published as
"Afterword" in the revised edition (see B5a).
Introduction reprinted in William Faulkner:
Three Decades of Criticism, edited by
Frederick J. Hoffman and O.W. Vickers (East
Lansing: Michigan State University Press,
1960), pp. 94-109; in Faulkner: A Collection
of Critical Essays, edited by Robert Penn
Warren (Englewood Cliffs, New Jersey:
Prentice-Hall, 1966), pp. 34-46; and in
American Literature: A Critical Survey,

vol. 2, edited by Thomas D. Young and
Ronald E. Fine (New York: American Book Co.,
1968), pp. 370-86.

B5a   Revised and expanded edition: New York: The
Viking Press, 1967. xxxvii, 724 pp.
Has more words to the page and some addition-
al Faulkner material. The introduction is
longer, and the book has an "Afterword" which
originally appeared in Critic (see G321).
This revised introduction is the basis for
chapter 7, "Faulkner: The Yoknapatawpha
Story," of A Second Flowering (see A13).
A German translation of the revised introduction appears in Über William Faulkner,
edited by Gerd Haffmans (Zürich: Diogenes
Verlag, 1973), pp. 36-61.

B5b   Italian edition: 664 Pagine di William
Faulkner, translated by Edoardo Bizzarri.
Milan: Il saggiatore, 1959. 652 pp.

B5c   English edition: The Essential Faulkner.
London: Chatto and Windus, 1967. xxxvii,
724 pp.

B6   The Portable Hawthorne. New York: The Viking
Press, 1948. vi, 634 pp.
Introduction appeared in part in the New
Republic (see G212).

B6a   Revised edition: 1969. vi, 698 pp.

B6b   English edition: Nathaniel Hawthorne: The
Selected Works. London: Chatto and Windus,
1971.

B7   The Complete Poetry and Prose of Walt Whitman.
New York: Pellegrini and Cudahy, 1948. Vol. 1,
xxxix, 482 pp.; Vol. 2, 538 pp.

Introduction originally appeared in the <u>New</u>
<u>Republic</u> (see G194-95, G207-8).

Introduction collected as "Whitman: The Poet
and the Mask," in <u>A</u> <u>Many-Windowed</u> <u>House</u>,
pp. 35-75 (see A12).

B7a   Reprinted in two volumes: <u>The</u> <u>Works</u> <u>of</u> <u>Walt</u>
<u>Whitman</u>: <u>The</u> <u>Deathbed</u> <u>Edition</u> <u>in</u> <u>Two</u> <u>Volumes</u>.
<u>Vol</u>. <u>1</u>, <u>The</u> <u>Collected</u> <u>Poetry</u>; <u>Vol</u>. <u>2</u>, <u>The</u>
<u>Collected</u> <u>Prose</u>. New York: Funk & Wagnalls,
1968.

(Vol. 1 contains a new foreword; Vol. 2 contains a newly added brief prefatory note,
both by MC.)

B8   <u>The</u> <u>Stories</u> <u>of</u> <u>F</u>. <u>Scott</u> <u>Fitzgerald</u>. New York:
Charles Scribner's Sons, 1951. xxv, 473 pp.

A collection of twenty-eight stories, with
notes by MC and with a long introduction
partly rewritten from two magazine pieces
(see G225 and G226).

Introduction revised for <u>The</u> <u>Bodley</u> <u>Head</u>
<u>Scott</u> <u>Fitzgerald</u>, vols. 5 and 6 (see B14).
Part of the introduction was later used in
the Fitzgerald chapter of <u>A</u> <u>Second</u> <u>Flowering</u>
(see A13).

B9   <u>Tender</u> <u>Is</u> <u>the</u> <u>Night</u>, by F. Scott Fitzgerald.
New York: Charles Scribner's Sons, 1951. xvii,
356 pp.

Text of the novel was revised by MC in ac-
cordance with the author's final instructions.
Introduction appeared in part in the <u>New</u>
<u>Republic</u> (see G229).

B10   <u>Three</u> <u>Novels</u> <u>of</u> <u>F</u>. <u>Scott</u> <u>Fitzgerald</u>: <u>The</u> <u>Great</u>
<u>Gatsby</u> . . . <u>Tender</u> <u>Is</u> <u>the</u> <u>Night</u> . . . <u>The</u> <u>Last</u>

Tycoon. New York: Charles Scribner's Sons,
1953. xx, 137 pp.; xii, 356 pp.; v, 163 pp.
  The first two novels are edited by MC, the
  last by Edmund Wilson.
  Introduction to The Great Gatsby originally
  appeared in Western Review (see G237). Intro-
  reprinted in Three Great American Novels
  (New York: Charles Scribner's Sons, 1967).

B11   Writers at Work: The Paris Review Interviews.
      New York: The Viking Press, 1958. xx, 309 pp.
        Interviews with sixteen writers: E.M. Forster,
        François Mauriac, Joyce Cary, Dorothy Parker,
        James Thurber, Thornton Wilder, William
        Faulkner, Georges Simenon, Frank O'Connor,
        Robert Penn Warren, Alberto Moravia, Nelson
        Algren, Angus Wilson, William Styron, Truman
        Capote, Françoise Sagan.
        A shorter version of the introduction origi-
        nally appeared in the Saturday Review (see
        G269, G271).

B11a English edition: 'Paris Review.' Writers at
      Work. London: Secker & Warburg, 1958. 276 pp.

B11b German edition: Wie sie schreiben, translated
      by Wilhelm Borgers and Günther Steinbrinker.
      Gütersloh: S. Mohn, 1959. 359 pp.

B11c Paperback edition: Reinbeck: Rowohlt, 1963.
      308 pp. (Bibliography updated.)

B12   Walt Whitman's Leaves of Grass: The First (1855
      Edition. New York: The Viking Press, 1959.
      xxxvii, 145 pp.
        There was also a limited edition of 475
        copies.
        Most of the introduction originally appeared

in the Saturday Review of Literature (see
G280).

Introduction reprinted in Sunrise XVIII
(October 1968): 9-20, and (abridged) in A
Century of Whitman Criticism, edited by Edwin
H. Miller (Bloomington: Indiana University
Press, 1968), pp. 231-46; also abridged in
Leaves of Grass, a Norton Critical Edition,
edited by Sculley Bradley and Harold W.
Blodgett (New York: W.W. Norton & Company,
1973), pp. 918-26.

B12a   English edition: Leaves of Grass: The First,
1855, Edition. London: Secker & Warburg,
1960. xxxvii, 145 pp.

B13   Winesburg, Ohio, by Sherwood Anderson. New
York: The Viking Press, 1960. xvii, 247 pp.
A shorter version of the introduction ap-
peared in the New Republic (see G282).
Collected as "Sherwood Anderson's Book of
Moments" in A Many-Windowed House, pp. 166-
77 (see A12).

B14   The Bodley Head Scott Fitzgerald. Vols. Five
and Six: Short Stories. London: Bodley Head,
1963. xxxiv, 488; 381 pp.
Revised and expanded edition of B8, with ad-
ditional stories, selected and introduced by
MC.
Newly added "Editor's Notes" appear in vol.
5, pp. 37-39, 283-85; and vol. 6, pp. 9-11,
173-75.

B15   Fitzgerald and the Jazz Age, edited by Malcolm
and Robert Cowley. New York: Charles Scribner's
Sons, 1966. xvii, 192 pp.

A collection of source material by MC and
others "designed to cast light on the cultural
and literary history of the dozen years that
followed the First World War."
Includes "Ambulance Service," pp. 27-32,
"Valuta," pp. 95-96, and "Epilogue: New Year's
Eve," pp. 175-77, from Exile's Return (see
A3a).
Excerpt printed in American Heritage (see
G318).

B16 (With Howard E. Hugo) The Lessons of the Masters: An Anthology of the Novel from Cervantes
to Hemingway. New York: Charles Scribner's
Sons, 1971. xii, 514 pp.

C.   INTRODUCTIONS TO BOOKS BY OTHERS

C1   Daughter of Earth, an Autobiography, by Agnes
Smedley. New York: Coward-McCann, 1935. "Foreword," pp. v-vii.

C2   The Selected Writings of Lafcadio Hearn, edited
by Henry Goodman. New York: The Citadel Press,
1949. "Introduction," pp. 1-15.
Introduction appeared in part in the New
Republic (see G217).
Collected as "Lafacadio Herun-san" in A Many-
Windowed House, pp. 100-115 (see A12).

C3   Great Tales of the Deep South. New York: Lion
Library Editions, 1955. "Introduction," pp. vii-
xii.

C4   The Ordeal of Mark Twain, by Van Wyck Brooks.
New York: Meridian Books, 1955. "Introduction,"

pp. 5-10.

A shorter version of the introduction originally appeared in the New Republic (see G259).

C5   A Thornton Wilder Trio: The Bridge of San Luis
Rey, The Cabala, The Woman of Andros. New York:
Criterion Press, 1956. "Introduction," pp. 1-
19.

A shorter version of the introduction appeared
in the Saturday Review of Literature (see
G263).

The introduction, in a somewhat revised form,
became chapter 6, "Wilder: Time Abolished,"
of A Second Flowering (see A13).

C6   Great Scenes from Great Novels, edited by
Robert Terrall. New York: Dell Publishing Co.,
1956. "The Limits of the Novel," pp. 9-18.

Introduction originally appeared in the New
Republic (see G261).

C7   Madame Bovary, by Gustave Flaubert. New York:
Bantam Books, 1959. "Introduction," pp. vii-
xii.

C8   Miss Lonelyhearts, by Nathanael West. New York:
Avon Publications, 1959. "Introduction," pp.
ii-iv, 96.

Introduction originally appeared in the New
York Times Book Review (see F510).

C9   The Outlaws on Parnassus, by Margaret Kennedy.
New York: The Viking Press, 1960. "Foreword,"
pp. ix-xvii.

Foreword originally appeared in the New
Republic (see F517).

C10   Anna Karenina, by Leo Tolstoy. New York: Bantam
Books, 1960. "Foreword," pp. v-xii.

C11   Fontamara, by Ignazio Silone. New York:
      Atheneum Press, 1960. "Foreword," pp. v-viii.

C12   American Literature Survey: The Twentieth
      Century, edited by Milton R. Stern and Seymour
      L. Gross. New York: The Viking Press, 1962.
      "Preface," pp. xv-xxi.

C13   Three Novels: The Sun Also Rises, A Farewell to
      Arms, The Old Man and the Sea, by Ernest
      Hemingway. New York: Charles Scribner's Sons,
      1962.

      The Sun Also Rises has an introduction by MC,
      "Commencing with the Simplest Things,"
      pp. ix-xxviii. This introduction was revised
      for sections 1, 3, and 4 of chapter 3,
      "Hemingway in Paris," of A Second Flowering
      (see A13).

C14   An Autobiography, by Van Wyck Brooks. New York:
      E.P. Dutton and Co., 1965. "Introduction,"
      pp. xvii-xxxvi.

      A shorter version of the introduction
      originally appeared in the Saturday Review
      (see G285, G298).
      Collected as "Van Wyck Brooks's 'Usable
      Past'," in A Many-Windowed House, pp. 213-28
      (see A12).

D.   CONTRIBUTIONS TO BOOKS EDITED BY OTHERS

D1   Eight More Harvard Poets (see L1).

D2   "Humanizing Society," in The Critique of
      Humanism: A Symposium, edited by C. Hartley
      Grattan. New York: Brewer and Warren, 1930,
      pp. 63-84.

Shorter version appeared in the New Republic
(see G63).

Reprinted in Men and Books, edited by M.S.
Maclean and E.K. Holmes (New York: Richard
R. Smith, Inc., 1930), pp. 287-300; collected
in Think Back on Us, pp. 3-13 (see A10).

D3   "Oedipus; or, The Future of Love," in Whither,
Whither; or, After Sex What? edited by Walter
S. Hankel (pseud.). New York: The Macaulay
Company, 1930, pp. 250-79.

Originally appeared in the New Republic (see
G65).

D3a   "Alfred Hayes," in Trial Balances, edited by
Ann Winslow (pseud. of Verna Elizabeth Grubbs).
New York: Macmillan Co., 1935, pp. 210-12.

Biographical sketch and critical notice of
the proletarian poet.

D4   "What the Revolutionary Movement Can Do for a
Writer," in American Writers' Congress, edited
by Henry Hart. New York: International
Publishers, 1935, pp. 59-65.

First appeared in New Masses (see G102).
Collected in Think Back on Us, pp. 87-94
(see A10).

D5   "The Seven Years of Crisis," in The Writer in
a Changing World, edited by Henry Hart. New
York: Equinox Cooperative Press, 1937, pp. 44-
47.

MC reconstructed this summary of extempora-
neous remarks he made at the Second Congress
of American Writers.

D6   "Faith and the Future," in Whose Revolution?
edited by Irving Dewitt Talmadge. New York:
Howell, Soskin, 1941, pp. 135-65.

Communism as a religion and its weaknesses
as compared with Christianity.

D6a   [Autobiographical sketch), in Twentieth
Century Authors, edited by Stanley J. Kunitz
and Howard Haycraft. New York: H.W. Wilson Co.,
1942, pp. 320-21.

The sketch consists mostly of quotations from
MC. For its sequel, see D12a.

D7   "William Faulkner's Legend of the South," in
A Southern Vanguard, edited by Allen Tate.
New York: Prentice-Hall, 1947, pp. 13-27.

Prize-winning essay (John Peale Bishop
Memorial Literary Prize Contest, sponsored
by the Sewanee Review and Prentice-Hall,
Inc.) excerpted from a longer manuscript,
"Introduction to William Faulkner," which
was not published in its entirety until
later (see D12).

Originally appeared in the Sewanee Review
(see G185).

Reprinted in Essays in Modern Literary Criticism, edited by Ray Benedict West (New
York: Rinehart, 1952), pp. 513-26.

D8   "If You Want To Write . . .," in A Man's Reach:
Some Choices Facing Youth Today, edited by
Thomas H. Johnson. New York: Putnam's, 1947,
pp. 35-53.

D9   "Creating an Audience" (with H.S. Canby; pp.
1119-34); "How Writers Lived" (pp. 1263-72);
"American Books Abroad" (pp. 1374-91) in
Literary History of the United States, edited
by Robert E. Spiller, Willard Thorp, Thomas H.
Johnson, and Henry Seidel Canby. New York: The
Macmillan Company, 1948.

"American Books Abroad" originally
appeared in part in the New Republic
(see G196) and in part in Life (see
G197).

D10   "Naturalism in American Literature," in Evolutionary Thought in America, edited by Stow
Persons. New Haven: Yale University Press,
1950, pp. 300-333.
    Part of this essay appeared in the Kenyon
    Review (see G205); another section appeared
    as part of a three-part piece in the New
    Republic (see G202).
    Reprinted in Critiques and Essays on Modern
    Fiction, 1920-1951, selected by John W.
    Aldridge (New York: The Ronald Press, 1952),
    pp. 370-87; collected as "A Natural History
    of American Naturalism" in A Many-Windowed
    House (see A12), pp. 116-52.

D11   "How the Writer Lives," in Twentieth Century
Unlimited, edited by Bruce Bliven. New York:
Lippincott, 1950, pp. 254-65.
    Abridged version appeared in the New Republic
    (see G199), and was reprinted in Writer LXIV
    (June 1951): 181-83.

D12   "Introduction to William Faulkner," in Critiques and Essays on Modern Fiction, selected
by John W. Aldridge. New York: The Ronald Press,
1952, pp. 427-46.
    This is the only complete version of MC's
    original essay on Faulkner. Selections from
    it were printed separately (see B5, D7, G184,
    G185).

D12a [Autobiographical sketch], in Twentieth
Century Authors: First Supplement, edited by

Stanely J. Kunitz. New York: H.W. Wilson Co.,
1955, p. 240.

Part of the sketch consists of a quotation
from MC. For its predecessor, see D6a.

D13 "Five Acts of The Scarlet Letter," in Twelve
Original Essays on Great American Novels,
edited by Charles Shapiro. Detroit: Wayne State
University Press, 1958, pp. 23-43.

A first, shorter version appeared in the New
York Herald Tribune Book Review (see G223).
Another short version appeared in College
English (see G268).

D14 "Thomas Wolfe: The Professional Deformation,"
in American Critical Essays (Twentieth Century),
edited by Harold Beaver. London: Oxford University Press, 1959, pp. 89-105.

Originally appeared in the Atlantic Monthly
(see G270).

Reprinted in This Is My Best, edited by Whit
Burnett (New York: Doubleday & Company, 1970),
pp. 636-48.

D15 "Ethics in the Arts," in Ethical Problems for
the Sixties, by Malcolm Cowley, Robert Lewis
Shayon, John Smith, and Charles Frankel. New
Britain: Central Connecticut State College,
1962, pp. 1-15.

A shorter version of "Ethics in the Arts" appeared in the Saturday Review (see G293).

D15a [Untitled tribute to Pascal Covici], in Pascal
Covici, 1888-1964. New York: The Viking Press,
1965, pp. 23-25.

A tribute from MC to Pascal Civici, sent
after the memorial service on October 16, 1964

D16   "The Beginning Writer in the University," in
      To the Young Writer: Hopwood Lectures, Second
      Series, edited by A.L. Rader. Ann Arbor:
      University of Michigan Press, 1965, pp. 68-84.
         First printed in Michigan Alumnus Quarterly
         Review (see G272).

D17   "Anderson's Lost Days of Innocence," in The
      Achievement of Sherwood Anderson, edited by
      Ray Lewis White. Chapel Hill: University of
      North Carolina Press, 1966, pp. 224-30.
         Shorter version appeared in the New Republic
         and in the London Magazine (see G282).
         Collected as "Sherwood Anderson's Book of
         Moments," in A Many-Windowed House, pp. 166-
         77 (see A12).

D18   "Postscript," in An Illustrated History of the
      United States, by André Maurois. New York:
      The Viking Press, 1969, pp. 266-88.

D19   "S. Foster Damon: The New England Voice," in
      William Blake: Essays for S. Foster Damon,
      edited by Alvin H. Rosenfeld. Providence:
      Brown University Press, 1969, pp. xv-xxviii.
         First printed in Southern Review (see G326).

D20   "A Note by Malcolm Cowley," in Robber Rocks:
      Letters and Memories of Hart Crane, by Susan
      Jenkins Brown. Middletown, Connecticut:
      Wesleyan Univeristy Press, 1969, pp. 102-7.
         First appeared as part of a review in Sewanee
         Review (see F533). See also K18.

D21   "Paul Valéry," in Atlantic Brief Lives, edited
      by Louis Kronenberger; associate editor, Emily
      Morison Beck. Boston: Atlantic-Little Brown,
      1971, pp. 819-22.

An account of Valéry's career.

E.   BOOKS TRANSLATED

E1   On Board the Morning Star, by Pierre MacOrlan
     (pseud. of Pierre Dumarchey). New York: Albert
     and Charles Boni, 1924. 120 pp.
        Fifth, eighth, twelfth, and sixteenth epi-
        sodes printed in Broom (see I1).
E2   Joan of Arc, by Joseph Delteil. New York:
     Minton, Balch, 1926. xix, 266 pp.
        With an introduction by MC.
E3   Variety, by Paul Valéry. New York: Harcourt,
     Brace, 1927. xv, 283 pp.
        Introduction by MC originally appeared in the
        New Republic (see G39).
E4   Jesus, by Henri Barbusse, translated by Solon
     Librescot, supervised by Malcolm Cowley. New
     York: The Macaulay Co., 1927. 235 pp.
E5   Catherine-Paris, by Princess Marthe Bibesco.
     New York: Harcourt, Brace, 1928. vi, 368 pp.
E6   The Green Parrot, by Princess Marthe Bibesco.
     New York: Harcourt, Brace, 1929. 246 pp.
E7   The Sacred Hill, by Maurice Barrès. New York:
     The Macaulay Co., 1929. x, 269 pp.
        With an introduction by MC.
E8   The Count's Ball, by Raymond Radiguet. New
     York: W.W. Norton, 1929. xiv, 243 pp.
E9   Imaginary Interviews, by André Gide. New York:
     Alfred A. Knopf, 1944. xvii, 172 pp.
        With introduction (see G176) and appendix
        (see G175) by MC, both of which appeared in
        part in the New Republic.

E10 Aragon, Poet of the French Resistance (see B4).

E11 Leonardo, Poe, Mallarmé. (The Collected Works
of Paul Valéry, volume 8). Translated by
Malcolm Cowley and James R. Lawler. Princeton:
Princeton University Press, 1972. 463 pp.

Mostly translated by MC. He did "Introduction
to the Method of Leonardo da Vinci"; "Note
and Digression"; "Leonardo and the Philoso-
phers"; "On Poe's Eureka"; "The Existence of
Symbolism" (see I13); "Letter about Mallarmé";
"I Would Sometimes Say to Stéphane Mallarmé
. . ." (see I15); "Concerning 'A Throw of the
Dice'"; "Last Visit to Mallarmé"; "Stéphane
Mallarmé."

E11a English edition: London: Routledge and Kegan
Paul, 1972.

PART 2: CONTRIBUTIONS TO PERIODICALS

F.   BOOK REVIEWS

1916

F1   [Review of The Darling, by Anton Chekhov,
     translated by Constance Garnett]. Harvard Advo-
     cate CII (November 22, 1916): 62-63.

F2   [Review of Of Human Bondage, by W. Somerset
     Maugham]. Harvard Advocate CII (November 22,
     1916): 63.

1917

F3   [Review of Casuals of the Sea, by William
     McFee]. Harvard Advocate CII (January 17, 1917):
     124.

F4   [Review of Egotism in German Philosophy, by
     George Santayana]. Harvard Advocate CIII
     (May 14, 1917): 73-74.

1919

F5   "Through Yellow Glasses." New Republic XIX
     (July 23, 1919): 401.
         Victorious, by Reginald Wright Kauffman
         (see Introduction).

F6   [Review of A Servant of Reality, by Phyllis

Bottome]. New Republic XXI (December 17, 1919):
86.

1920

F7   "Necromancy." Harvard Advocate CVI (January 29,
      1920): 181.
         Poems, First Series, by J.C. Squire.
F8   [Reviews of Storm in a Teacup, by Eden Phill-
      potts, and The Builders, by Ellen Glasgow]. New
      Republic XXI (February 18, 1920): 364,366.
F9   "The Woman of Thornden." Dial LXVIII (February
      1920): 259-62.
         A Challenge to Sirius and The Four Roads, by
         Sheila Kaye-Smith (see Introduction).
F10   [Review of The Little Daughter of Jerusalem, by
      Myriam Harry]. New Republic XXII (March 31,
      1920): 168.
F11   [Review of Short Stories from the Balkans,
      translated by Edna Worthley Underwood]. New
      Republic XXII (April 17, 1920): 192.
F12   "Colas Breugnon." Dial LXVIII (April 1920): 513-16.
         Colas Breugnon: Burgundian, by Romain
         Rolland, translated by Katherine Miller.
F13   "Against Nightingales." Dial LXVIII (May 1920):
      621-25.
         Picture Show and The War Poems, by Siegfried
         Sassoon.
F14   [Review of Masks, by George Middleton]. New
      Republic XXIV (September 1, 1920): 26.
F15   "Georgians and Post-Georgians." New Republic
      XXIV (September 15, 1920): 77-78.
         Wheels 1919, Fourth Cycle, edited by Edith
         Sitwell.
F16   "Mme. Duclaux on France." Literary Review of the

New York Evening Post I (October 2, 1920): 3.

Twentieth Century France, by Mary Duclaux.

F17   "Gaucho Drama." Literary Review of the New York
Evening Post I (November 13, 1920): 3.

Three Plays of the Argentine, edited with an
introduction by Edward Hale Bierstadt.

F18   "The Era of Disillusion." Literary Review of th
New York Evening Post I (November 20, 1920): 4.

Youth and Egolatry, by Pio Baroja, translated
Jacob S. Fassett, Jr., and Frances L. Phillip

F19   "The World's Timber." Literary Review of the
New York Evening Post I (November 27, 1920): 4.

A Manual of the Timbers of the World, by
Alexander L. Howard.

F20   "Woman of Japan." Literary Review of the New
York Evening Post I (December 24, 1920): 9.

Diaries of Court Ladies of Old Japan, translated by Annie Shepley Omori and Kochi Doi.

F21   "Entertaining Plays." Literary Review of the
New York Evening Post I (December 31, 1920): 5.

Plays for Merry Andrews, by Alfred Kreymborg.

F22   "Motley Verse." Literary Review of the New York
Evening Post I (December 31, 1920): 9.

Poems, by Haniel Long.

1921

F23   "The Chinless Age." Dial LXX (January 1921): 73
Leda, by Aldous Huxley.

F24   "A War-Time Squad." Literary Review of the New
York Evening Post I (March 26, 1921): 6.

Wooden Crosses, by Roland Dorgelès.

F25   "Random Reflections." Literary Review of the
New York Evening Post I (May 21, 1921): 6.

Things That Have Interested Me, by Arnold
Bennett.

F26 "These Things Are Banal . . ." Dial LXX (June
1921): 700-704.

Breakers and Granite, by John Gould Fletcher,
and Punch: The Immortal Liar, by Conrad
Aiken.

F27 "A Liberal Policy." Literary Review of the New
York Evening Post I (July 9, 1921): 5.

The Problem of Foreign Policy, by Gilbert
Murray.

F28 "Adam & Eve & Pinch Me." Dial LXXI (July 1921):
93-95.

Adam & Eve & Pinch Me, by A.E. Coppard.

F29 "Programme Music." Dial LXXI (August 1921):
222-26.

Legends, by Amy Lowell.

F30 "Page Dr. Blum!" Dial LXXI (September 1921):
365-67.

Bliss, by Katherine Mansfield.

1922

F31 "Bonded Translation." Dial LXXII (May 1922):
517-21.

Fir-Flower Tablets, poems translated from the
Chinese by Florence Ayscough, English versions
by Amy Lowell.

F32 "In Vindication of Mr. Horner." Freeman X (June
7, 1922): 308-9.

William Wycherley: sa vie, son oeuvre, by
Charles Perromat.

F33 "Colloquial French." Literary Review of the
New York Evening Post II (July 1, 1922): 776.

Traité pratique de prononciation française,
by Maurice Grammont.

F34 "Keats and Hearst." Dial LXXIII (July 1922):
108-11

Poems: Second Series, by J.C. Squire, and
Music: Lyrical and Narrative Poems, by John
Freeman.

F35 "The Author of Bliss." Dial LXXIII (August
1922): 230-32.

The Garden Party and Other Stories, by
Katherine Mansfield.

F36 "Euphues." Dial LXXIII (October 1922): 446-48.

Introducing Irony, by Maxwell Bodenheim.

F37 "Two American Poets." Dial LXXIII (November
1922): 563-67.

Priapus and the Pool, by Conrad Aiken, and
Slabs of the Sunburnt West, by Carl Sandburg.

1923

F38 "The Owl and the Nightingale." Dial LXXIV
(June 1923): 624-26.

Black Armour, by Elinor Wylie.

F39 "Phantasus." Dial LXXV (August 1923): 196-99.

Contemporary German Poetry, translated by
Babette Deutsch and Avrahm Yarmolinsky.

F40 "Family Adventures." Literary Review of the New
York Evening Post IV (September 22, 1923): 61.

The Nuptial Flight, by Edgar Lee Masters.

F41 "Properties." Dial LXXV (September 1923):
296-98.

The Hundred and One Harlequins, by Sacheverell
Sitwell.

F42 "The Best of Medicine." Literary Review of the

New York Evening Post IV (October 27, 1923):
184.

 Oh, Doctor! by Harry Leon Wilson.

1924

F43 "Black and White." Literary Review of the New
 York Evening Post IV (February 16, 1924): 520.
  The Color of a Great City, by Theodore
  Dreiser.

F44 "Portrait of a Genius." Literary Review of the
 New York Evening Post IV (June 7, 1924): 805.
  The Grand Tour, by Romer Wilson

F45 "St. Apollinaire." Literary Review of the New
 York Evening Post IV (June 21, 1924): 835.
  The Poet Assassinated, by Guillaume
  Apollinaire, translated with a biographical
  notice by Matthew Josephson.

F46 "The Village Smell." Literary Review of the New
 York Evening Post IV (June 21, 1924): 844.
  The Eleventh Virgin, by Dorothy Day.

F47 "A Lamb among Wolves." Saturday Review of
 Literature I (November 15, 1924): 279-80.
  Professor, How Could You! by Harry Leon
  Wilson.

F48 "Gulliver." Dial LXXVII (December 1924): 520-
 22.
  The White Oxen, by Kenneth Burke.

1925

F49 "Festoons of Fishes." Dial LXXVIII (April 1925):
 326-29.
  Less Lonely, by Alfred Kreymborg.

F50 "The Dark City." Saturday Review of Literature

I (June 27, 1925): 851.

    Bring! Bring! and Other Stories, by Conrad
Aiken.

F51 "Mr. Moore's Golden Treasury." New York Herald
Tribune Books, August 2, 1925, p. 5.

    An Anthology of Pure Poetry, edited with an
introduction by George Moore (see Introduction).

F52 "An Excellent Manual." Saturday Review of
Literature II (August 8, 1925): 22.

    Contemporary French Literature, by René
Lalou, translated by William Aspinwall Bradley.

F53 "A Few Books Well Worth Keeping." Charm IV
(August 1925): 52-53.

    The Life of Abraham Lincoln, by William E.
Barton; The Adventures of Wrangel Island, by
Vilhjalmur Stefansson; and Jefferson and
Monticello, by Paul Wilstach. (Includes notes
on the roles of book reviewers and critics.)

F54 "Some Interesting Biographies." Charm IV
(September 1925): 28, 86.

    Brigham Young, by M.R. Werner; Life and Times,
by Meade Minnegerode; and The Man Christ
Jesus, by Dr. W.J. Dawson.

F55 "Icy Fire." New York Herald Tribune Books,
October 11, 1925, p. 5.

    Collected Poems of H.D. (Hilda Doolittle
Aldington).

F56 "Some Books for Fall Reading." Charm IV (October
1925): 38, 92.

    A Player under Three Reigns, by Sir Johnston
Forbes-Robertson; Anatole France Himself, by
Jean Jacques Brousson, translated by John

Pollock; and Original Letters from India,
by Eliza Fay.

F57   "Frankenstein; or, the Poetical Faculty." New
York Herald Tribune Books, November 1, 1925,
p. 10.

Doctor Transit, by I.S. (Isidor Schneider).

F58   "Urbanites." New York Herald Tribune Books,
November 15, 1925, p. 8.

Lectures to Living Authors, text by Lacon
(E.H. Lacon Watson), caricatures by Quiz.
The English Novel of Today, by Gerald Gould.

F59   "Exact Fancy." New York Herald Tribune Books,
November 22, 1925, p. 8.

Doodab, by Harold Loeb.

F60   "Cocteau's First Novel." Saturday Review of
Literature II (November 28, 1925): 335.

The Grand Écart, by Jean Cocteau, translated
by Lewis Galantière.

F61   "An Ikon." New York Herald Tribune Books,
December 6, 1925, p. 7.

Peter the Czar, by Klabund (Alfred Henschke),
translated by Herman George Scheffauer.

F62   "The Orange Moth." Dial LXXIX (December 1925):
507-9.

Bring! Bring! and Other Stories, by Conrad
Aiken.

1926

F63   "A Man of Letters." New York Herald Tribune
Books, January 17, 1926, pp. 4-5.

The Vatican Swindle, by André Gide, translated by Dorothy Bussy.

F64   "Fraulein Ophelia." New York Herald Tribune

Books, January 31, 1926, p. 7.

    Fräulein Else, by Arthur Schnitzler, translated by F.H. Lyon.

F65 "Untranslatable Genius." New York Herald Tribune Books, January 31, 1926, p. 19. [Unsigned.]

    Claire Lenoir, by Villiers de l'Isle Adam, translated by Arthur Symons.

F66 "A Miscellany of Winter Books." Charm IV (January 1926): 50, 78.

    Story of the World's Literature, by John Macy; Possession, by Louis Bromfield; and The Professor's House, by Willa Cather.

F67 "The Road of Excess." New York Herald Tribune Books, February 7, 1926, p. 17.

    Chains, by Henri Barbusse, translated by Stephen Haden Guest.

F68 "Murder, Piracy and Justice." New Republic XLV (February 17, 1926): 362-63.

    Murder, Piracy and Treason, by Raymond Postgate.

F69 "Two Anthologies." New York Herald Tribune Books, February 21, 1926, p. 6.

    The Best Short Stories of 1925, edited by Edward J. O'Brien and John Cournos, and The World's Best Short Stories of 1925, selected by editors of leading American magazines.

F70 "A Pedlar of the King." New York Herald Tribune Books, February 28, 1926, p. 4

    Memoirs of Léon Daudet, edited and translated by Arthur Kingsland Griggs.

F71 "Two Novels from the French." New York Herald Tribune Books, April 4, 1926, p. 11.

    Aricie Brun, by Emile Henriot, translated by

Henry Longan Stuart, and <u>Comes</u> <u>the</u> <u>Blind</u>
<u>Fury</u>, by Raymond Escholier, translated by
J. Lewis May.

F72 "French Verse in English." <u>New</u> <u>York</u> <u>Herald</u>
<u>Tribune</u> <u>Books</u>, April 25, 1926, p. 12.

<u>Modern</u> <u>French</u> <u>Poetry</u>: <u>An</u> <u>Anthology</u>, compiled
and translated by Joseph T. Shipley.

F73 "Books of the Spring Season." <u>Charm</u> V (April
1926): 34, 84.

<u>Abraham</u> <u>Lincoln</u>: <u>The</u> <u>Prairie</u> <u>Years</u>, by Carl
Sandburg; <u>Verdi</u>, by Franz Werfel; <u>Appas-</u>
<u>sionata</u>, by Fannie Hurst; and <u>The</u> <u>Diary</u> <u>of</u> <u>a</u>
<u>Young</u> <u>Lady</u> <u>of</u> <u>Fashion</u> <u>in</u> <u>the</u> <u>Year</u> <u>1764-1765</u>,
by Cleone Knox [pseud. of Magdelen King-Hall].

F74 "Haloes for the Damned." <u>New</u> <u>York</u> <u>Herald</u> <u>Tri-</u>
<u>bune</u> <u>Books</u>, May 9, 1926, p. 10.

<u>Four</u> <u>Novelists</u> <u>of</u> <u>the</u> <u>Old</u> <u>Regime</u>, by John
Garber Palache.

F75 "Stendhal Complete." <u>New</u> <u>York</u> <u>Herald</u> <u>Tribune</u>
<u>Books</u>, May 23, 1926, p. 12.

<u>The</u> <u>Charterhouse</u> <u>of</u> <u>Parma</u>, by Stendhal, trans-
lated by C.K. Scott Moncrieff.

F76 "Now the Age of Cuckoo Humor." <u>Charm</u> V (May
1926): 46, 80-81.

<u>Gentlemen</u> <u>Prefer</u> <u>Blondes</u>, by Anita Loos; <u>The</u>
<u>Love</u> <u>Nest</u>, by Ring Lardner; <u>Three</u> <u>Rousing</u>
<u>Cheers</u> <u>for</u> <u>the</u> <u>Rollo</u> <u>Boys</u>, by Corey Ford; <u>All</u>
<u>the</u> <u>Sad</u> <u>Young</u> <u>Men</u>, by F. Scott Fitzgerald;
and <u>Pluck</u> <u>and</u> <u>Luck</u>, by Robert Benchley.

F77 "The Mirror of Innocence." <u>Dial</u> LXXX (May
1926): 415-16.

<u>Beatrice</u> <u>Cenci</u>, by Corrado Ricci, translated
by Morris Bishop and Henry Longan Stuart.

F78   "Four Books about Ourselves." Charm V (June
      1926): 33, 72.
         The Mauve Decade, by Thomas Beer; Our Times,
         by Mark Sullivan; Fix Bayonets! by John W.
         Thomason; and The Intimate Papers of Colonel
         House, edited by Charles Seymour.
F79   "Errors and Asterisks." New York Herald Tribune
      Books, September 5, 1926, p. 17.
         The Best French Short Stories of 1924-25,
         edited by Richard Eaton.
F80   "Fiction, Philosophy and Bandits." Charm VI
      (September 1926): 36.
         The Story of Philosophy, by Will Durant, and
         The Arcturus Adventure, by William Beebe.
F81   "What Is a Show Boat, Anyway?" Charm VI (Novem-
      ber 1926): 31, 76.
         Show Boat, by Edna Ferber; The Cabala, by
         Thornton Wilder; and Nigger Heaven, by Carl
         Van Vechten.
F82   "Good Books for Christmas Giving." Charm VI
      (December 1926): 52, 86.
         Abraham Lincoln, by Carl Sandburg; Notes on
         Democracy, by H.L. Mencken; The Conquest of
         Civilization, by James H. Breasted; and The
         Story of Philosophy, by Will Durant.

      1927
F83   "From 'Flowers of Evil' to the Super Realists."
      Literary Review of the New York Evening Post
      VII (January 29, 1927): 1, 14.
         Baudelaire: Prose and Poetry, translated by
         Arthur Symons, and Modern French Poetry: An
         Anthology, compiled and translated by Joseph

T. Shipley.

F84 "Four Biographies and a Novel." <u>Charm</u> VI (Janu-
     ary 1927): 49, 80.

     <u>George</u> <u>Washington</u>: <u>The</u> <u>Image</u> <u>of</u> <u>the</u> <u>Man</u>, by
     W.E. Woodward; <u>Benjamin</u> <u>Franklin</u>: <u>The</u> <u>First</u>
     <u>Civilized</u> <u>American</u>, by Phillips Russell;
     <u>Darwin</u>, by Gamaliel Bradford; <u>You</u> <u>Can't</u> <u>Win</u>,
     by Jack Black; and <u>The</u> <u>World</u> <u>of</u> <u>William</u>
     <u>Clissold</u>, by H.G. Wells.

F85 "A Few Translations and Reprints." <u>Charm</u> VII
     (March 1927): 39, 84, 87.

     <u>Napoleon</u>, by Emil Ludwig, translated by Eden
     and Cedar Paul; <u>Power</u>, by Lion Feuchtwanger,
     translated by Willa and Edwin Muir; <u>The</u>
     <u>Thibaults</u>, by Roger Martin du Gard, trans-
     lated by Madeleine Boyd; and <u>Sutter's</u> <u>Gold</u>,
     by Blaise Cendrars, translated by Henry
     Longan Stuart.

F86 "The Art of Visible Things." <u>Dial</u> LXXXII
     (March 1927): 247-49.

     <u>Gautier</u> <u>and</u> <u>the</u> <u>Romantics</u>, by John Garber
     Palache.

F87 "Lightning in a Mist." <u>New</u> <u>York</u> <u>Herald</u> <u>Tribune</u>
     <u>Books</u>, April 10, 1927, p. 2.

     <u>A</u> <u>Call</u> <u>to</u> <u>Order</u>, by Jean Cocteau, translated
     by Rollo H. Myers.

F88 "The Vanguard of Spring Novels." <u>Charm</u> VII
     (April 1927): 37, 66-67.

     <u>Tomorrow</u> <u>Morning</u>, by Anne Parish; <u>Jill</u>, by
     E.M. Delafield; <u>East</u> <u>Side</u>, <u>West</u> <u>Side</u>, by
     Felix Reisenberg; <u>The</u> <u>Plutocrat</u>, by Booth
     Tarkington; and <u>Mr</u>. <u>Gilhooley</u>, by Liam
     O'Flaherty.

F89 "Genji, Aging, Disports Himself Sedately in
     This Third Volume." Literary Review of the New
     York Evening Post VII (May 21, 1927): 3.
        A Wreath of Cloud, by Lady Murasaki, trans-
     lated by Arthur Waley.

F90 "Much Stranger Than Ficiton." Charm VII (June
     1927): 33, 86.
        Revolt in the Desert, by T.E. Lawrence; The
     South Africans, by Sarah G. Millin; Anthony
     Comstock: Roundsman of the Lord, by Heywood
     Broun and Margaret Leech; and Palmerston, by
     Philip Guedalla.

F91 "The Margins of Infinity." Dial LXXXII (June
     1927): 516-17.
        Streets in the Moon, by Archibald MacLeish.

F92 "Reading America First." Charm VIII (August
     1927): 53, 76.
        The Rise of American Civilization, by Charles
     R. and Mary R. Beard; Thomas Paine: Prophet
     and Martyr of Democracy, by Mary Agnes Best;
     Marching On, by James Boyd; and The Girl from
     Rectors, by George Rector.

F93 "Israfel." Dial LXXXIII (August 1927): 168-71
        Israfel: The Life and Times of Edgar Allan
     Poe, by Hervey Allen.

F94 "The Coin of Greatness." New York Herald Tri-
     bune Books, September 25, 1927, pp. 1-2.
        The Counterfeiters, by André Gide, translated
     by Dorothy Bussy.

F95 "Midsummer Fiction and Biography." Charm VIII
     (September 1927): 50, 76.
        Giants in the Earth, by O.E. Rölvaag; A Good
     Woman, by Louis Bromfield; and Blue Voyage,

by Conrad Aiken.

F96   "Poets March in the Van." <u>New</u> <u>York</u> <u>Herald</u> <u>Tri-</u>
<u>bune</u> <u>Books</u>, October 16, 1927, p. 4.

<u>Since</u> <u>Victor</u> <u>Hugo</u>: <u>French</u> <u>Literature</u> <u>of</u>
<u>Today</u>, by Bernard Faÿ, translated by Paul
Rice Doolin.

F97   "A Fourth Bronte." <u>New</u> <u>York</u> <u>Herald</u> <u>Tribune</u>
<u>Books</u>, October 23, 1927, p. 5.

<u>Avarice</u> <u>House</u>, by Julien Green, translated by
Marshall A. Best.

F98   "Desert, Jungle and Prairie." <u>Charm</u> VIII (October 1927): 35, 74.

<u>Adventures</u> <u>in</u> <u>Arabia</u>, by W.B. Seabrook;
<u>Trader</u> <u>Horn</u>, by Ethelreda Lewis; <u>America</u>
<u>Comes</u> <u>of</u> <u>Age</u>, by André Siegfried; and <u>Henry</u>
<u>Ward</u> <u>Beecher</u>: <u>An</u> <u>American</u> <u>Portrait</u>, by Paxton
Hibben. (Includes a preview of fall books.)

F99   "The Golden House." <u>Dial</u> LXXXIII (October 1927):
339-42.

<u>Lotus</u> <u>and</u> <u>Chrysanthemum</u>, <u>an</u> <u>Anthology</u> <u>of</u>
<u>Chinese</u> <u>and</u> <u>Japanese</u> <u>Poetry</u>, selected by
Joseph Lewis French.

F100 "Aspects of the American Scene." <u>Charm</u> VIII
(November 1927): 30, 86.

<u>The</u> <u>American</u> <u>Caravan</u>, edited by Van Wyck
Brooks, Paul Rosenfeld, Alfred Kreymborg, and
Lewis Mumford.

F101 "The Geographer of Love." <u>New</u> <u>York</u> <u>Herald</u> <u>Tri-</u>
<u>bune</u> <u>Books</u>, December 4, 1927, pp. 6-7.

<u>Nothing</u> <u>but</u> <u>the</u> <u>Earth</u>, by Paul Morand, trans-
lated by Lewis Galantière.

F102 "Death of a Nobody." <u>New</u> <u>York</u> <u>Herald</u> <u>Tribune</u>
<u>Books</u>, December 18, 1927, p. 5.

The Man Who Conquered Death, by Franz Werfel,
translated by Clifton Fadiman and William A.
Drake.

1928

F103 "As Told in a Bazaar." New York Herald Tribune
Books, January 8, 1928, p. 13.
Uncle Anghel, by Panaït Istrati, translated
by Maude Valerie White.

F104 "Humbert Wolfe." New Republic LIII (February 1,
1928): 304.
Kensington Gardens, Requiem, Lampoons, and
News of the Devil, by Humbert Wolfe.

F105 "The Apron-Strings of Vice." New Republic LIII
(February 8, 1928): 328.
The Letters of Baudelaire, translated by
Arthur Symons.

F106 "The Wild Body." New Republic LIV (April 11,
1928): 253.
The Wild Body, by Wyndham Lewis.

F107 "Style and Fashion." New Republic LIV (April
18, 1928): 278.
Alger: A Biography without a Hero, by Herbert
R. Mayes, and Buccaneers of the Pacific, by
George Wycherley.

F108 "Babbilogues." New Republic LIV (April 25,
1928): 302.
The Man Who Knew Coolidge, by Sinclair Lewis.

F109 "Junketing for Science." New Republic LIV (May
16, 1928): 393-94.
Pheasant Jungles and The Arcturus Adventure,
by William Beebe.

F110 "The Peasants of New York." New Republic LV

(June 6, 1928): 74-75.

Tammany Hall, by M.R. Werner, and The Gangs
of New York, by Herbert Asbury.

F111 "Alastor." Dial LXXXIV (June 1928): 475-78.

Shelley: His Life and Work, by Walter Edwin
Peck.

F112 "The Caged Osprey." New Republic LV (July 4,
1928): 179.

The Closed Garden, by Julien Green, translated by Henry Longan Stuart.

F113 "Dynamic Liberalism." New Republic LV (July 11,
1928): 204.

The Inquiring Mind, by Zechariah Chafee, Jr.

F114 "Grosse Margot's Lover." New York Herald Tribune
Books, July 15, 1928, p. 3.

The Complete Works of François Villon, translated with an introduction by J.U. Nicolson.

F115 "The Chaos of English Grammar." New Republic LV
(July 18, 1928): 232.

Crowell's Dictionary of English Grammar and
Handbook of American Usage, by Maurice H.
Weseen.

F116 "A Talented Subaltern." New York Herald Tribune
Books, August 26, 1928, p. 4.

The Pure in Heart, by Joseph Kessel.

F117 "That Excellent Blackguard." New York Herald
Tribune Books, September 9, 1928, p. 3.

François Villon, by D.B. Wyndham Lewis.

F118 "Biography and Legend." New Republic LVI (September 19, 1928): 132.

La Fayette, by Henry Dwight Sedgwick, and
La Fayette, by Joseph Delteil, translated by
Jacques Le Clercq.

F119 "'I Am the Prison'." New Republic LVI (October
3, 1928): 183.

Condemned to Devils Island: The Biography of
an Unknown Convict, by Blair Niles.

F120 "Backstairs." New York Herald Tribune Books,
October 7, 1928, p. 4.

Theresa: The Chronicle of a Woman's Life, by
Arthur Schnitzler, translated by William A.
Drake.

F121 "A Messiah of the Skeptics." New York Herald
Tribune Books, October 21, 1928, p. 7.

Remy de Gourmont: Selections from All His
Works, chosen and translated by Richard
Aldington.

F122 "Gongorism." New Republic LVI (October 24, 1928)
281.

Gongorism and the Golden Age, by Elisha K.
Kane.

F123 "The Haunted Castle." New Republic LVI (October
31, 1928): 300-1.

The Haunted Castle, by Eino Railo.

F124 "As If Written by Starlight." New York Herald
Tribune Books, December 2, 1928, p. 4.

The Wanderer, by Alain-Fournier, translated
by Françoise Delisle.

F125 "Patriot and Expatriate." New York Herald
Tribune Books, December 30, 1928, pp. 1, 4.

The Diary of Dostoyevsky's Wife, edited by
René Fülöp-Miller and Friedrich Eckstein,
translated by Madge Pemberton.

1929

F126 "The Voyager of Dreams." New York Herald Tribune Books, February 10, 1929, p. 3.

Charles Baudelaire, by François Porché.

F127 "Hearts of Whipped Cream." New York Herald
Tribune Books, May 26, 1929, p. 3.

Molinoff; or, the Count in the Kitchen, by
Maurice Bedel, translated by Lawrence S.
Morris.

F128 "The Curse of Beauty." New York Herald Tribune
Books, June 16, 1929, p. 4.

Destinies, by François Mauriac, translated by
Eric Sutton.

F129 "The Men of the Road." New York Herald Tribune
Books, July 7, 1929, p. 4.

The Road, by André Chamson, translated by
Van Wyck Brooks.

F130 "Lycidas and Thanatopsis." New Republic LIX
(August 14, 1929): 346.

The Winged Horse Anthology, edited by Joseph
Auslander and Frank Ernest Hill.

F131 "A Theologian of Letters." New York Herald
Tribune Books, September 1, 1929, p. 5.

Style and Form in American Prose, by Gorham
B. Munson.

F132 "Not Yet Demobilized." New York Herald Tribune
Books, October 6, 1929, pp. 1, 6.

A Farewell to Arms, by Ernest Hemingway.
This was the first of a series of four
leading essay-reviews commissioned by Irita
Van Doren for her book section. The others
were F134, F136, and G62.

F133 "Albumblatt." New York Herald Tribune Books,
October 20, 1929, pp. 5-6.

The School for Wives, by André Gide, translated by Dorothy Bussy.

F134 "Machine-Made America." New York Herald Tribune
Books, November 3, 1929, pp. 1, 6.

Our Business Civilization, by James Truslow
Adams; This Ugly Civilization, by Ralph
Borsodi; and Dance of the Machines, by
Edward J. O'Brien.

F135 "Hard-Boiled and Romantic." New Republic LX
(November 6, 1929): 326-27.

The New American Caravan, edited by Alfred
Kreymborg, Lewis Mumford, and Paul Rosenfeld.

F136 "The Business of Being a Poet." New York
Herald Tribune Books, November 17, 1929, pp. 1,
6.

Our Singing Strength: An Outline of American
Poetry, 1620-1930, by Alfred Kreymborg.

1930

F137 "The Sex Boys in a Balloon." New Republic LXI
(January 15, 1930): 227-28.

Our Changing Human Nature, by Samuel D.
Schmalhausen; The Riddle of Sex, by Joseph
Tenenbaum; and Critique of Love, by Fritz
Wittels.

F138 "Ford or Lenin." New York Herald Tribune Books
February 9, 1930, p. 7.

The Two Frontiers, by John Gould Fletcher.

F139 "Not Stendhal." New York Herald Tribune Books,
April 6, 1930, p. 17.

Stendhal; or, the Life of an Egotist, by
Rudolf Kayser, translated by Geoffrey Dunlop

F140 "The Victim of a Mask." New York Herald Tribun
Books, April 13, 1930, p. 8.

Baudelaire, by Lewis Piaget Shanks.

F141 "A Preface to Hart Crane." New Republic LXII
(April 23, 1930): 276-77.

The Bridge: A Poem, by Hart Crane.
Collected in Think Back on Us, pp. 199-202
(see A10).

F142 "Happiness Made Easy." New Republic LXII (April
30, 1930): 304-5.

Love in the Machine Age, by Floyd Dell.

F143 "A Pedagogue's Love Affair." New York Herald
Tribune Books, June 8, 1930, pp. 3-4.

Philine. Selections from the Unpublished
Journals of Henri-Frédéric Amiel, translated
by Van Wyck Brooks.

1931

F144 "Resurrection of a Poet." New York Herald
Tribune Books, March 8, 1931, pp. 1, 6.

Poems of Gerard Manley Hopkins, edited by
Robert Bridges; A Vision of the Mermaids, by
Gerard Manley Hopkins; and Gerard Manley
Hopkins, by G.F. Lahey.

F145 "The Real Tragedy of the Farmer." New York
Herald Tribune Books, April 12, 1931, p. 5.

Jonathan Gentry, by Mark Van Doren.

F146 "Two Judgments of American Earth." New Republic
LXVII (June 17, 1931): 130-32.

American Earth, by Erskine Caldwell.
Cowley's part of this double review is on
pp. 131-32.

F147 "'Nigger Fever'." New Republic LXIX (December
9, 1931): 107-8.

Slave Trading in the Old South, by Frederic

Bancroft.

1932

F148 "Local Color." New Republic LXIX (January 13,
    1932): 248.

    A Buried Treasure, by Elizabeth Madox Roberts.

F149 "The Last of Lyric Poets." New Republic LXIX
    (January 27, 1932): 299-300.

    VV (Viva), by E.E. Cummings.

    Collected in Think Back on Us, pp. 203-8 (see
    A10).

F150 "Unwilling Novelist." New Republic LXX (February
    17, 1932): 23-24.

    Towards a Better Life, by Kenneth Burke.

    Collected as "Kenneth Burke: Unwilling
    Novelist" in Think Back on Us, pp. 208-11
    (see A10).

F151 "The Poet and the World." New Republic LXX
    (April 27, 1932): 303-5.

    1919, by John Dos Passos.

    Reprinted with G112 in Literary Opinion in
    America, edited by Morton Dauwen Zabel (New
    York: Harper, 1937), pp. 495-505.

    Collected in Think Back on Us, pp. 212-19
    (see A10).

    Rewritten with G112 as "Dos Passos: Poet a-
    gainst the World" in After the Genteel
    Tradition, pp. 168-85 (see A4).

F152 "Sermon against War." New Republic LXX (May 4,
    1932): 333.

    The Horror of It: Camera Records of War's
    Gruesome Glories, arranged by Frederick A.
    Barber.

Collected in Think Back on Us, pp. 18-21 (see
A10).

F153 "The Enchanted Castle." New Republic LXXI (July
27, 1932): 293.

The Fountain, by Charles Morgan.

F154 "Decline and Fall." New Republic LXXIII
(November 16, 1932): 22-23.

Decline and Fall, Vile Bodies, They Were
Still Dancing, and Black Mischief, by
Evelyn Waugh.

F155 "A Farewell to Spain." New Republic LXXIII
(November 30, 1932): 76-77.

Death in the Afternoon, by Ernest Hemingway.
Reprinted as "Ernest Hemingway: A Farewell
to Spain" in Literary Opinion in America,
edited by Morton Dauwen Zabel (New York:
Harper, 1937), pp. 506-11.
Collected as "Hemingway: A Farewell to Spain"
in Think Back on Us, pp. 219-25 (see A10).

F156 "Nobel Prizeman." New Republic LXXIII (December
14, 1932): 133-34.

Flowering Wilderness, by John Galsworthy.

1933

F157 "The Sea Jacobins." New Republic LXXIII
(February 1, 1933): 327-29.

The History of Piracy, by Philip Gosse.

F158 "Tired Feminist." New Republic LXXIV (February
15, 1933): 22-23.

Ann Vickers, By Sinclair Lewis.

F159 "World's End Tomorrow." New Republic LXXIV
(March 15, 1933): 138-39.

When Worlds Collide, by Edwin Balmer and

Philip Wylie.

F160 "The Art of Insurrection." New Republic LXXIV
(April 12, 1933): 248-50.

The History of the Russian Revolution, by
Leon Trotsky, translated by Max Eastman.
Collected as "Trotsky and the Art of Insur-
rection" in Think Back on Us, pp. 27-35 (see
A10).

F161 "A Primer of Fascism." New Republic LXXVI
(November 1, 1933): 339-40.

The Menace of Fascism, by John Strachey.

F162 "To a Revolutionary Critic." New Republic LXXVI
(November 8, 1933): 368-69.

The Great Tradition, by Granville Hicks.
Collected in Think Back on Us, pp. 47-51 (see
A10).

F163 "No Prophet." New Republic LXXVII (November 15,
1933): 22-23.

The Intelligent Man's Review of Europe Today,
by G.D.H. Cole and Margaret Cole.

F164 "Homesteads, Inc." New Republic LXXVII (November
29, 1933): 77-78.

Flight from the City, by Ralph Borsodi.
Collected in Think Back on Us, pp. 51-55 (see
A10).

F165 "Panorama." New Republic LXXVII (December 20,
1933): 172-73.

Radetzky March, by Joseph Roth, translated by
Geoffrey Dunlop; The Kaiser Goes, the General
Remain, by Theodor Plivier, translated by
A.W. Wheen; Karl and the Twentieth Century,
by Rudolf Brunngraber, translated by Eden and
Cedar Paul; and Time, Forward! by Valentine

Kataev, translated by Charles Malamuth.

1934

F166 "Figures in a Crowd." New Republic LXXVII
(February 7, 1934): 369-70.
Yesterday's Burdens, by Robert M. Coates.

F167 "Breakdown." New Republic LXXIX (June 6, 1934):
105-6.
Tender Is the Night, by F. Scott Fitzgerald.
Collected as "Fitzgerald's Goodbye to His
Generation" in Think Back on Us, pp. 225-28
(see A10); reprinted as "Tender Is the Night:
Breakdown" in F. Scott Fitzgerald in His Own
Time, edited by Matthew J. Bruccoli and
Jackson R. Bryer (Kent, Ohio: Kent State
University Press, 1971), pp. 387-90.

F168 "Holocaust." New Republic LXXIX (June 13, 1934):
132-33.
A Chinese Testament: The Autobiography of
Tan Shih-hua as told to Sergei Tretiakov.
Collected as "A Russo-Chinese Documentary" in
Think Back on Us, pp. 63-66 (see A10).

F169 "Primitive Peoples." New Republic LXXIX (June
20, 1934): 160-61.
Rebel Destiny, by Melville J. and Frances
Herskovits, and Beyond the Mexique Bay, by
Aldous Huxley.

F170 "Man's Solitude." New Republic LXXIX (July 4,
1934): 214-15.
Man's Fate, by André Malraux, translated by
Haakon M. Chevalier.
Collected as "Malraux on Man's Solitude" in
Think Back on Us, pp. 228-32 (see A10).

F171 "The Problems of André Gide." <u>New York Herald</u>
<u>Tribune Books</u>, July 22, 1934, p. 4.
 <u>André Gide: His Life and His Work</u>, by Leon
Pierre-Quint, translated by Dorothy M.
Richardson.

F172 "Benefit Show." <u>New Republic</u> LXXIX (August 8,
1934): 350-51. <u>Modern American Prose</u>, edited by
Carl Van Doren.

F173 "Midsummer Medley." <u>New Republic</u> LXXX (August 15
1934): 24-25.
 <u>Becoming a Writer</u>, by Dorothea Brande, and
<u>Dynamite</u>, by Louis Adamic. (Includes notes on
the demise of <u>Hound & Horn</u>.)

F174 "Good Reading." <u>New York Herald Tribune</u>, August
17, 1934, p. 11.
 A list with brief comments of six books MC
had reread: <u>The Enormous Room</u>, by E.E.
Cummings; <u>The Time of Man</u>, by Elizabeth Madox
Roberts; <u>The Great Gatsby</u>, by F. Scott Fitzgerald; <u>The Sun Also Rises</u>, by Ernest Hemingway; <u>Zola and His Time</u>, by Matthew Josephson;
and <u>Axel's Castle</u>, by Edmund Wilson.

F175 "Angry Author's Complaint." <u>New Republic</u> LXXX
(August 22, 1934): 51-52.
 <u>East and West: The Collected Short Stories of</u>
<u>W. Somerset Maugham</u>.

F176 "Eagle Orator." <u>New Republic</u> LXXX (August 29,
1934): 79-80.
 <u>American Song: A Book of Poems</u>, by Paul
Engle.
 Reprinted in <u>Proletarian Literature in the</u>
<u>United States</u>, edited by Granville Hicks and
others (New York: International Publishers,

1935), pp. 346-49.

Collected in Think Back on Us, pp. 66-70 (see
A10).

F177 "Malthus Was Wrong." New Republic LXXX (September 5, 1934): 107-8.

The Twilight of Parenthood, by Enid Charles.

F178 "A Handbook for Demagogues." New Republic LXXX
(September 12, 1934): 134-35.

An Introduction to Pareto, His Sociology, by
George C. Homans and Charles P. Curtis, Jr.

F179 "The Golden Legend of Li Ning." New Republic
LXXX (September 19, 1934): 163.

China's Red Army Marches, by Agnes Smedley.

F180 "Spender and Auden." New Republic LXXX (September 26, 1934): 189-90.

Poems, by Stephen Spender, and Poems, by
W.H. Auden.

Collected in Think Back on Us, pp. 232-36
(see A10).

F181 "Travels with a Mirror." New Republic LXXX
(October 3, 1934): 219-20.

One's Company: A Journey to China, by Peter
Fleming.

F182 "Donkey Town." New Republic LXXX (October 10,
1934): 247-48.

Fontamara, by Ignazio Silone, translated by
Michael Wharf.

Collected as "Silone's Villagers" in Think
Back on Us, pp. 237-40 (see A10).

F183 "Pilgrim's Progress." New Republic LXXX (October
17, 1934): 279-80.

The Death and Birth of David Markand, by Waldo
Frank.

F184 "Man with a Hoe." New Republic LXXX (October
     31, 1934): 342-43.
          Man with a Bull Tongue Plow, by Jesse Stuart.
          Collected as "Jesse Stuart: Man with a Hoe"
          in Think Back on Us, pp. 240-42 (see A10).
F185 "The Man Who Would Be King." New Republic LXXX
     (November 7, 1934): 370-71.
          The Proud and the Meek (Men of Good Will,
          Vol. III), by Jules Romains, translated by
          W.B. Wells.
F186 "Outline of Wells' History." New Republic LXXXI
     (November 14, 1934): 22-23.
          Experiment in Autiobiography, by H.G. Wells.
          Collected in Think Back on Us, pp. 244-47
          (see A10).
F187 "Schlaraffenland." New Republic LXXXI (November
     28, 1934): 80.
          February Hill, By Victoria Lincoln.
F188 "Valuta Girl." New Republic LXXXI (December 5,
     1934): 107-8.
          Prelude to the Past: The Autobiography of a
          Woman, by R.G. (Rosie Goldschmidt).
          Collected in Think Back on Us, pp. 74-77 (see
          A10).
F189 "Marcel Proust's Unfinished Symphony." New
     Republic LXXXI (December 12, 1934): 134-40.
          Remembrance of Things Past, by Marcel Proust,
          translated by C.K. Scott Moncrieff and
          Frederick A. Blossom.
F190 "Books in Brief." New Republic LXXXI (December
     26, 1934): 200.
          The Concise Oxford French Dictionary, compile
          by Abel and Marguerite Chevalley.

1935

F191 "Literature and Politics." New Republic LXXXI
    (January 2, 1935): 224.
        Literature and Dialectical Materialism, by
        John Strachey.
        Collected in Think Back on Us, pp. 78-80 (see
        A10).

F192 "Europe Was a Success." New Republic LXXXI
    (January 9, 1935): 253-54.
        Was Europe a Success? by Joseph Wood Krutch.

F193 "The Smart Set Legend." New Republic LXXXI
    (January 16, 1935): 281.
        The Smart Set Anthology, edited by Burton
        Rascoe and Groff Conklin.
        Collected in Think Back on Us, pp. 248-50
        (see A10).

F194 "The Good Earthling." New Republic LXXXI
    (January 23, 1935): 309-10.
        A House Divided, by Pearl Buck.
        Collected in Think Back on Us, pp. 251-54
        (see A10).

F195 "The March on Berlin." New Republic LXXXI
    (February 6, 1935): 364.
        A History of National Socialism, by Konrad
        Heiden.

F196 "The Long View." New Republic LXXXII (February
    20, 1935): 50-51.
        Personal History, by Vincent Sheean.

F197 "A Hope for Poetry." New Republic LXXXII
    (February 27, 1935): 79.
        Vienna, by Stephen Spender, and Poems, by
        C. Day Lewis.
        Collected in Think Back on Us, pp. 258-61

(see A10).

F198 "The Forty Days of Thomas Wolfe." New Republic
     LXXXII (March 20, 1935): 163-64.
     Of Time and the River, by Thomas Wolfe.
     Collected in Think Back on Us, pp. 261-64
     (see A10).

F199 "Men and Ghosts." New Republic LXXXII (March
     27, 1935): 190-91.
     Panic: A Play in Verse, by Archibald MacLeish
     Collected as "MacLeish's Poetic Drama" in
     Think Back on Us, pp. 264-68 (see A10).

F200 "Everyday Life in Hell." New Republic LXXXII
     (April 3, 1935): 218.
     Fatherland, by Karl Billinger (pseud. of Paul
     W. Massing).

F201 "Voodoo Dance." New Republic LXXXII (April 10,
     1935): 254-55.
     Pylon, by William Faulkner.
     Collected as "Faulkner: Voodoo Dance" in
     Think Back on Us, pp. 263-71 (see A10).

F202 "Wells in the Kremlin." New Republic LXXXII
     (April 24, 1935): 317.
     Marxism vs. Liberalism: An Interview between
     Joseph Stalin and H.G. Wells.
     Collected as "H.G. Wells in the Kremlin" in
     Think Back on Us, pp. 84-86 (see A10).

F203 "Fellow Traveler." New Republic LXXXII (May 1,
     1935): 345-46.
     I Change Worlds: The Remaking of an American,
     by Anna Louise Strong.

F204 "Muddletown." New Republic LXXXIII (May 15,
     1935): 23.
     Greenwich Village 1920-1930: A Comment on

American Civilization in the Post-War Years,
by Caroline F. Ware.

F205 "News from New Guinea." New Republic LXXXIII
(June 5, 1935): 107.

Sex and Temperament in Three Primitive
Societies, by Margaret Mead.
Collected in Think Back on Us, pp. 94-97 (see
A10).

F206 "Not without Bias." New Republic LXXXIII (June
12, 1935): 142.

The Russian Revolution, 1917-1921, by William
Henry Chamberlin.

F207 "Bread and Butter Letter." New Republic LXXXIV
(August 14, 1935): 23-24.

The Intelligentsia of Great Britain, by
Dmitri Mirsky, translated by Alec Brown.

F208 "Hell under England." New Republic LXXXIV
(August 21, 1935): 51.

Land under England, by Joseph O'Neill.

F209 "Oregon Trail." New Republic LXXXIV (September
4, 1935): 107-8.

Honey in the Horn, by H.L. Davis.

F210 "Class Enemy." New Republic LXXXIV (September
11, 1935): 134.

Prisoner of the Ogpu, by George Kitchin.

F211 "The Last Days of Pompeii." New Republic LXXXIV
(September 25, 1935): 191.

Europa: The Days of Ignorance, by Robert
Briffault.

F212 "Men of Good Intentions." New Republic LXXXIV
(October 2, 1935): 219-20.

The World from Below (Men of Good Will, Vol.
IV), by Jules Romains, translated by Gerard

Hopkins.

F213 "The Road to Damascus." New Republic LXXXIV
(October 9, 1935): 248-49.

Seven Pillars of Wisdom, by T.E. Lawrence.

F214 "Hemingway Mixed with Hearst." New Republic
LXXXV (December 4, 1935): 108-9.

Butterfield 8, by John O'Hara.

F215 "Rain in the Cumberlands." New Republic LXXXV
(December 11, 1935): 148.

Fish on the Steeple, by Ed Bell.

F216 "Two Items for Reference." New Republic LXXXV
(December 25, 1935): 203.

The Columbia Encyclopedia, edited by Charles
F. Ansley, and a series of five articles in
the Nation, "Our Critics, Right or Wrong,"
by Margaret Marshall and Mary McCarthy.

1936

F217 "Poem for Amy Lowell." New Republic LXXXV
(January 8, 1936): 258-59.

Amy Lowell: A Chronicle, by S. Foster Damon.
Collected in Think Back on Us, pp. 278-82
(see A10).

F218 "Monsieur de Montherlant." New Republic LXXXV
(January 22, 1936): 315.

Perish in Their Pride, by Henry de Montherlant, translated by Thomas McGreevy.

F219 "It Could Happen There." New Republic LXXXV
(January 29, 1936): 343.

In the Second Year, by Storm Jameson.

F220 "The Personal Element." New Republic LXXXVI
(February 12, 1936): 22-23.

Inside Europe, by John Gunther.

F221 "Footnotes to a Life of Marx." New Republic
LXXXVI (February 26, 1936): 79-80.
Karl Marx: The Story of His Life, by Franz
Mehring, translated by Edward Fitzgerald.
Collected in Think Back on Us, pp. 104-9 (see
A10).

F222 "Homage to Ancestors." New Republic LXXXVI
(March 4, 1936): 114.
The Destructive Element: A Study of Modern
Writers and Beliefs, by Stephen Spender.

F223 "Million Dollar Baby." New Republic LXXXVI
(March 11, 1936): 142.
The Thinking Reed, by Rebecca West.

F224 "The Making of an Englishman." New Republic
LXXXVI (March 18, 1936): 170.
Antony: A Record of Youth, by the Earl of
Lytton.

F225 "Public Speakers." New Republic LXXXVI (April 1,
1936): 226.
Break the Heart's Anger, by Paul Engle, and
Public Speech, by Archibald MacLeish.

F226 "Comrade Trotsky." New Republic LXXXVI (April
8, 1936): 254.
My Life, by Leon Trotsky.
Collected in Think Back on Us, pp. 109-12
(see A10).

F227 "Baudelaire as Revolutionist." New Republic
LXXXVI (April 15, 1936): 287-88.
Flowers of Evil, by Charles Baudelaire,
translated by George Dillon and Edna St.
Vincent Millay.
Collected in Think Back on Us, pp. 283-87
(see A10).

F228 "The Making of a Writer." New Republic LXXXVI
      (April 22, 1936): 319.

      John Reed: The Making of a Revolutionary, by
      Granville Hicks.
      Collected as "Hicks's Life of John Reed" in
      Think Back on Us, pp. 112-15 (see A10).

F229 "A Game of Chess." New Republic LXXXVI (April
      29, 1936): 348-49.

      Reactionary Essays on Poetry and Ideas, by
      Allen Tate.

F230 "Two Books about the Negro." New Republic
      LXXXVII (May 13, 1936): 22.

      Alien Americans: A Study of Race Relations,
      by B. Schrieke, and The Negro Question in
      the United States, by James S. Allen.

F231 "Afterthoughts on T.S. Eliot." New Republic
      LXXXVII (May 20, 1936): 49.

      Collected Poems 1909-35, by T.S. Eliot.
      Collected in Think Back on Us, pp. 288-90
      (see A10).

F232 "Flight from the Masses." New Republic LXXXVII
      (June 3, 1936): 106, 108.

      Travels in Two Democracies, by Edmund Wilson.
      Collected with F233 as "Edmund Wilson in
      Russia" in Think Back on Us, pp. 115-22 (see
      A10).

F233 "Postscript to a Paragraph." New Republic
      LXXXVII (June 10, 1936): 134-35.

      Travels in Two Democracies, by Edmund Wilson.
      Collected with F232 as "Edmund Wilson in
      Russia" in Think Back on Us, pp. 115-22 (see
      A10).

F234 "The Rebirth of Tragedy." New Republic LXXXVII

(June 17, 1936): 181-82.

Days of Wrath, by André Malraux, translated
by Haakon M. Chevalier.

F235 "The Last Great European." New Republic LXXXVII
(June 24, 1936): 213-14.

Stories of Three Decades, by Thomas Mann,
translated by H.T. Lowe-Porter.
Collected as "The Last Great European:
Thomas Mann" in Think Back on Us, pp. 291-94
(see A10).

F236 "The End of a Trilogy." New Republic LXXXVIII
(August 12, 1936): 23-24.

The Big Money, by John Dos Passos.

F237 "The Puritan Legacy." New Republic LXXXVIII
(August 26, 1936): 79-80.

The Flowering of New England, 1815-1865, by
Van Wyck Brooks.
Collected as "Van Wyck Brooks and the New
England Legacy" in Think Back on Us, pp. 294-
98 (see A10).

F238 "Spain in Revolt." New Republic LXXXVIII
(September 2, 1936): 107.

The Olive Field, by Ralph Bates.

F239 "The Waste Land." New Republic LXXXVIII
(September 23, 1936): 187.

Rich Land, Poor Land, by Stuart Chase.

F240 "Louis Aragon." New Republic LXXXVIII (October
7, 1936): 258.

The Bells of Basel, by Louis Aragon, transla-
ted by Haakon M. Chevalier.
Collected in Think Back on Us, pp. 301-4 (see
A10).

F241 "Unfinished Symphony." New Republic LXXXVIII

(October 28, 1936): 356.

An American Testament: A Narrative of Rebels
and Romantics, by Joseph Freeman.

F242 "Poe in Mississippi." New Republic LXXXIX
(November 4, 1936): 22.

Absalom, Absalom! by William Faulkner.

F243 "Portrait of the Artist." New Republic LXXXIX
(November 18, 1936): 79-80.

A World I Never Made, by James T. Farrell.
Collected as "A Portrait of James T. Farrell
as a Young Man" in Think Back on Us, pp. 304-
7 (see A10).

F244 "Fable for Russian Children." New Republic
LXXXIX (November 25, 1936): 120, 122.

Movers and Shakers, by Mabel Dodge Luhan.
Collected in Think Back on Us, pp. 123-26
(see A10).

F245 "A Poet's Anthology." New Republic LXXXIX
(December 16, 1936): 221-22.

The Oxford Book of Modern Verse, chosen by
W.B. Yeats.
Collected as "Yeats as Anthologist" in
Think Back on Us, pp. 307-10 (see A10).

F246 "Hymn of Hate." New Republic LXXXIX (December
23, 1936): 249-50.

Interregnum: Drawings by George Grosz, with
an introductory comment by John Dos Passos.

F247 "Marx and Plekhanov." New Republic LXXXIX
(December 30, 1936): 277-78.

Sur la litterature et l'art: Karl Marx,
Friedrich Engels, edited by Jean Fréville,
and Art and Society, by George V. Plekhanov,
translated by Paul S. Leitner, Alfred

Goldstein, and C.H. Crout.
Collected with F248 in Think Back on Us,
pp. 130-35 (see A10).

1937
F248 "Marx and Plekhanov: II." New Republic LXXXIX
(January 6, 1937): 306.
Art and Society, by George V. Plekhanov,
translated by Paul S. Leitner, Alfred Gold-
stein, and C.H. Crout.
Collected with F247 in Think Back on Us,
pp. 130-35 (see A10).
F249 "The Boys." New Republic XC (March 10, 1937):
142-43.
Army without Banners: Adventures of an Irish
Volunteer, by Ernie O'Malley.
F250 "Retreat from Moscow." New Republic XC (March
17, 1937): 172-73.
Retour de l'U.R.S.S., by André Gide.
Collected as "André Gide's Retreat from
Moscow" in Think Back on Us, pp. 135-39
(see A10).
F251 "The Record of a Trial." New Republic XC
(April 7, 1937): 267-70.
The Case of the Anti-Soviet Trotskyite Center:
A Verbatim Report Published by the People's
Commissariat of Justice of the USSR.
F252 "Still Middletown?" New Republic XCI (May 12,
1937): 23-24.
Middletown in Transition: A Study in Cultural
Conflicts, by Robert S. Lynd and Helen Merrell
Lynd.
Collected in Think Back on Us, pp. 139-44

(see A10).

F253 "Freud in Fiction." New Republic XCI (May 19,
1937): 51.

The Outward Room, by Millen Brand, and
Trumpet of Jubilee, by Ludwig Lewisohn

F254 "Muse at the Microphone." New Republic XCI
(May 26, 1937): 78.

The Fall of the City, by Archibald MacLeish.

F255 "Perspectives." New Republic XCI (June 2, 1937)
106.

Progress and Catastrophe, by Stanley Casson.

F256 "The Roaring Boy." New Republic XCI (June 9,
1937): 134.

Hart Crane: The Life of an American Poet, by
Philip Horton.

F257 "Hemingway: Work in Progress." New Republic
XCII (October 20, 1937): 305-6.

To Have and Have Not, by Ernest Hemingway.
Collected in Think Back on Us. pp. 310-14
(see A10).

F258 "Benton of Missouri." New Republic XCII
(November 3, 1937): 375.

An Artist in America, by Thomas Hart Benton.

F259 "Pictures Tell the Story." New Republic XCIII
(November 10, 1937): 23.

The United States: A Graphic History, text by
Louis M. Hacker; pictorial statistics by
Rudolf Modley and George R. Taylor.

F260 "Fall Catalogue." New Republic XCIII (November
24, 1937): 78-79.

You Have Seen Their Faces, by Erskine Caldwel
and Margaret Bourke-White.

F261 "Nobel Prize Novel." New Republic XCIII (December 29, 1937): 232-33.

L'Eté 1914, by Roger Martin du Gard.

1938

F262 "Red China." New Republic XCIII (January 12,
1938): 287-88.

Red Star over China, by Edgar Snow.

F263 "Mr. Huxley's New Jerusalem." New Republic XCIII
(January 19, 1938): 315-16.

Ends and Means, by Aldous Huxley.

F264 "George F. Babbitt's Revenge." New Republic
XCIII (January 26, 1938): 342-43.

The Prodigal Parents, by Sinclair Lewis.

F265 "Reviewers on Parade." New Republic XCIII
(February 2, 1938): 371-72.

A review of the reviewers of U.S.A., by
John Dos Passos.

F266 "Reviewers on Parade: II:" New Republic XCIV
(February 9, 1938): 23-24.

More about the incompetent reviews of U.S.A.,
by John Dos Passos.

F267 "Abyssinia and Spain." New Republic XCIV
(February 16, 1938): 50-51.

Arthur Rimbaud in Abyssinia, by Enid Starkie,
and Two Wars and More To Come, by Herbert L.
Matthews.

F268 "Apocalypse." New Republic XCIV (March 2,
1938): 106-7.

L'Espoir, by André Malraux.

F269 "Civil War Movie." New Republic XCIV (March 9,
1938): 138-40.

Action at Aquila, by Hervey Allen.

F270 "The Golden Legend." New Republic XCIV (March

16, 1938): 170-71.

Joseph in Egypt, by Thomas Mann.
Collected with F271 as "Thomas Mann's Joseph
Legend" in Think Back on Us, pp. 314-20 (see
A10).

F271 "Second Thoughts on 'Joseph'." New Republic
XCIV (March 23, 1938): 198-99.

Joseph in Egypt, by Thomas Mann.
Collected with F270 as "Thomas Mann's Joseph
Legend" in Think Back on Us, pp. 314-20 (see
A10).

F272 "The Ascent of Man." New Republic XCIV (May 4,
1938): 401-2.

The Conquest of Civilization, by James Henry
Breasted.

F273 "The Maugham Enigma." New Republic XCIV (March
30, 1938): 227-28.

The Summing Up, by W. Somerset Maugham.
Collected in Think Back on Us, pp. 321-24
(see A10).

F274 "Long Black Song." New Republic XCIV (April 6,
1938): 280.

Uncle Tom's Children, by Richard Wright.

F275 "The Arts in Russia." New Republic XCIV
(April 13, 1938): 309-10.

The Seven Soviet Arts, by Kurt London.

F276 "Heavenly City." New Republic XCIV (April 20,
1938): 337-38.

The Culture of Cities, by Lewis Mumford.

F277 "Moscow Trial: 1938." New Republic XCV (May
18, 1938): 50-51.

The Case of the Anti-Soviet Bloc of Rights
and Trotskyites. A Verbatim Report Published

by the People's Commissariat of Justice of
the USSR.
An article on the subject appeared the following week (see G126).

F278 "Eastern Front: 1918." New Republic XCV (June
1, 1938): 106.

The Crowning of a King, by Arnold Zweig,
translated by Eric Sutton.

F279 "Adamic Omnibus." New Republic XCV (June 8,
1938): 135.

My America, by Louis Adamic.

F280 "Poetry Tomorrow." New Republic XCV (August 3,
1938): 368-69.

A New Anthology of Modern Poetry, edited by
Selden Rodman.

F281 "Fable in Slang." New Republic XCVI (August 10,
1938): 25-26.

The World is Mine, by William Blake.

F282 "Dickens and the Revolution." New Republic XCVI
(August 24, 1938): 81.

Charles Dickens: The Progress of a Radical,
by T.A. Jackson.

F283 "Poet in Politics." New Republic XCVI (September 21, 138): 191-92.

The Autobiography of William Butler Yeats.
Collected as "Yeats and the 'Baptism of the
Gutter'" in Think Back on Us, pp. 324-28 (see
A10).

F284 "Tribute to Ben Franklin." New Republic XCVI
(October 26, 1938): 338-39.

Benjamin Franklin, by Carl Van Doren.
Reprinted in Essay Annual, 1939, edited by
Erich Albert Walter (New York: Scott,

Foresman and Company, 1939), pp. 158-61.
Collected in Think Back on Us, pp. 333-36
(see A10).

F285 "Hemingway in Madrid." New Republic XCVI
(November 2, 1938): 367-68.

The Fifth Column and the First Forty-Nine
Stories, by Ernest Hemingway.

F286 "The Real World." New Republic XCVII (November
23, 1938): 78.

Residential Quarter, by Louis Aragon, translated by Haakon M. Chevalier.

F287 "Tract for Our Times." New Republic XCVII
(November 30, 1938): 105-6.

It Is Later Than You Think: The Need for a
Militant Democracy, by Max Lerner.

F288 "Lord of These Elements." New Republic XCVII
(December 28, 1938): 235-36.

The Notebooks of Leonardo da Vinci, edited
and translated with an introduction by
Edward MacCurdy.

1939

F289 "The Dream of the Great Bird." New Republic
XCVII (January 4, 1939): 263-64.

Leonardo da Vinci: The Tragic Pursuit of
Perfection, by Antonina Vallentin, translated by E.W. Dickes.

F290 "Sanctuary." New Republic XCVII (January 25,
1939): 349.

The Wild Palms, by William Faulkner.

F291 "Collective Novel." New Republic XCVIII
(February 22, 1939): 77.

Industrial Valley, by Ruth McKenney.

F292 "Dahomey." New Republic XCVIII (March 1, 1939):
      110-11.
      Dahomey: An Ancient West African Kingdom, by
      Melville J. Herskovits.
F293 "American Tragedy." New Republic XCVIII (May
      3, 1939): 382-83.
      The Grapes of Wrath, by John Steinbeck.
F294 "Wang Lung's Children." New Republic XCIX (May
      10, 1939): 24-25.
      The Patriot and House of Earth, by Pearl Buck.
F295 "Episodes in a Poet's Life." New Republic XCIX
      (June 7, 1939): 135-36.
      Huntsman, What Quarry? by Edna St. Vincent
      Millay.
F296 "Disillusionment." New Republic XCIX (June 14,
      1939): 163.
      Adventures of a Young Man, by John Dos Passos.
F297 "Thomas Wolfe's Legacy." New Republic XCIX
      (July 19, 1939): 311-12.
      The Web and the Rock, by Thomas Wolfe.
      Collected in Think Back on Us, pp. 342-47
      (see A10).
F298 "Lost Battalion." New Republic C (October 25,
      1939): 345-46.
      Men in Battle, by Alvah Bessie.
F299 "Essay in Ideas." New Republic CI (December 20,
      1939): 264.
      Ideas are Weapons: The History and Uses of
      Ideas, by Max Lerner.

1940
F300 "Krivitsky." New Republic CII (January 22,
      1940): 120-23.

In *Stalin's Secret Service*, by W.G. Krivitsky

F301 "The Eighth Volume." *New Republic* CII (January 29, 1940): 153-54.

Verdun (*Men of Good Will*, *Vol. VIII*), by Jules Romains, translated by Gerard Hopkins.

F302 "Swan into Swami." *New Republic* CII (February 12, 1940): 216-17.

After Many a Summer Dies the Swan, by Aldous Huxley.

F303 "Yesterbook." *New Republic* CII (March 4, 1940): 315-16.

Since Yesterday: The 1930's in America, by Frederick Lewis Allen.

F304 "The Case of Bigger Thomas." *New Republic* CII (March 18, 1940): 382-83.

Native Son, by Richard Wright.
Collected as "Richard Wright: The Case of Bigger Thomas" in *Think Back on Us*, pp. 355-57 (see A10).

F305 "Faulkner by Daylight." *New Republic* CII (April 15, 1940): 510.

The Hamlet, by William Faulkner.
Collected in *Think Back on Us*, pp. 358-60 (see A10).

F306 "The Other England." *New Republic* CII (April 29, 1940): 580-82.

Failure of a Mission: Berlin 1937-1939, by Sir Nevile Henderson.

F307 "Samson." *New Republic* CII (June 10, 1940): 797-98.

Chart for Rough Water: Our Role in a New World, by Waldo Frank.

F308 "Tract for the Times." *New Republic* CII (June

17, 1940): 829-30.

The Idea of a Christian Society, by T.S.
Eliot.

Collected as "Mr. Eliot's Tract for the
Times" in Think Back on Us, pp. 174-77 (see
A10).

F309 "In Memoriam." New Republic CIII (August 12,
1940): 219-20.

Fighting Words, by Donald Ogden Stewart, an
account of the Third American Writers'
Congress in June 1939.

F310 "New America's Primer." New Republic CIII
(August 19, 1940): 250-51.

North America: Its People and the Resources,
Development and Prospects of the Continent as
the Home of Man, by J. Russell Smith and M.
Ogden Phillips.

F311 "Shipwreck." New Republic CIII (September 9,
1940): 357-58.

Faith for Living, by Lewis Mumford.

F312 "From the Finland Station." New Republic CIII
(October 7, 1940): 478-80.

To the Finland Station: A Study in the Writing
and Acting of History, by Edmund Wilson.
Collected in Think Back on Us, pp. 178-84
(see A10).

1941

F313 "The People's Theatre." New Republic CIV
(January 13, 1941): 57-58.

Arena, by Hallie Flanagan, director of the
abolished Federal Theater Project.
Collected in Think Back on Us, pp. 184-88

(see A10).

F314 "Death of a Hero." New Republic CIV (January
20, 1941): 89-90.

For Whom the Bell Tolls, by Ernest Hemingway.
Collected as "Hemingway's 'Nevertheless'" in
Think Back on Us, pp. 361-64 (see A10).

F315 "Man of Good Will." New Republic CIV (January
27, 1941): 121-22.

Seven Mysteries of Europe, by Jules Romains,
translated by Germaine Brée.

F316 "Jeremiad." New Republic CIV (February 3, 1941)
153-54.

Night over Europe: The Diplomacy of Nemesis,
1939-1940, by Frederick L. Schuman.

F317 "1919." New Republic CIV (February 10, 1941):
187-88.

Aftermath (Men of Good Will, Vol. IX), by
Jules Romains, translated by Gerard Hopkins.

F318 "What New Directions?" New Republic CIV
(February 17, 1941): 218-20.

New Directions in Prose and Poetry, 1940,
edited by James Laughlin.

F319 "The Boston Story." New Republic CIV (March 3,
1941): 314-15.

H.M. Pulham, Esquire, by John P. Marquand.

F320 "The Next-to-Longest Novel." New Republic CIV
(March 10, 1941): 346-47.

The World of the Thibaults, by Roger Martin
du Gard, translated by Stuart Gilbert.
Collected as "Roger Martin du Gard: The Next-
to-Longest Novelist" in Think Back on Us,
pp. 364-68 (see A10).

F321 "The Reconquest of Europe." New Republic CIV

(March 24, 1941): 409-10.

War by Revolution, by Francis Williams.

F322 "Miss Glasgow's Purgatorio." New Republic CIV
(March 31, 1941): 441-42.

In This Our Life, by Ellen Glasgow.

F323 "Auden in America." New Republic CIV (April 7,
1941): 473-74.

The Double Man, by W.H. Auden.

F324 "Mr. Churchill Speaks." New Republic CIV
(April 21, 1941): 537-38.

Blood, Sweat and Tears, by Winston S.
Churchill.
Collected in Think Back on Us, pp. 368-71
(see A10).

F325 "Where the World Is Going." New Republic CIV
(April 28, 1941): 607-8.

The Managerial Revolution: What Is Happening
in the World, by James Burnham.

F326 "Impersonal History." New Republic CIV (May 12,
1941): 669-70.

Men and Politics: An Autobiography, by Louis
Fischer.

F327 "Marginalia." New Republic CIV (May 19, 1941):
701-2.

On Literature Today, by Van Wyck Brooks.
(Includes comments on Horizon and T.S. Eliot.)

F328 "No Defense." New Republic CIV (May 26, 1941): 732-34.

United We Stand! Defense of the Western
Hemisphere, by Hanson W. Baldwin.

F329 "Punishment and Crime." New Republic CIV (June
2, 1941): 766-67.

Darkness at Noon, by Arthur Koestler, translated by Daphne Hardy.

F330 "The Birth of a World." New Republic CIV (June
      16, 1941): 828-29.

      France, My Country, through the Disaster,
      by Jacques Maritain.

F331 "Finger Exercise." New Republic CIV (June 23,
      1941): 862.

      The Transposed Heads: A Legend of India, by
      Thomas Mann, translated by H.T. Lowe-Porter.

F332 "William L. Shirer Speaking." New Republic CIV
      (June 30, 1941): 893-94.

      Berlin Diary: The Journal of a Foreign Cor-
      respondent, by William L. Shirer.

F333 "The Longest Book Review." New Republic CV
      (July 14, 1941): 60-61.

      What Mein Kampf Means to America, by Francis
      Hackett.

F334 "The Michael Golden Legend." Decision II, no. 1
      (July 1941): 40-45.

      The Hollow Men, by Michael Gold.
      Collected in Think Back on Us, pp. 189-96
      (see A10).

F335 "Black Earth." New Republic CV (August 18,
      1941): 225-25.

      The Silent Don, by Mikhail Sholokhov, trans-
      lated by Stephen Garry.
      Collected in Think Back on Us, pp. 378-81
      (see A10).

F336 "The Unholy Alliance." New Republic CV (August
      25, 1941): 260.

      The Conservative Revolution, by Hermann
      Rauschning.

F337 "Sandburg's Ties, Speech, Forelocks, etc."
      PM, August 31, 1941, p. 45.

Carl Sandburg: A Study in Personality, by
Karl Detzer.

F338 "Ancestors." New Republic CV (September 1,
1941): 282-83.

The Ground We Stand On: Some Examples from
the History of a Political Creed, by John
Dos Passos.

F339 "The Triumphant Lie." New Republic CV
(September 8, 1941): 313-14.

My New Order: Speeches by Adolf Hitler,
edited with a commentary by Raoul de Roussy
de Sales.

F340 "Personal Histories." New Republic CV
(September 15, 1941): 345-46.

A Thousand Shall Fall, by Hans Habe, translated by Norbert Guterman.

F341 "Not All Our Poetry." New Republic CV
(September 22, 1941): 377-78.

The Viking Book of Poetry of the English-
Speaking World, edited by Richard Aldington.

F342 "Fadiman, the I.P. Man, Sums Up His Reading."
PM, September 28, 1941, p. 39.

Reading I've Liked, edited by Clifton
Fadiman.

F343 "Democrats All." New Republic CV (September 29,
1941): 409-10.

The Democratic Spirit: A Collection of
American Writings from the Earliest Times to
the Present Day, edited by Bernard Smith.

F344 "England under Glass." New Republic CV (October
6, 1941): 440.

Between the Acts, by Virginia Woolf.
Collected as "Virginia Woolf: England under

Glass" in Think Back on Us, pp. 382-84 (see A10).

F345 "The Saint in Politics." New Republic CV (October 20, 1941): 516.

Grey Eminence: A Study in Religion and Politics, by Aldous Huxley.

F346 "Three Poets." New Republic CV (November 10, 1941): 625-26.

Poems and New Poems, by Louise Bogan; What Are Years, by Marianne Moore; and Selected Poems, by George Barker.

F347 "Rebecca West Has Found Clue to Europe's Sickness." PM, November 16, 1941, p. 60.

Black Lamb and Grey Falcon: A Journey Through Yugoslavia, by Rebecca West.

F348 "Mr. Brooks Dissenting." New Republic CV (November 24, 1941): 705-6.

Opinions of Oliver Allston, by Van Wyck Brooks.

"Mr. Brooks Dissenting: II." New Republic CV (December 1, 1941): 738-39.

Opinions of Oliver Allston, by Van Wyck Brooks.

F349 "Decline and Fall." New Republic CV (December 8, 1941): 768-69.

Scum of the Earth, by Arthur Koestler; Pierre Laval, by Henry Torrès, translated by Norbert Guterman; and The Century Was Young, by Louis Aragon, translated by Hannah Josephson.

1942

F350 "Geopolitik." New Republic CVI (April 20,

1942): 546-47.

America's Strategy in World Politics: The
United States and the Balance of Power, by
Nicholas John Spykman.

F351 "Laval's Republic." New Republic CVI (April 27,
1942): 578-79.

The Last Time I Saw Paris, by Elliot Paul;
Prisoners of Hope, by Howard L. Brooks; and
The France of Tomorrow, by Albert Guérard.

F352 "Chicago Poem." New Republic CVI (May 4, 1942):
613-14.

Never Come Morning, by Nelson Algren.

F353 "This War and Peace." New Republic CVI (May 11,
1942): 642-43.

War and Peace, by Leo Tolstoy, translated by
Louise and Aylmer Maude.

F354 "Bad Company." New Republic CVI (May 25, 1942):
737.

The Company She Keeps, by Mary McCarthy.

F355 "Washington Is Like Hell." New Republic CVI
(June 1, 1942): 769-70.

Washington Is Like That, by W.M. Kiplinger.

F356 "Victory When?" New Republic CVI (June 15,
1942): 834.

Strategy for Victory, by Hanson W. Baldwin.

F357 "The Dispossessed." New Republic CVI (June 22,
1942): 865-66.

Today We Are Brothers: The Biography of a
Generation, by Leo Lania.

F358 "Go Down to Faulkner's Land." New Republic CVI
(June 29, 1942): 900.

Go Down, Moses, and Other Stories, by William
Faulkner.

F359 "Success Story: 1930-39." New Republic CVII
      (July 6, 1942): 25-26.
         Writers in Crisis: The American Novel between
         Two Wars, by Maxwell Geismar.

F360 "Tribute to Mary Vorse." New Republic CVII
      (July 13, 1942): 59-60.
         Time and the Town: A Provincetown Chronicle,
         by Mary Heaton Vorse.

F361 "Koestler: The Disenchanted." New Republic CVII
      (July 20, 1942): 89-90.
         The Gladiators, translated by Edith Smith;
         Darkness at Noon, translated by Daphne Hardy.
         Scum of the Earth and Dialogue with Death,
         translated by Trevor and Phyllis Blewitt.
         All by Arthur Koestler.

F362 "America the So Beautiful." New Republic CVII
      (July 27, 1942): 122-23.
         Fair Is Our Land, edited by Samuel Chamber-
         lain.

F363 "The Red and the Black." New Republic CVII
      (August 2, 1942): 146-47.
         French Literature and Thought since the
         Revolution, edited by Ramon Guthrie and
         George E. Diller.

F364 "No More Damned Nonsense." New Republic CVII
      (August 10, 1942): 178.
         Prelude to Victory, by James B. Reston.

F365 "The Death of Debunking." New Republic CVII
      (August 17, 1942): 203.
         The Unvanquished, by Howard Fast.

F366 "The Man Who Lived Twice." New Republic CVII
      (August 24, 1942): 234-35.
         The Seed beneath the Snow, by Ignazio Silone

translated by Frances Frenaye.

F367 "The State Department Story." New Republic CVII
(August 31, 1942): 260-61.

How War Came: An American White Paper from
the Fall of France to Pearl Harbor, by
Forrest Davis and Ernest K. Lindley.

F368 "Inside Germany." New Republic CVII (September
7, 1942): 289-90.

Last Train from Berlin, by Howard K. Smith.

F369 "The Dynamics of Peace." New Republic CVII
(September 21, 1942): 353-54.

Conditions of Peace, by Edward Hallett Carr.

F370 "The Soldier and the Saint." New Republic CVII
(September 28, 1942): 385-86.

The Seventh Cross, by Anna Seghers.

F371 "Spender, Auden and After." New Republic CVII
(October 5, 1942): 418-19.

Auden and After: The Liberation of Poetry
1930-41, by Francis Scarfe.

F372 "Journey in the Slave States." New Republic
CVII (October 12, 1942): 470-71.

No Day of Triumph, by J. Saunders Redding.

F373 "The Banquet." New Republic CVII (October 19,
1942): 505-6.

American Harvest: Twenty Years of Creative
Writing in the United States, edited by
Allen Tate and John Peale Bishop.

F374 "The Singapore Story." New Republic CVII
(October 26, 1942): 550-51.

Suez to Singapore, by Cecil Brown.

F375 "Lost Worlds." New Republic CVII (November 9,
1942): 614-15.

I Came out of the Eighteenth Century, by

John Andrew Rice.

F376 "Notes on the Enemy." New Republic CVII (November 23, 1942): 684-86.

Balcony Empire, by Reynolds and Eleanor Packard; This Is the Enemy, by Frederick Oechsner and the United Press Berlin Staff; and Government by Assassination, by Hugh Byas.

F377 "First Blood." New Republic CVII (November 30, 1942): 718-19.

Blood for a Stranger, by Randall Jarrell.

F378 "From Hegel to Hitler." New Republic CVII (December 7, 1942): 759-60.

Egotism in German Philosophy, by George Santayana; German Philosophy and Politics, by John Dewey; and Imperial Germany and the Industrial Revolution, by Thorstein Veblen.

F379 "Japan after the War." New Republic CVII (December 21, 1942): 830-31.

Government by Assassination, by Hugh Byas; Report from Tokyo: A Message to the American People, by Joseph C. Grew; and Basis for Peace in the Far East, by Nathaniel Peffer.

F380 "But Listen, Dorothy." New Republic CVII (December 28, 1942): 861-62.

Listen, Hans, by Dorothy Thompson.

1943

F381 "Men of Good Will." New Republic CVIII (January 11, 1943): 58.

Wide Is the Gate, by Upton Sinclair.

F382 "The Imp of the Perverse." New Republic CVIII (January 18, 1943): 88, 90.

The Secret Life of Salvador Dali, by Salvador
Dali, translated by Haakon M. Chevalier.

F383 "Europe: Death and Rebirth." New Republic CVIII
(January 25, 1943): 122-23.

The Conspirators, by Frederic Prokosch.

F384 "The Hosting of the Shee." New Republic CVIII
(February 8, 1943): 185-86.

W.B. Yeats, 1865-1939, by Joseph Hone.

F385 "Stepmother Congress." New Republic CVIII
(February 15, 1943): 214.

This Is Congress, by Roland Young.

F386 "Lives and Times." New Republic CVIII (February
22, 1943): 257-58.

Twentieth Century Authors, edited by Stanley
J. Kunitz and Howard Haycraft.

F387 "A Lively and Deadly Wit." Poetry LXI (February
1943): 620-22.

Person, Place and Thing, by Karl Jay Shapiro.

F388 "Who Was Right about Spain?" New Republic CVIII
(March 1, 1943): 288-89.

Appeasement's Child: The Franco Regime in
Spain, by Thomas J. Hamilton.

F389 "Mencken and Mark Twain." New Republic CVIII
(March 8, 1943): 321-22.

Heathen Days: 1890-1936, by H.L. Mencken.

F390 "The Book of Martyrs." New Republic CVIII
(March 22, 1943): 386-87.

Never Call Retreat, by Joseph Freeman.

F391 "Personal History, Cont'd." New Republic CVIII
(April 5, 1943): 450-51.

Between the Thunder and the Sun, by Vincent
Sheean.

F392 "Last Man around the World." New Republic CVIII

(April 19, 1943): 513.

One World, by Wendell L. Willkie.

F393 "Thunder over Aldanov." New Republic CVIII (May 10, 1943): 641-42.

The Fifth Seal, by Mark Aldanov, translated by Nicholas Wreden.

F394 "The Newest Machiavelli." New Republic CVIII (May 17, 1943): 673-74.

The Machiavellians: Defenders of Liberty, by James Burnham.

F395 "Graham Greene." New Republic CVIII (May 24, 1943): 706.

The Ministry of Fear, by Graham Greene.

F396 "Beyond Poetry." New Republic CVIII (June 7, 1943): 767-68.

Four Quartets, by T.S. Eliot.

F397 "Russian Turnabout." New Republic CVIII (June 14, 1943): 800-1.

Moscow Dateline, 1941-43, by Henry C. Cassidy Round Trip to Russia, by Walter Graebner; Mother Russia, by Maurice Hindus; and The Last Days of Sevastopol, by Boris Voyetekhov, translated by Ralph Parker and V.M. Genne.

F398 "Revolution by Consent." New Republic CVIII (June 21, 1943): 833-34.

Reflections on the Revolution of Our Time, by Harold J. Laski.

F399 "American Scholar." New Republic CIX (July 19, 1943): 81-82.

Pioneer to the Past: The Story of James Henry Breasted, by Charles Breasted.

F400 "The Grammar of Facts." New Republic CIX (July 26, 1943): 113-14.

McSorley's Wonderful Saloon, by Joseph
Mitchell.

F401 "Duce, Duce!" New Republic CIX (August 16,
1943): 226-27.

We Cannot Escape History, by John T. Whitaker.

F402 "Luke Lea's Empire." New Republic CIX (August
23, 1943): 258.

At Heaven's Gate, by Robert Penn Warren.

F403 "Escape from the Galleys." New Republic CIX
(August 30, 1943): 289-90.

They Shall Not Have Me, by Jean Hélion.

F404 "Tell Your Countrymen." New Republic CIX
(September 13, 1943): 366-67.

Battle Hymn of China, by Agnes Smedley.

F405 "Vansittartism." New Republic CIX (October 25,
1943): 586-88.

Lessons of My Life, by Lord Vansittart.

F406 "Port of Refuge." New Republic CIX (November
22, 1943): 721-22.

Arrival and Departure, by Arthur Koestler.

F407 "E.M. Forster's Answer." New Republic CIX
November 29, 1943): 749-50.

Indigo, by Christine Weston.

F408 "Chesterton's Later Years." New Republic CIX
(December 20, 1943): 889-90.

Gilbert Keith Chesterton, by Maisie Ward.

F409 "Chesterton's Later Years: II." New Republic
CIX (December 27, 1943): 921-22.

Gilbert Keith Chesterton, by Maisie Ward.

1944

F410 "Santayana at Harvard." New Republic CX
(January 17, 1944): 88, 90.

Persons and Places: The Background of My
Life, by George Santayana.

F411 "Europe in Exile." New Republic CX (January
24, 1944): 120-21.

Heart of Europe: An Anthology of Creative
Writing in Europe, 1920-1940, edited by
Klaus Mann and Hermann Kesten.

F412 "The Führer's Followers." New Republic CX
(January 31, 1944): 152, 154.

Der Führer: Hitler's Rise to Power, by
Konrad Heiden.

F413 "Novels after the War." New Republic CX (February 14, 1944): 216-17.

A Bell for Adano, by John Hersey.

F414 "Who's Fascist Now?" New Republic CX (February
1944): 246-48.

As We Go Marching, by John T. Flynn.

F415 "The Assassinated Poet." New Republic CX
(February 28, 1944): 284, 286.

The Silence of the Sea, by Vercors (Jean Brul

F416 "Southways." New Republic CX (March 6, 1944):
320, 322.

Strange Fruit, by Lillian Smith.

F417 "Cassandra's Children." New Republic CX (March
13, 1944): 352-53.

American Negro Slave Revolts, by Herbert
Aptheker; The Hunted, by Albert J. Guérard;
and The Passing of the European Age, by Eric
Fischer.

F418 "Rattling around the War." New Republic CX (Mar
20, 1944): 383-84.

Wingate's Raiders, by Charles J. Rolo; Tarawa
The Story of a Battle, by Robert Sherrod; and
D-Day, by John Gunther.

F419 "Peace and the Pundits." New Republic CX
      (April 10, 1944): 504-5.
      How To Think about War and Peace, by
      Mortimer J. Adler.
F420 "In Defense of the 1920's." New Republic CX
      (April 24, 1944): 564-65.
      The Literary Fallacy, by Bernard DeVoto.
F421 "The Devil a Monk Was He." New Republic CX
      (May 1, 1944): 609.
      The Razor's Edge, by W. Somerset Maugham.
F422 "Brooks in Progress." New Republic CXI (October
      9, 1944): 463, 465.
      The World of Washington Irving, by Van Wyck
      Brooks.
F423 "The Two Erskine Caldwells." New Republic CXI
      (November 6, 1944): 599-600.
      Tragic Ground, by Erskine Caldwell.
F424 "Twenty Lessons in How To Write like Saroyan,
      Who Says It's Easy." PM, November 12, 1944,
      Magazine Section, p. 15.
      Dear Baby, by William Saroyan.

1945
F425 "Steinbeck Delivers a Mixture of Farce and
      Freud." PM, January 14, 1945, Magazine Section,
      p. 15.
      Cannery Row, by John Steinbeck.
F426 "The Return of Henry James." New Republic CXII
      (January 22, 1945): 121-22.
      Criticism in American Periodicals of the Works
      of Henry James from 1866 to 1916, by Richard
      Nicholas Foley; The Great Short Novels of
      Henry James, edited by Philip Rahv; Stories
      of Writers and Artists, by Henry James,

edited by F.O. Matthiessen; and Henry James:
The Major Phase, by F.O. Matthiessen.
Collected with F427 as "The Two Henry Jameses"
in A Many-Windowed House, pp. 89-99 (see A12)

F427 "The Two Henry Jameses." New Republic CXII
(February 5, 1945): 177-78, 180.

Criticism in American Periodicals of the
Works of Henry James from 1866 to 1916, by
Richard Nicholas Foley; The Great Short
Novels of Henry James, edited by Philip Rahv;
Stories of Writers and Artists, by Henry
James, edited by F.O. Matthiessen; and Henry
James: The Major Phase, by F.O. Matthiessen.
Collected with F427 as "The Two Henry Jameses"
in A Many-Windowed House, pp. 89-99 (see A12)

F428 "Virtue and Virtuosity: Notes on W.H. Auden."
Poetry LXV (January 1945): 202-9.

For the Time Being, by W.H. Auden.

F429 "Gertrude Stein for the Plain Reader." New York
Times Book Review, March 11, 1945, pp. 1, 22.

Wars I Have Seen, by Gertrude Stein.

F430 "James Thurber's Dream Book." New Republic CXII
(March 12, 1945): 362-63.

The Thurber Carnival, written and illustrated
by James Thurber.

F431 "Santayana in Society." New Republic CXII
(April 30, 1945): 591-92.

The Middle Span: Persons and Places, Vol. 2,
by George Santayana.

F432 "Auden's a Better Poet Than Editor in Collectin
His Own Works." PM, May 20, 1945, Magazine
Section, pp. 7-8.

The Collected Poetry of W.H. Auden.

F433 "Third Act and Epilogue." New Yorker XXI,

no. 2 (June 30, 1945): 49-52.

The Crack-Up, by F. Scott Fitzgerald, edited
by Edmund Wilson.
Reprinted, slightly expanded, in F. Scott
Fitzgerald: The Man and His Work, edited by
Alfred Kazin (Cleveland: World, 1951),
pp. 146-53, and in F. Scott Fitzgerald; A
Collection of Critical Essays, edited by
Arthur Mizener (Englewood Cliffs, New Jersey:
Prentice-Hall, 1963), pp. 64-69.

F434 "How Do We Talk American?" New Republic CXIII
(July 9, 1945): 50-51.

A Dictionary of American English on Historical
Principles, edited by Sir William Craigie and
James R. Hulbert.

F435 "War and the Poets." New Republic CXIII
(August 27, 1945): 258-60.

The War Poets: An Anthology of the War Poetry
of the Twentieth Century, edited by Oscar
Williams.

F436 "Mencken Adds a 789-Page Rider to His American
Language." PM, September 2, 1945, Magazine
Section, p. 15.

The American Language: Supplement One, by
H.L. Mencken.

F437 "The Alger Story." New Republic CXIII (September 10, 1945): 319-20.

Struggling Upward and Other Works, by
Horatio Alger.
Collected with G188 and G328 as "The Real
Horatio Alger Story" in A Many-Windowed
House, pp. 76-88 (see A12).

F438 "Stuart Little; or, New York through the Eyes
of a Mouse." New York Times Book Review,

October 28, 1945, p. 7.

Stuart Little, by E.B. White.

F439 "Aidgarpo." New Republic CXIII (November 5, 1945): 607-10.

Edgar Allan Poe, edited by Philip Van Doren Stern.

1946

F440 "Walt Whitman: Poet of America?" New York Times Book Review, February 24, 1946, pp. 1, 36.

Leaves of Grass, by Walt Whitman with a preface by Bernard Smith, and Walt Whitman Handbook, by Gay Wilson Allen.

F441 "Limbo-by-the-Sea." New Republic CXIV (March 25, 1946): 418-19.

Memoirs of Hecate County, by Edmund Wilson.

F442 "Cowley Finds Cain's New Novel Smothered in Celluloid." PM, June 2, 1946, Magazine Section, p. 14.

Past All Dishonor and Three Novels, by James M. Cain.

F443 "An American Patriot by Remote Control." New York Herald Tribune Books, July 21, 1946, p. 5.

Brewsie and Willie, by Gertrude Stein.

F444 "Whose Housatonic?" New Republic CXV (August 19, 1946): 205-6.

The Housatonic: Puritan River, by Chard Powers Smith.

F445 "DeVoto, with Chipless Shoulders, Edits Portable Mark Twain." PM, September 15, 1946, Magazine Section, p. 7.

The Portable Mark Twain, selected with an

introduction by Bernard DeVoto.

F446 "Gertrude Stein, Writer or Word Scientist?"
New York Herald Tribune Weekly Book Review,
November 24, 1946, p. 1.

Selected Writings of Gertrude Stein, edited
by Carl Van Vechten.

F447 "Hicksborough." New Republic CXV (December 9,
1946): 766, 768.

Small Town, by Granville Hicks.

1947

F448 "Dos Passos and His Predecessors." New York
Times Book Review, January 19, 1947, pp. 1, 29.

U.S.A., by John Dos Passos, reconsidered.

F449 "Steinbeck Brings 'em Back under Glass." PM,
February 16, 1947, Magazine Section, p. 13.

The Wayward Bus, by John Steinbeck.

F450 "Voices from the Nazi Rubble Pile." New York
Times Book Review, June 8, 1947, pp. 1, 29.

The Hidden Damage, by James Stern.

F451 "Books and Things." New York Herald Tribune,
September 15, 1947, p. 13.

The Journal of André Gide, translated from
the French with an introduction and notes by
Justin O'Brien.

F452 "Books and Things." New York Herald Tribune,
September 16, 1947, p. 19.

Mixed Train Daily, by Lucius Beebe.

F453 "Books and Things." New York Herald Tribune,
September 17, 1947, p. 27.

Gus the Great, by Thomas W. Duncan.

F454 "Books and Things." New York Herald Tribune,
September 18, 1947, p. 23.

Still-Life Painting in America, by Wolfgang
Born; Treasury of American Drawings, by
Charles E. Slatkin and Regina Shoolman;
Tchelitchew Drawings, edited by Lincoln
Kirstein; Hieronymus Bosch, by Howard Daniel;
and Daumier, by Jacques Lassaigne.

F455 "Books and Things." New York Herald Tribune,
September 19, 1947, p. 23.

An Explorer Comes Home, by Roy Chapman
Andrews.

F456 "Books and Things." New York Herald Tribune,
September 22, 1947, p. 13.

End of a Berlin Diary, by William L. Shirer.

F457 "Books and Things." New York Herald Tribune,
September 23, 1947, p. 23.

Lucky Forward, by Colonel Robert S. Allen.

F458 "Books and Things." New York Herald Tribune,
September 24, 1947, p. 23.

The Needle's Eye, by Timothy Pember, and
Anna Collett, by Barbara Lucas.

F459 "Books and Things." New York Herald Tribune,
September 25, 1947, p. 27.

The Kingdom of Adventure: Everest, by James
Ramsey Ullman.

F460 "Books and Things." New York Herald Tribune,
September 26, 1947, p. 21.

The Great Forest, by Richard G. Lillard.

F461 "Sherwood Anderson, Still Fresh and New." New
York Herald Tribune Books, November 9, 1947,
pp. 1-2.

The Sherwood Anderson Reader, edited by Paul
Rosenfeld.

F462 "Brooks and the 'Usable Past'." New Republic

CXVII (November 10, 1947): 25-27.

The Times of Melville and Whitman, by Van
Wyck Brooks.

F463 "Novelists, Pioneers of the New Generation."
New York Herald Tribune Books, November 16,
1947, p. 5.

The Last of the Provincials: The American
Novel, 1915-1925, by Maxwell Geismar.

F464 "Ending Dreiser's 'Trilogy of Desire'." New
York Times Book Review, November 23, 1947,
pp. 7, 57.

The Stoic, by Theodore Dreiser.

F465 "Classics and Best-Sellers." New Republic CXVII
(December 22, 1947): 25-27.

Golden Multitudes, by Frank Luther Mott.

1948

F466 "Career of a Great Teacher and Liberal Editor."
New York Herald Tribune Books, May 30, 1948,
p. 3.

All Our Years: The Autobiography of Robert
Morss Lovett.

F467 "The European Travel Diary of a Humanist." New
York Herald Tribune Books, September 12, 1948,
p. 5.

From the Heart of Europe, by F.O. Matthiessen.

F468 "In Love with Germany." New Republic CXIX
(September 27, 1948): 33-34.

Last of the Conquerors, by William Gardner
Smith, and The Crusaders, by Stefan Heym.

F469 "William Faulkner's Nation." New Republic CXIX
(October 18, 1948): 21-22.

Intruder in the Dust, by William Faulkner.

F470 "Two Men of Letters." New Republic CXIX
      (November 8, 1948): 21-22.
         Henry David Thoreau, by Joseph Wood Krutch,
         and Nathaniel Hawthorne: A Biography, by
         Randall Stewart.
F471 "Edwin Arlington Robinson: Defeat and Triumph."
      New Republic CXIX (December 6, 1948): 26-30.
         Edwin Arlington Robinson, by Emery Neff.
         Collected as "Edward Arlington Robinson" in
         After the Genteel Tradition, revised edition,
         pp. 28-36 (see A4a).

      1949
F472 "Washington Wasn't Like That." New Republic CXX
      (January 17, 1949): 23-24.
         The Grand Design, by John Dos Passos.
F473 "A New American War Novel That May Stand the
      Test of Time." New York Times Book Review,
      March 20, 1949, p. 3.
         The Girl on the Via Flaminia, by Alfred
         Hayes.
F474 "Hawthorne as Tragic Artist: A Fine Study."
      New York Herald Tribune Book Review, May 8,
      1949, p. 3.
         Nathaniel Hawthorne, by Mark Van Doren.
F475 "The External Emerson." New Republic CXX
      (June 13, 1949): 17-18.
         The Life of Ralph Waldo Emerson, by Ralph
         L. Rusk.
F476 "Sex, Censorship and Superman." New Republic
      CXXI (October 10, 1949): 18-19.
         Love & Death: A Study in Censorship, by G.
         Legman.

F477 "Faulkner Stories, in Amiable Mood." New York
Herald Tribune Book Review, November 6, 1949,
p. 7.
Knight's Gambit, by William Faulkner.

1950

F478 "Prolegomena to Kenneth Burke." New Republic
CXXII (June 5, 1950): 18-19.
A Rhetoric of Motives, by Kenneth Burke.

F479 "Mr. Warren's New Novel Is His Longest and
Richest." New York Herald Tribune Book Review,
June 25, 1950, p. 1.
World Enough and Time, by Robert Penn Warren.

F480 "Survival by Co-operation." New York Herald
Tribune Book Review, July 9, 1950, p. 11.
On Being Human, by Ashley Montagu.

F481 "Hemingway's Portrait of an Old Soldier Pre-
paring To Die." New York Herald Tribune Book
Review, September 10, 1950, pp. 1, 16.
Across the River and into the Trees, by
Ernest Hemingway.

F482 "Mythology and Melville." New Republic CXXIII
(October 30, 1950): 24-26.
Herman Melville, by Newton Arvin, and Herman
Melville: A Critical Study, by Richard Chase.

F483 "Mad about Poetry: And Other Things Too." New
York Herald Tribune Book Review, November 12,
1950, p. 4.
The Letters of Ezra Pound 1907-1941, edited
by D.D. Paige.

1951

F484 "The Last Flight from Main Street." New York

Times Book Review, March 25, 1951, pp. 1, 16.

World So Wide, by Sinclair Lewis.

Reprinted in Highlights of Modern Literature,
edited by Francis Brown (New York: New
American Library, 1954), pp. 146-49.

F485 "No Rules for What Sherwood Anderson Tried To
Do." New York Herald Tribune Book Review,
April 8, 1951, p. 3.

Sherwood Anderson, by Irving Howe.

F486 "From A to Zymurgy." New Republic CXXIV (April
16, 1951): 27-28.

Thorndike-Barnhart Comprehensive Desk
Dictionary, by Clarence L. Barnhart.

F487 "Today's Young Writers: Are They Doomed to
Failure?" New York Herald Tribune Book Review,
May 27, 1951, pp. 1, 18.

After the Lost Generation: A Critical Study
of the Writers of Two Wars, by John W.
Aldridge.

F488 "In Which Mr. Faulkner Translates Past into
Present." New York Herald Tribune Book Review,
September 30, 1951, pp. 1, 14.

Requiem for a Nun, by William Faulkner.

F489 "The Faulkner Pattern." New Republic CXXV
(October 8, 1951): 19-20.

Lie Down in Darkness, by William Styron.

F490 "An Indispensable Guide to a Fuller Under-
standing of Herman Melville." New York Herald
Tribune Book Review, November 11, 1951, p. 7.

The Melville Log: A Documentary Life of
Herman Melville, by Jay Leyda.

F491 "The Religion of Humanity." New Republic CXXV
(November 19, 1951): 17-18.

The Conduct of Life, by Lewis Mumford.

F492 "Not Evil Enough." New Republic CXXV (November 26, 1951): 20-21.

Evil under the Sun, by Anton Myrer.

1952

F493 "Van Wyck Brooks' Great Evocation of Our Literary Past." New York Herald Tribune Book Review, January 6, 1952, pp. 1, 13.

The Confident Years: 1885-1915; Makers and Finders. (A History of the Writer in America, 1800-1915, Vol. V), by Van Wyck Brooks.

F494 "Sex Murder Incorporated." New Republic CXXVI (February 11, 1952): 17-18.

The Big Kill, by Mickey Spillane.

F495 "What Are the Qualities That Make an Author Modern?" New York Herald Tribune Book Review, July 27, 1952, pp. 1, 10.

Baudelaire, by P. Mansell Jones; Benedetto Croce--Man and Thinker, by Cecil Spriggs; Paul Valéry: The Mind in the Mirror, by Elizabeth Sewell; and Rainer Maria Rilke-- A Study of His Later Poetry, by Hans Egon Holthusen, translated by J.P. Stern.

F496 "Hemingway's Novel Has the Rich Simplicity of a Classic." New York Herald Tribune Book Review, September 7, 1952, pp. 1, 17.

The Old Man and the Sea, by Ernest Hemingway.

F497 "Conrad Aiken's Autobiography." New Republic CXXVII (October 6, 1952): 20-22.

Ushant: An Essay, by Conrad Aiken.

F498 "Edmund Wilson's Specimen Days." New Republic CXXVII (November 10, 1952): 17-18, 22.

The Shores of Light, by Edmund Wilson.

F499 "Farrell's Time Obliterated." New Republic
    CXXVII (December 1, 1952): 17-18.
        Yet Other Waters, by James T. Farrell.

1953

F500 "A Faith for Writing." New Republic CXVIII
    (March 9, 1953): 19-20.
        The Writer in America, by Van Wyck Brooks.

F501 "A Critic's First Principle." New Republic
    CXXIX (September 14, 1953): 16-17.
        Counter-Statement, by Kenneth Burke.

F502 "American Social Revolt as Mirrored in the Work
    of Five Novelists." New York Herald Tribune
    Book Review, September 20, 1953, p. 5.
        Rebels and Ancestors: The American Novel,
        1890-1915, by Maxwell Geismar.

1954

F503 "Faulkner's Powerful New Novel: Biblical Over-
    tones, Daring Symbols." New York Herald Tribune
    Book Review, August 1, 1954, pp. 1, 8.
        A Fable, by William Faulkner.

F504 "English Eyes upon Us." Saturday Review of
    Literature XXXVII (October 30, 1954): 16-17.
        "American Writing Today: Its Independence
        and Vigour, " in Times Literary Supplement,
        edited by Alan Pryce-Jones, September 17,
        1954. (For MC's contribution, see G257.)

1955

F505 "Walt Whitman, Champion of America." New York
    Times Book Review, February 6, 1955, pp. 1, 22

The Solitary Singer: A Critical Biography of
Walt Whitman, by Gay Wilson Allen.
F506 "Life of the Hunter." New York Times Book
Review, October 16, 1955, pp. 4, 44.
Big Woods, by William Faulkner.
F507 "Mr. Mailer Tells a Tale of Love, Art, Corrup-
tion." New York Herald Tribune Book Review,
October 23, 1955, p. 5.
The Deer Park, by Norman Mailer.

1956
F508 "The Life and Death of Thomas Wolfe." New
Republic CXXXV (November 19, 1956): 17-21.
The Letters of Thomas Wolfe, collected and
edited by Elizabeth Nowell.
Parts 1 and 5 of a long essay on Thomas Wolfe
first published integrally in A Second
Flowering (see A13).
F509 "Lions and Lemmings, Toads and Tigers."
Reporter XV (December 13, 1956): 42-44.
Further Fables for Our Time, by James
Thurber.

1957
F510 "It's the Telling That Counts." New York Times
Book Review, May 12, 1957, pp. 4-5.
The Complete Works of Nathanael West, intro-
duction by Alan Ross.
Reprinted as "Introduction" to Miss Lonely-
hearts, by Nathanael West (New York: Avon
Publications, 1959), pp. ii-iv, 96 (see C8).
F511 "The World of Arthur Winner, Jr." New York
Times Book Review, August 25, 1957, pp. 1, 18.

By Love Possessed, by James Gould Cozzens.

1958

F512 "Success That Somehow Led to Failure." New York
Times Book Review, April 13, 1958, pp. 4-5, 45.
The Great Days, by John Dos Passos.

F513 "Twenty by Scott Fitzgerald." New York Herald
Tribune Book Review, April 27, 1958, p. 5.
Afternoon of an Author--A Selection of Uncol-
lected Stories and Essays, by F. Scott
Fitzgerald, edited by Arthur Mizener.

F514 "There's Always a Point of No Return." New York
Times Book Review, September 28, 1958, pp. 4-5
Women and Thomas Harrow, by John P. Marquand

F515 "Triangle, Pentagon, Square." New Republic
CXXXIX (December 22, 1958): 16-17.
Water Music, by Bianca Van Orden.

1959

F516 "The Life and Death of a Fire Eater." New York
Times Book Review, June 7, 1959, pp. 1, 33.
The Light Infantry Ball, by Hamilton Basso.

F517 "Storyteller Strikes Back." New Republic CXLI
(October 12, 1959): 15-17.
The Outlaws on Parnassus, by Margaret Kenned
Reprinted as "Introduction" to The Outlaws
on Parnassus (New York, The Viking Press,
1960), pp. ix-xvii (see C9).

F518 [Review of Graffiti, by Ramon Guthrie]. New
York Herald Tribune Book Review, November 8,
1959, p. 8

F519 "Flem Snopes Gets His Come-Uppance." New York
Times Book Review, November 15, 1959, pp. 1, 1

The <u>Mansion</u>, by William Faulkner.

<u>1960</u>

F520 "Exploring a World of Nightmares." <u>New</u> <u>York</u>
     <u>Times</u> <u>Book</u> <u>Review</u>, March 27, 1960, pp. 1, 40.

     <u>Love</u> <u>and</u> <u>Death</u> <u>in</u> <u>the</u> <u>American</u> <u>Novel</u>, by
     Leslie A. Fiedler.

F521 "The Ideas of an Artist." <u>New</u> <u>York</u> <u>Times</u> <u>Book</u>
     <u>Review</u>, May 29, 1960, pp. 4, 16.

     <u>The</u> <u>Landscape</u> <u>and</u> <u>the</u> <u>Looking</u> <u>Glass</u>: <u>Willa</u>
     <u>Cather's</u> <u>Search</u> <u>for</u> <u>Value</u>, by John H. Randall.

<u>1963</u>

F522 "Dear Scottie, Zelda & Max." <u>New</u> <u>York</u> <u>Times</u>
     <u>Book</u> <u>Review</u>, October 20, 1963, pp. 1, 56-57.

     <u>The</u> <u>Letters</u> <u>of</u> <u>F.</u> <u>Scott</u> <u>Fitzgerald</u>, edited
     by Andrew Turnbull.

<u>1965</u>

F523 "Genius in the Raw." <u>Book</u> <u>Week,</u> April 25, 1965,
     pp. 1, 8-9.

     <u>Dreiser</u>, by W.A. Swanberg.

F524 "Yankee Crusader on the Left." <u>New</u> <u>York</u> <u>Times</u>
     <u>Book</u> <u>Review</u>, August 1, 1965, pp. 1, 18.

     <u>Part</u> <u>of</u> <u>the</u> <u>Truth</u>, by Granville Hicks.

F525 "The Well-Bred Borzoi." <u>Book</u> <u>Week</u>, October 31,
     1965, pp. 1, 34.

     <u>Fifty</u> <u>Years</u>: <u>Borzoi</u> <u>Books</u> <u>1915-1965</u>, <u>a</u>
     <u>Retrospective</u> <u>Collection</u>, edited by Clifton
     Fadiman.

<u>1966</u>

F526 "Gide as Friend and Colleague." <u>Book</u> <u>Week</u>,

May 1, 1966, p. 2.

Self Portraits: The Gide/Valéry Letters,
1890-1942, edited by Robert Mallet, and
Conversations with André Gide, by Claude
Mauriac, translated by Michael Lebeck.

F527 "Jargon and Its Discontents." Book Week,
November 20, 1966, p. 3.

Modern American Usage: A Guide, by Wilson
Follett, edited and completed by Jacques
Barzun.

1967

F528 "A Unique Case." Book Week, April 2, 1967,
pp. 1-2.

The Eighth Day, by Thornton Wilder.

1968

F529 "Those Paris Years." New York Times Book
Review, June 9, 1968, p. 1.

Being Geniuses Together, by Robert McAlmon,
revised and with supplementary chapters by
Kay Boyle.

F530 "American Fables." New York Times Book Review,
August 4, 1968, pp. 1, 26, 27.

How We Live--Contemporary Life in Contemporary Fiction, an Anthology, edited by
Penney Chapin Hills and L. Rust Hills.

F531 "The Soviet Socialist Republic of the Dead."
Book World (Washington Post, Chicago Tribune)
II (September 22, 1968): 1, 3.

The Great Terror: Stalin's Purge of the
Thirties, by Robert Conquest.

1969

F532 "Her Name Was a Singing Line of Verse." Book
World (Washington Post, Chicago Tribune) III
(May 18, 1969): 5.
The Poet and Her Book: A Biography of Edna
St. Vincent Millay, by Jean Gould.

1970

F533 "Hart Crane: The Evidence in the Case."
Sewanee Review LXXVIII (Winter 1970): 176-84.
Voyager: A Life of Hart Crane, by John
Unterecker.
Reprinted in part in Robber Rocks: Letters
and Memories of Hart Crane, 1923-1932, by
Susan Jenkins Brown (see D20).

F534 "They Cheered One Another On." New York Times
Book Review, July 26, 1970, pp. 4, 23.
The Van Wyck Brooks--Lewis Mumford Letters;
the Record of a Literary Friendship, 1921-
1963, edited by Robert E. Spiller.

F535 "A Double Life, Half Told." Atlantic CCXXVI
(December 1970): 105-8.
Islands in the Stream, by Ernest Hemingway.
Revised and used in chapter 10 of A Second
Flowering, pp. 216-23 (see A13).

1971

F536 "Mizener on Ford Madox Ford: Sad, but Not the
'Saddest'." Chicago Daily News, Panorama,
May 1-2, 1971, p. 11.
The Saddest Story: The Biography of Ford
Madox Ford, by Arthur Mizener.

F537 "Editing Eliot." Book World (Washington Post,
     Chicago Tribune) V (November 7, 1971): 3, 14.
     The Waste Land: A Facsimile and Transcript
     of the Original Drafts Including the Annota-
     tions of Ezra Pound, by T.S. Eliot, edited
     by Valerie Eliot.

F538 "We Had Such Good Times." New Republic CLXV
     (December 25, 1971): 27-28.
     Memoirs of Montparnasse, by John Glassco.

     1972

F539 "Federal Writers' Project." New Republic CLXVII
     (October 21, 1972): 23-26.
     The Dream and the Deal: The Federal Writers'
     Project, 1935-1943, by Jerre Mangione.

F540 "Leading His Flock of Long-Legged, Flat-Chested
     Flappers." New York Times Book Review, Novem-
     ber 19, 1972, pp. 5, 35.
     The Most of John Held, Jr., with an intro-
     duction by Carl J. Weinhardt.

     1973

F541 "He Wrote Honestly and Well, He Told the Truth
     about His Time." New York Times Book Review,
     March 18, 1973, pp. 3-4.
     O'Hara: A Biography, by Finis Farr.

F542 "The Wilder Side of Life." Book World, October
     21, 1973, p. 5.
     Theophilus North, by Thornton Wilder.

G.   ESSAYS AND ARTICLES

1918

G1   "U.S. Volunteer Tells of French Battle Front
      Visit--No Union Hours." Pittsburgh Gazette
      Times, January 6, 1918, 5th section, p. 3.
         Cowley has written, " I received for it a
         check for $5, that being the first money I
         earned by writing for publication." Illus-
         trated with five photographs, including a
         picture of Cowley.

G2   "The History of a Push." Harvard Advocate CIV
      (January 1918): 240.
         An on-the-scene report from the French Trans-
         port service.

1920

G3   "Agassiz and Agony." Harvard Advocate CVI
      (March 1, 1920): 219.
         Review of a production by "The 47 Workshop,"
         a Harvard theatre group.

G4   "Colonizing Manhattan's Lower West Side."
      New York Evening Post, April 10, 1920, Magazine,
      p. 5. (Signed David Malcolm.)
         Manhattan house-seekers are pushing westward
         as the demands for housing grow.

1921

G5   "This Youngest Generation." Literary Review of
      the New York Evening Post II (October 15,
      1921): 81-82.
         On literary trends espoused by the young
         writers in 1921.

G6   "Rabelais Returns to His Own Home Town." New
      York Tribune, November 21, 1921, p. 3.
          A Rabelais monument by Villeneuve was unveile
      November 6, 1921, at Montpellier by the Presi
      dent of France.

      1922

G7   "The French and Our New Poetry." Literary Revie
      of the New York Evening Post II (May 6, 1922):
      641.
          On the tendency of the French to appreciate
      American poetry before Americans do.

G8   "A Brief History of Bohemia." Freeman V
      (July 19, 1922): 439.
          "Bohemia" as it was in 1850 and as it is in
          1920.

G9   "Henri Barbusse." Bookman LVI (October 1922):
      180-82.
          Barbusse became famous overnight with Under
          Fire, a literarily and politically provoca-
          tive novel (see Introduction).

      1923

G10   "Pascin's America." Broom IV (January 1923):
      136-37.
          Jules Pascin's sketches present a particular
          conception of America.

G11   "André Salmon and His Generation." Bookman LVI
      (February 1923): 714-17.
          Salmon's generation created a new ideal of
          the artistic life.

G12   "A Monument to Proust." Dial LXXXIV (March
      1923): 234-40.

On Remembrance of Things Past.

G13 "Duhamel, M.D." Bookman LVII (April 1923):
160-62.

Georges Duhamel, French writer and army
surgeon, owes his reputation to the war.

G14 "Charles Vildrac." Bookman LVII (May 1923):
291-94.

A personal look at Vildrac, writer and ini-
tiator of the Abbey, a unique writing and
publishing venture.

G15 "Racine." Freeman VIII (October 10, 1923): 104-6.
The tragedies of Jean Racine are perfect
expressions of seventeenth-century France.
Had first appeared with G16 as a pamphlet
(see A1).

G16 "Racine." Freeman VIII (October 17, 1923):
132-33.

Had first appeared with G15 as a pamphlet
(see A1).

G17 "Paul Fort." Bookman LVIII (November 1923):
253-54.

A profile of the French "prince of poets."

1924

G18 (With Slater Brown) "To the Editors of the
Dial." Broom VI (January 1924): 30-31.
A challenge to the editors of the Dial to
defend their choices for annual awards.

G19 "Parnassus-on-the-Seine." Charm I (July 1924):
19, 80, 83.

"Montparnasse, the art student quarter of
Paris, is the rendezvous of the world."

G20 "James Joyce." Bookman LIX (July 1924): 518-21.

A survey of reactions to Joyce's Ulysses two
years after its publication.

G21 "Do Artists Make Good Husbands?" Charm II
(August 1924): 28-29, 83, 91.

"Contrary to popular fiction stories, an
artist's marriage is usually successful."
(See Introduction.)

G22 "How Do You Do Your Reading?" Charm II (October
1924): 34-35, 72.

On reading habits.

1925

G23 "Pierre MacOrlan." Bookman LX (January 1925):
585-89.

This "piece" on MacOrlan (pseud. of Pierre
Dumarchey) is the last of seven profiles of
French writers (and of James Joyce) with
portraits of each by Ivan Opffer (see G9,
G11, G13, G14, G17, G20).

G24 "To Whom It May Concern." Aesthete: 1925 I
(February 1925): 28.

A rejoinder to Ernest Boyd's article,
"Aesthete: Model 1924," in the American
Mercury I (January 1924): 51-56.
Aesthete 1925 was edited by W.S. Hankel
(pseud.).

G25 "In Defense of Sherlock Holmes." Charm III
(July 1925): 34-35.

"It is only in mediums like the detective
story that we can find the imaginative power
which all of us desire."

G26 "Beavers, Builders and Lakes." Charm IV
(August 1925): 14-17, 83, 90.

"Lakes of all sizes and depths, single and
in clusters are in northern New Jersey."

G27 "A Few Novels Worth Keeping." Charm IV
(November 1925): 34, 64.
On the modern novel, with a quotation from
Kenneth Burke.

G28 "Churches Which Remember the Revolution."
Charm IV (December 1925): 12-17, 78.
A description of churches remaining from
colonial times in New Jersey.

G29 "Books for Your Christmas List." Charm IV
(December 1925): 42, 84-85.
Mostly about reprints of standard works.

1926

G30 "The Foundations of a Library." Charm V
(February 1926): 30, 84-85
"An ideal library is one which comes nearest
to expressing one's own personal judgment."
On choosing an edition of Dickens, encyclo-
pedias, English poets, Poe, and English
novels.

G31 "Doing Your Play-Going at Home." Charm V
(March 1926): 32, 78.
"Few forms of reading are more enjoyable than
a good play published in book form." On
Eugene O'Neill, Noël Coward, John Galsworthy,
George Kelly, Patrick Kearney.

G32 "Lost! A Lady. Found! An Artist." Brentano's
Book Chat V (March-April 1926): 19-23.
A "pen-portrait" of Willa Cather.

G33 "Garcong! Garcong!" Brentano's Book Chat V
(May-June 1926): 24-29.

A "pen-portrait" of Sinclair Lewis.

G34   "Low Bridge and Lock Ahead." Charm V (July
      1926): 18-21.

      A history of the Morris Canal, which ran
      from Phillipsburg, New Jersey, to Newark.

G35   "Two Kinds of Travel Books." Charm V (July
      1926): 41, 76.

      Suggested books to carry abroad and others
      to be read at home.

G36   "Eugene O'Neill, Writer of Synthetic Drama."
      Brentano's Book Chat V (July-August 1926):
      17-21.

      A "pen-portrait" of Eugene O'Neill.

G37   "The Real Jungle King." Brentano's Book Chat V
      (September-October 1926): 17-21.

      On William Beebe.

G38   "How To Interview Ring Lardner." Brentano's
      Book Chat V (November-December 1926): 25-30.

      Impressions of Lardner formed during an
      interview.

G39   "Toward a Universal Mind." New Republic XLIX
      (December 8, 1926): 69-71.

      On Paul Valéry.

      Reprinted as "Introduction" to Variety, by
      Paul Valéry (New York: Harcourt, Brace, 1927)
      pp. v-xv (see E3).

1927

G40   "Wowsers on the Run." Brentano's Book Chat VI
      (January-February 1927): 30-33.

      On H.L. Mencken.

G41   "The Reviewer Cleans House." Charm VII (Febru-
      ary 1927): 33, 75, 81.

Reflections on books published in 1926.

G42   "Edwin Arlington Robinson: The Person and the
      Poet." Brentano's Book Chat VI (March-April
      1927): 24-28.

      "I had found a poet--one I could add to the
      very limited number of those I deeply admire."

G43   "The Role of the Hero in Hair-Pants Romances."
      Literary Review of the New York Evening Post
      VII (April 16, 1927): 6, 12.

      Western stories and their resemblance to
      Arthurian legend.

G44   "French Poetry and the New Spirit." Saturday
      Review of Literature III (May 7, 1927): 810.

      "Poetry, in France, is still the basis of
      all the literary arts."

G45   "Decadent Spring." Brentano's Book Chat VI
      (May-June 1927): 37-41.

      A spoof of old-fashioned poems about the
      coming of spring.

G46   "Nick Carter." Brentano's Book Chat VI (July-
      August 1927): 34-37.

      A brief history of the Nick Carter adventure
      stories and the men who wrote them.

G47   "Fisherman's Luck on Barnegat Bay." Charm VIII
      (September 1927): 13-15, 72.

      A description of the plentiful fishing off
      Long Beach Island, New Jersey.

G48   "Conrad Aiken: A Man of Letters." Brentano's
      Book Chat VI (September-October 1927): 29-32.

      A "pen-portrait."

G49   "Smash Your Guitar." Brentano's Book Chat VI
      (November-December 1927): 33-36.

      A "pen-portrait" of Carl Sandburg.

G50   "The Oldest Quaker Colony." Charm VIII (Decem-
      ber 1927): 11-13, 83-84.
          An historical guide to the Quaker settlements
      in western New Jersey.

      1928
G51   "Novelized Biography." Charm VIII (January
      1928): 52, 77.
          On a new type of biography.
G52   "On Giving Books." Brentano's Book Chat VII
      (January-February 1928): 38-40.
          Rules to follow when choosing books as gifts
G53   "Our Last Royal Governor." Charm IX (February
      1928): 18-20, 77-78.
          "William Franklin, Benjamin Franklin's son,
      whose story is the tragedy of a New Jersey
      Loyalist."
G54   "Last Veterans of the Revolution." Charm IX
      (May 1928): 24, 76, 78.
          A survey of trees that date from revolution-
      ary times in New Jersey.
G55   "The Hemingway Legend." Brentano's Book Chat
      VII (September-October) 1928): 25-29.
          An early "pen-portrait" of Ernest Hemingway.
G56   "The Edgar Allan Poe Tradition." Outlook CXLIX
      (July 25, 1928): 497-99, 511.
          A reevaluation of Poe.

      1929
G57   "My Countryside, Then and Now." Harper's
      CLVIII (January 1929): 239-45.
          MC's Pennsylvania countryside provides "a
      study in American evolution."

G58   "Portrait of a Publisher." New Masses IV
      (January 1929): 5-6.
      Satirical portrait of a fashionable publisher.
G59   "Our Own Generation," New York Herald Tribune
      Books, June 23, 1929, pp. 1, 6.
      "Already it seems that this wartime genera-
      tion will be rather important in the history
      of American letters."
G60   "The New Primitives," New York Herald Tribune
      Books, June 30, 1929, pp. 1, 6.
      A new group of young writers represent a
      break with the literary traditions valued by
      Oswald Spengler and Joseph Wood Krutch.
G61   "The Literary Business." New Republic LIX
      (July 3, 1929): 172-74.
      An evaluation of publishing.
G62   "The Escape from America," New York Herald
      Tribune Books, November 10, 1929, pp. 1, 6.
      Many writers leave America to achieve their
      independence from mass production and uni-
      formity. (Third in a series of leading es-
      say-reviews. The others were F132, F134, and
      F136.)

      1930
G63   "Angry Professors." New Republic LXII (April 9,
      1930): 207-11.
      An evaluation of the "New Humanism" of More
      and Babbitt.
      Reprinted in Men and Books, edited by Malcolm
      S. Maclean and Elizabeth Katz Holmes (New
      York: Richard R. Smith, Inc., 1930), pp. 287-
      300.

Collected in Think Back on Us, pp. 3-13
(see A10).
A longer version was published as "Humanizing
Society" in The Critique of Humanism: A
Symposium, edited by C. Hartley Grattan,
pp. 63-84 (see D2).

G64   "The Vice Squad Carries On." New Republic LXII
(June 25, 1930): 147-49.
The trial of Mrs. Oscar Hammerstein provokes
an investigation into the enforcement of laws
against prostitution in New York.

G64a "The Vice Squad Carries On: II." New Republic
LXIII (July 2, 1930): 177-80.
More ugly facts about the New York City
vice squad.

G65   "Oedipus: The Future of Love." New Republic
LXIV (August 20, 1930): 14-16.
Speculations, funny or pathetic, on the
future of love, "as foreshadowed by that
science or religion known to its adherents
as the New Sexology."
Later appeared as "Oedipus; or, The Future
of Love" in Whither, Whither; or, After Sex,
What? edited by Walter S. Hankel (pseud.)
(New York: Macaulay, 1930), pp. 250-70 (see
D3).

G66   "Cheaper and Better Books." Forum and Century
LXXXIV (September 1930): 167-70.
A debate with Walter B. Pitkin on the
feasibility of marketing books at $1 instead
of the traditional $2.50.

G67   "Emperor Hughes." New Republic LXIV (October 1
1930): 180.

Review of the film "Hell's Angels," produced
and directed by Howard Hughes.

1931

G68   "Connecticut Valley." New Republic LXV (January
      28, 1931): 297-99.
      How "summer people" live in what used to be
      farming country.
      Rewritten for chpater 7, "The Age of Islands,"
      of Exile's Return (see A3).

G69   "Rosalie Evans' Ranch." New Republic LXVI
      (February 18, 1931): 10-12.
      Tribute to an American woman shot from am-
      bush while defending her ranch against the
      agrarian revolutionaries in Mexico, 1924.

G70   "Continental Highway." New Republic LXVI
      (February 25, 1931): 34-37.
      The effects of industrialization, drought,
      and progress on the rich farming areas of
      Pennsylvania, Ohio, and Tennessee.
      Collected as "Drought" in Think Back on Us,
      pp. 14-15 (see A10).

G71   "Twenty-Four Youngsters." New Republic LXVII
      (July 8, 1931): 205-6.
      Twenty-four young writers were tortured and
      killed in the campaign to suppress the
      Chinese revolution.

G72   "Played Straight." New Republic LXVII (July 22,
      1931): 262-63.
      Review of the "Ziegfeld Follies," 1931.

G73   "Exile's Return." New Republic LXVIII (Septem-
      ber 23, 1931): 150-53.
      First of a series of five articles rewritten

for chapters 5 and 6 of Exile's Return (see
A3).

G74   "Exile's Return: Significant Gesture." New
Republic LXVIII (September 30, 1931): 172-76.
MC describes his encounter with Paris police,
his trial, and the unusual repercussions.
Rewritten for chapter 5, "The Death of
Dada," of Exile's Return (see A3).

G75   "Is the Small Farmer Dying?" New Republic
LXVIII (October 7, 1931): 211-13.
Michael Gold's review of Red Bread by
Maurice Hindus and Red Villages by Y.A.
Yakovlev includes footnote by MC on pp.
212-13.

G76   "Exile's Return: Coffee and Pistols for Two."
New Republic LXVIII (October 21, 1931): 259-62.
In an effort to keep Broom alive, MC calls
a meeting of the returned exiles. The meeting
dissolves in private squabbles and has as
its sequel a bout of fisticuffs between
Josephson and Munson.
"Coffee and Pistols for Two" includes a
contemptuous portrait of Munson, which was
softened and shortened when the article was
rewritten for chapter 6 of Exile's Return
(see A3). For Munson's equally scathing reply
to the article, see his "The Fledgeling
Years" (O2).

G77   "Exile's Return: Women Have One Breast." New
Republic LXVIII (November 11, 1931): 345-48.
In the midst of a farcical dispute with
Ernest Boyd, postal censorship leads to the
death of Broom.

Rewritten for chapter 6 of Exile's Return
(see A3).

G78   "Manhattan Melody." New Republic LXIX (November 18, 1931): 14-17.

As echoes of Montparnasse grow fainter,
the returned exiles readjust themselves to
a quieter life in New York. Fifth and last
article in the series "Exile's Return."
Rewritten for chapter 6 of Exile's Return
(see A3).

1932

G79   "Manifesto to the Trade." New Republic LXIX (February 3, 1932): 326-27.

Reactions to an economic survey of the book industry.

G80   "'Let's Build a Railroad'." New Republic LXIX (February 10, 1932): 351.

Review of the first Russian sound film shown
in this country, Road to Life.
Collected in Think Back on Us, pp. 16-18
(see A10).

G81   "Kentucky Coal Town." New Republic LXX (March 2, 1932): 67-70.

An on-the-scene account of class warfare in
the mining towns of Kentucky.

G82   "The Biography of a Strike." New Republic LXX (March 9, 1932): 98-99.

Review of the play "Mill Shadows" by Tom
Tippett, a chronicle of the textile strike
in Marion, North Carolina, and an example
of the new "theater of labor."

G83   "The Flight of the Bonus Army." New Republic

LXXII (August 17, 1932): 13-15.

What happened after the bonus marchers were
driven out of Washington.

Reprinted in The New Republic Anthology:
1915-1935, edited by Groff Conklin (New
York: Dodge Publishing Co., 1936), pp. 429-
34, and in The Thirties: A Time to Remember,
edited by Don Congdon (New York: Simon and
Schuster, 1962), pp. 118-22.

Collected in Think Back on Us, pp. 21-26
(see A10).

G84   "The Homeless Generation: Mansions in the Air."
New Republic LXXII (October 26, 1932): 281-85.

The high-school and college education of MC
and his friends. The first of two articles.

Rewritten for chapter 1, "Mansions in the
Air," of Exile's Return (see A3).

G85   "Ambulance Service." New Republic LXXII (November 2, 1932): 325-28.

MC joins the American Ambulance Service in
France, 1917. The second of two articles on
the homeless generation.

Rewritten for chapter 1, "Mansions in the
Air," of Exile's Return (see A3).

G86   "Red Day in Washington." New Republic LXXIII
(December 21, 1932): 153-55.

On the use of police force to restrain the
"hunger marchers."

MC wrote "King Mob and John Law," the second
part of this article, pp. 154-55.

1933

G87   "War in Bohemia." Scribner's Magazine XCIII

(January 1933): 56-59.

Greenwich Village, 1919.

Rewritten for chapter 2, "War in Bohemia,"
of Exile's Return (see A3).

Revised version reprinted in A Preface to
Our Times, edited by William E. Buckler
(New York: American Book Co., 1968), pp. 313-
22.

G88 "How Far Back to the Land." New Republic LXXV
(August 9, 1933): 336-39.

People returning to farms are going to
mountain and scrub areas with the poorest
soil because the rich agricultural areas
are heavily mortgaged. MC wrote "Mountain
Slum," the second part of this article,
pp. 337-39.

G89 [Untitled]. New Republic LXXVI (September 20,
1933): 160-61.

A reply to Archibald MacLeish's review (in
the same issue) of The First World War,
edited by Laurence Stallings (see K6).
Collected with K6 as "MacLeish vs. Cowley:
Lines for an Interment" in Think Back on Us,
pp. 35-47 (see A10).

1934

G90 "The Religion of Art: Readings from the Lives
of the Saints." New Republic LXXVII (January 3,
1934): 216-18.

On Eliot, Joyce, Proust, and Valéry.
Rewritten for chapter 4, "Paris Pilgrimages,"
of Exile's Return (see A3).
The Eliot section of the chapter was re-

printed in T.S. Eliot: A Selected Critique,
edited by Leonard Unger (New York: Rinehart,
1948), pp. 30-33.

G91 "The Religion of Art." New Republic LXXVII
(January 10, 1934): 246-49.
Part 2, "A Discourse over the Grave of
Dada." On the Symbolist movement as a way
of life, and how it led to Dadaism.
Rewritten for chapter 5, "The Death of Dada,"
of Exile's Return (see A3).

G92 "The Religion of Art." New Republic LXXVII
(January 17, 1934): 272-75.
Part 3, "The Death of a Religion."
Rewritten for chapter 5, "The Death of
Dada," of Exile's Return (see A3).

G93 "Ivory Towers To Let." New Republic LXXVIII
(April 18, 1934): 260-63.
An explanation of the American writer's
change in position from political indif-
ference to political action.

G94 "Good Books That Almost Nobody Has Read." New
Republic LXXVIII (April 18, 1934): 281-83.
Some neglected books recommended by John Dos
Passos, Sinclair Lewis, Edmund Wilson,
Clara G. Stillman, John Chamberlain, Isidor
Schneider, Suzanne LaFollette, Thornton
Wilder, Horace Gregory, F. Scott Fitzgerald,
T.S. Matthews, and Conrad Aiken.

G95 "Art Tomorrow." New Republic LXXIX (May 23,
1934): 34-36.
On the artist's role in society.
Included as "Epilogue" in the first edition
of Exile's Return (see A3); omitted from

1951 edition.

Collected in Think Back on Us, pp. 56-62
(see A10).

G96 "More about Neglected Books." New Republic
LXXIX (May 23, 1934): 49-50.

Some neglected books recommended by Newton
Arvin, Mary M. Colum, Robert M. Coates,
Clifton Fadiman, Harry Hansen, Robert Cant-
well, and Lewis Gannett; and comments on
Lee J. Smits' novel The Spring Flight.

G97 "Former Fugleman." New Republic LXXXI (November
21, 1934): 50-51.

Inconsistencies in H.L. Mencken's criticism
of the young writers.

Collected in Think Back on Us, pp. 70-74
(see A10).

G98 "More about Romains." New Republic LXXXI
(December 19, 1934): 170-71.

On Men of Good Will, by Jules Romains.

1935

G99 "Letter from the States." Time and Tide XVI
(January 12, 1935): 50-51.

On the Smart Set Anthology, edited by Burton
Rascoe, and contemporary American literature.
Reprinted in the New Republic LXXXII (February
13, 1935): pp. 22-23, as "Letter to England";
collected in Think Back on Us, pp. 254-58
(see A10).

G100 "A Note on Marxian Criticism." New Republic
LXXXI (January 30, 1935): 337.

A request that the American Writers' Congress
carefully define the limits of revolutionary

criticism.

Collected in <u>Think</u> <u>Back</u> <u>on</u> <u>Us</u>, pp. 81-83
(see A10).

G101 "Strictly Private." <u>New</u> <u>Republic</u> LXXXII (March
6, 1935): 106.

Notes for a personal collection of good
American prose.

G102 "What the Revolutionary Movement Can Do for a
Writer." <u>New</u> <u>Masses</u> XV, no. 6 (May 7, 1935):
20-22.

A paper read at the American Writers' Congres
Reprinted in <u>American</u> <u>Writers'</u> <u>Congress</u>,
edited by Henry Hart (New York: International
Publishers, 1935), pp. 59-65 (see D4);
collected in <u>Think</u> <u>Back</u> <u>on</u> <u>Us</u>, pp. 87-94 (see
A10).

G103 "In Congress Here Assembled." <u>New</u> <u>Republic</u>
LXXXII (May 8, 1935): 371.

MC comments on American Writers' Congress.
Includes program for International Congress
of Writers for the Defense of Culture to be
held in Paris on June 3.
Reprinted in <u>The</u> <u>New</u> <u>Republic</u> <u>Anthology</u>:
<u>1915-1935</u>, edited by Groff Conklin (New York:
Dodge Publishing Co., 1936), pp. 510-13.

G104 "The Mid Victoria Cross." <u>New</u> <u>Republic</u> LXXXIII
(May 22, 1935): 51-52.

The Pulitzer prizes in literature, 1935.
Collected in <u>Think</u> <u>Back</u> <u>on</u> <u>Us</u>, pp. 271-74
(see A10).

G105 "Conscience Fund." <u>New</u> <u>Republic</u> LXXXIII (May
29, 1935): 79.

On recent books, good and bad, that MC hadn't
reviewed.

G106 "Directions for Making a Genius." New Republic
      LXXXIII (July 24, 1935): 311-12.
      The problems facing a writer who seeks wide
      recognition in his own time.
      Collected in Think Back on Us, pp. 274-78 (see
      A10).
G107 "The Writers' International." New Republic
      LXXXIII (July 31, 1935): 339.
      Issues and ideas discussed at the Writers'
      International Congress for the Defense of
      Culture.
      Collected in Think Back on Us, pp. 98-101
      (see A10).
G108 "Echoes of a Crime." New Republic LXXXIV
      (August 28, 1935): 79.
      The effect of the Sacco-Vanzetti case upon
      the American intelligentsia.
      Rewritten for chapter 7 of revised edition
      of Exile's Return (A3a), pp. 218-21.
G109 "The Poet's Privacy." New Republic LXXXIV
      (September 18, 1935): 163.
      Conrad Aiken's concept of the artist and his
      anonymity.
      Collected in Think Back on Us, pp. 101-4
      (see A10).

      1936
G110 "Two Sides of the Barricades." New Republic
      LXXXV (January 15, 1936): 287.
      French intellectuals and Fascism.
G111 "Nobel Prize Oration." New Republic LXXXVIII
      (August 19, 1936): 36-38.
      A reevaluation of the literary school
      represented by Sinclair Lewis.

Revised for "Foreword" of After the Genteel
Tradition (see A4).

G112 "Afterthoughts on Dos Passos." New Republic
LXXXVIII (September 9, 1936): 134.

A reevaluation of the values held by Dos
Passos' heroes.

Collected in Think Back on Us, pp. 298-301
(see A10).

Rewritten with B151 as "Dos Passos: Poet
against the World" in After the Genteel
Tradition, pp. 168-85 (see A4).

G113 "Going with the Wind." New Republic LXXXVIII
(September 16, 1936): 161-62.

Comments on the huge success of Gone with
the Wind, by Margaret Mitchell. Contains
press releases from Macmillan.

G114 "On Literature and Revolution." New Republic
LXXXIX (December 2, 1936): 147-48.

The fate of writers during and after a
revolutionary struggle.

Collected in Think Back on Us, pp. 126-29
(see A10).

1937

G115 "Stalin or Satan?" New Republic LXXXIX (January
20, 1937): 348-50.

Rebuttal to Edmund Wilson's attack (in the
same issue) on the American left-wing
writers.

G116 "A Literary Calendar: 1911-1930." New Republic
XC (February 24, 1937): 78-80, 82.

A year-by-year list of books, literary
fashions, and political events that

determined the literary climate of the
twenty years ending in 1930.
Included in After the Genteel Tradition,
pp. 183-98 (see A4).

G117 "Twenty Years of American Letters." New
Republic XC (March 3, 1937): 101-4.
Rewritten for "Postscript: Twenty Years of
American Literature [1910-1930]" in After
the Genteel Tradition, pp. 167-82 (see A4).

G118 "Congress in Madrid." New Masses XXIV (August
10, 1937): 16.
A report on the Second International Writers'
Congress, Madrid. Page 2 of same issue con-
tains excerpts from MC's address to the
Congress.

G119 "To Madrid: I." New Republic XCII (August 25,
1937): 63-65.
Spain during the Spanish Civil War.

G120 "To Madrid: II." New Republic XCII (September
1, 1937): 93-96.
Second article of the series.

G121 "Spanish War Posters." New Republic XCII
(September 8, 1937): 122-23.
Photographs of eight posters designed and
printed in Madrid, with notes by MC.

G122 "To Madrid: III: Offensive on Two Fronts."
New Republic XCII (September 15, 1937):
153-55.
Third article of the series.

G123 "To Madrid: IV: Three Spanish Kids." New
Republic XCII (September 22, 1937): 179-82.
Fourth article of the series, attacking
U.S. immigration policy.

Collected in Think Back on Us, pp. 144-52
(see A10).

G124 "To Madrid: V: International Brigade." New
Republic XCII (October 6, 1937): 233-38.
Last article of the series, on the activities
of the International Brigade.

1938

G125 "There Have To Be Censors." New Republic XCIV
(April 27, 1938): 364-65.
Concerning political censorship of art.
Collected in Think Back on Us, pp. 152-56
(see A10).

G126 "Moscow Trial: II." New Republic XCV (May 25,
1938): 79-80.
Even on the assumption that the defendants
were guilty, the trial gives a bleak impres-
sion of a Communist society.
For a review on the same subject, see F277.

G127 "Poetry Project." Poetry LII (July 1938): 224-
27.
A plea for the kind of federal assistance
for poets that will enable them to write
poetry.

G128 "Socialists and Symbolists." New Republic XCVI
(September 28, 1938): 218-19.
The Symbolist techniques used by Yeats,
Rukeyser and Spender do not mix well with
social themes.
Collected in Think Back on Us, pp. 328-32
(see A10).

G129 "Partisan Review." New Republic XCVI (October
19, 1938): 311-12.

Political criticism of the Partisan Review.
Reprinted in Years of Protest: A Collection
of American Writings of the 1930's, edited
by Jack Salzman (New York: Pegasus, 1967),
pp. 297-304.

G130 "Books That Changed Our Minds." New Republic
XCVII (December 7, 1938): 135-37.

Books chosen by Carl Becker, Morris R.
Cohen, Thurman Arnold, Felix Frankfurter,
Kenneth Burke, Harold Laski, John Chamberlain,
and Granville Hicks.
Included in Books That Changed Our Minds, as
part of the "Foreword" (see B2).

G131 "The Business of Book Reviewing." Publishers'
Weekly CXXXIV (December 17, 1938): 2090-92.
Changes in book reviewing during the past
twenty years.

G132 "Books That Changed Our Minds: II." New
Republic XCVII (December 21, 1938): 205-7.
Books chosen by Paul Weiss, Lewis Mumford,
Clifton Fadiman, I.F. Stone, Newton Arvin,
and Robert S. Lynd.
Included in Books That Changed Our Minds, as
part of the "Foreword" (see B2).

1939

G133 "Transatlantic View." New Republic XCVII
(January 18, 1939): 318-20.
The New Republic compared with the New
Statesman.
Collected as "American and English Journals
of Opinion" in Think Back on Us, pp. 156-62
(see A10).

G134 "Yeats and O'Faolain." New Republic XCVIII
(February 15, 1939): 49-50.
     "Marxist" criticism vs. the "New" criticism.
     Collected in Think Back on Us, pp. 336-42
     (see A10).
G135 "Epitaph for Scribner's." New Republic XCIX
(May 24, 1939): 77.
     On the death of Scribner's Magazine.
G136 "Exiles of the Arts." New Republic XCIX
(May 31, 1939): 105-6.
     Artist-refugees who flocked to America in
     the 1930s.
     Collected in Think Back on Us, pp. 163-67
     (see A10).
G137 "Notes on a Writers' Congress." New Republic
XCIX (June 21, 1939): 192-93.
     Report on the educational and humanitarian
     accomplishments of the Third American
     Writers' Congress.
     Collected in Think Back on Us, pp. 167-70
     (see A10).
G138 "The End of the Reasoning Man." New Republic
C (October 4, 1939): 237-240.
     Part of the series "Books That Changed
     Our Minds."
     Rewritten with G138a for the "After-
     word" of Books That Changed Our Minds
     (see B2).
G138a"The End of the Reasoning Man: II." New
Republic C (October 11, 1939): 264-67.
     Last of the series "Books That Changed
     Our Minds."
     Rewritten with G138 for the "Afterword"

of Books That Changed Our Minds (see B2).

G139 "A Farewell to the 1930's." New Republic CI
(November 8, 1939): 42-44.

An appraisal of the literature of the
1930s and some predictions for the 1940s.
Collected in Think Back on Us, pp. 347-54
(see A10).

1940

G140 "Sixteen Propositions." New Republic CII
(February 26, 1940): 264-65.

An unsigned editorial by Cowley suggesting
new foundations for the American Progressive
movement.
Collected in Think Back on Us, pp. 170-74
(see A10).

G141 "This Man's Army." New Republic CIII (September 23, 1940): 406-7.

On the newly-passed conscription bill, with
suggestions to correct injustices that have
existed in American armies.

1941

G142 "Poets as Reviewers." New Republic CIV
(February 24, 1941): 281-82.

On the subjective nature of criticism.

G143 "Of Clocks and Calendars." New Republic CIV
(March 17, 1941): 376-77.

Notes on F. Scott Fitzgerald, poetry
reviewing, and mystery stories.

G144 "Remembering Hart Crane." New Republic CIV
(April 14, 1941): 504-6.

Included in chapter 7, "The Age of Islands,"

of the revised edition of Exile's Return
(see A3a).

Reprinted in The Creative Process: A Symposium, edited by Brewster Ghiselin (Berkeley:
University of California Press, 1952),
pp. 148-50.

G145 "What Poets Are Saying." Saturday Review of
Literature XXIV (May 3, 1941): 3-4, 18.

Some predictions for poetry in the 1940s.
Collected as "What the Poets Are Saying:
1941" in Think Back on Us, pp. 372-77 (see
A10).

G146 "Poets and Prophets." New Republic CIV (May 5,
1941): 639-40.

On Archibald MacLeish and the political
weakness of the intellectuals.

G147 "Marginalia." New Republic CIV (June 9, 1941):
798-99.

The effects of war on books and publishing.

G148 "Marginalia." New Republic CV (July 7, 1941):
25.

Notes on Louise Bogan, Winston Churchill, and
vegetable gardens.

G149 "Marginalia." New Republic CV (October 13,
1941): 480-81.

Notes on the current best-seller list,
Margaret Leech, and the critics' use of
psychology.

G150 "Wolfe and the Lost People." New Republic CV
(November 3, 1941): 592-94.

On Thomas Wolfe and the "artistic temperament."

G151 "Writing in Wartime." New Republic CV

(November 17, 1941). 674.

Prospects for the professional writer during
the defense emergency.

1942

G152 "Reading in Wartime." New Republic CVII
(September 14, 1942): 321-22.

Two types of reading that interest MC in
wartime: accurate reports and honest statements of feeling.

G153 "Town Report: 1942." New Republic CVII
(November 23, 1942): 674-76.

MC's New England town--here called "Sheridan"--has been rapidly changing since the
war began.

1943

G154 "Marginalia." New Republic CVIII (January 4,
1943): 25-26.

Notes on Hart Crane, literary trends,
and politicians.

G155 "Ferrero in Washington." New Republic CVIII
(February 1, 1943): 152-53.

An imaginary conversation based upon The
Principles of Power by Guglielmo Ferrero.

G156 "Books Are Too Long." New Republic CVIII
(March 29, 1943): 417-18.

On paper-rationing, and Generation of Vipers,
by Philip Wylie.

G157 "The Haunted House." New Republic CVIII
(April 12, 1943): 481-82.

Ghost writing and writers.

G158 "The Sorrows of Elmer Davis." New Republic

CVIII (May 3, 1943): 591-93.

The Office of War Information and its policie

G159 "The End of the New Deal." New Repbulic CVIII
(May 31, 1943): 729-32.

The last New Deal agencies have been abolishe
what will come next?

G160 "Poet of This War." New Republic CIX (July 5,
1943): 23-25.

Louis Aragon's effective war poems.

G161 "Marginalia." New Republic CIX (July 12, 1943)

On Sidney Hook's essay, "The New Failure of
Nerve," and The Fifth Seal, by Mark Aldanov.

G162 "Mr. Cholerton's Beard." New Republic CIX
(August 2, 1943): 145-56.

On the kinds of books correspondents come
home from Russia to write.

G163 "The Streets of Palermo." New Republic CIX
(August 9, 1943): 188-89.

On the rejoicing when American soldiers
landed in Sicily.

G164 "The Literary Business in 1943." New Republic
CIX (September 27, 1943): 417-19.

The first of two articles on publishing
during wartime.

G165 "Books by the Millions." New Republic CIX
(October 11, 1943): 482-85.

The second article on publishing during wart

G166 "For Otis." New Republic CIX (November 1,
1943): 625-26.

In memory of Otis Ferguson, lost when his
ship went down off Anzio Beach.

G167 "Books and People." New Republic CIX
(November 15, 1943): 689-90.

Reminiscences of Philip Littell and notes

on Ezra Pound.

G168 "American Literature in Wartime." New Republic
CIX (December 6, 1943): 800-803.

First of a series of articles by various
writers on American civilization in wartime.

1944

G169 "The Generation That Wasn't Lost." College
English V (February 1944): 233-39.

Significant qualities of the "lost generation."
Reprinted in College English XXII (November
1960): 93-98.

G170 "Marginalia." New Republic CX (March 27, 1944):
412-14.

Notes on The Silence of the Sea, by Vercors
(Jean Bruller), and Writers Take Sides, a
pamphlet published by the League of American
Writers, 1938.

G171 "Unshaken Friend: I." New Yorker XX (April 1,
1944): 28-32, 35-36.

Profile of a great editor, Maxwell Perkins.

G172 "Unshaken Friend: II." New Yorker XX (April 8,
1944): 30-34, 36, 39-40.

Profile of Maxwell Perkins concluded.

G173 "Marginalia." New Republic CX (April 17, 1944):
537-38.

Notes on Bernard DeVoto and on the eleventh
and fourteenth editions of The Encyclopaedia
Britannica.

G174 "The War against Writers." New Republic CX
(May 8, 1944): 631-32.

A rebuttal to Bernard DeVoto's attack on the
serious American writers of his time.

G175 "A Footnote on French Prosody." New Republic

CX (May 22, 1944): 714, 716.

The rules for writing poetry in French.
Revised as appendix to André Gide's
Imaginary Interviews (see E9).

G176 "André Gide in Wartime." New Republic CX
(June 5, 1944): 766-68.

On the political judgments expressed by
Gide in his literary criticism.
Revised for introduction to André Gide's
Imaginary Interviews (see E9).

G177 "Hemingway at Midnight." New Republic CXI
(August 14, 1944): 190-95.

Hemingway continues the tradition of Poe,
Hawthorne and Melville.
Extracted from the introduction to The
Portable Hemingway (see B3).
French translation: Revue internationale
(June-July 1947), pp. 549-54.
German translation: Umstrau II (1947) 542-50

G178 "Frost: A Dissenting Opinion." New Republic
CXI (September 11, 1944): 312-13.

Frost has been receiving political rather
than poetical accolades.
Reprinted in Robert Frost: A Collection of
Critical Essays, edited by James M. Cox
(Englewood Cliffs, New Jersey: Prentice-Hall
1962), pp. 36-45.
Collected with G179 as "Robert Frost: A
Dissenting Opinion" in A Many-Windowed
House, pp. 201-12 (see A12).

G179 "The Case against Mr. Frost: II." New Republic
CXI (September 18, 1944): 345-47.

Collected with G178 as "Robert Frost: A

Dissenting Opinion" in A Many-Windowed
House, pp. 201-12 (see A12).

G180 "Notes for a Hemingway Omnibus." Saturday
Review of Literature XXVII (September 23,
1944): 7-8, 23-25.

"The pattern of his work and its relation to
his life."
Extracted and revised from notes to various
sections of The Portable Hemingway (see B3).

G181 "William Faulkner's Human Comedy." New York
Times Book Review, October 29, 1944, p. 4.

"It is time to make a plea for the work of
William Faulkner."

G182 "Election Night in Sheridan." New Republic
CXI (November 20, 1944): 652-54.

The vote-counting procedures of a small
town in Connecticut.

G183 "Hemingway and the Hero." New Republic CXI
(December 4, 1944): 754, 756, 758.

One legend runs throughout Hemingway's four
novels.

1945

G184 "William Faulkner Revisited." Saturday Review
of Literature XXVIII (April 14, 1945): 13-16.

"He [Faulkner] deserves a much more important place in American literature than almost
any of his critics have been willing to
grant."
Extracted and revised from a longer essay on
Faulkner not published as a whole until
later (see D12).

G185 "William Faulkner's Legend of the South."

Sewanee Review LIII (Summer 1945): 343-61.
Prizewinning essay (John Peale Bishop
Memorial Contest), excerpted from a long
manuscript Introduction to William Faulkner,
which was not published complete until later
(see D12).
Reprinted in A Southern Vanguard, edited by
Allen Tate (New York: Prentice-Hall, 1947),
pp. 13-27, and in Essays in Modern Literary
Criticism, edited by Ray B. West (New York:
Rinehart, 1952), pp. 513-26.

G186 "The Middle American Style: D. Crockett to
E. Hemingway." New York Times Book Review,
July 15, 1945, pp. 3, 14.
Traces the history of the "exaggeratedly
simple style" from Davy Crockett through
Gertrude Stein.

G187 "One Poet and the War." New Republic CXIII
(August 13, 1945): 193-94.
". . . Aragon is the only poet of the
western countries who has left a complete
record of wartime emotions. . . ."
Revised with G190 as "Poet of This War" as
introduction to Aragon: Poet of the French
Resistance (see B4).

G188 [Unsigned] "Holy Horatio." Time XLVI (August
13, 1945): 98, 100, 102.
The life of Horatio Alger.
Collected with F437 and G328 as "The Real
Horatio Alger Story" in A Many-Windowed
House, pp. 76-88 (see A12).

G189 [Edited with an introduction by MC] "Aragon:
A Little Anthology." Sewanee Review LIII

(Autumn 1945): 609-29.

Selections from translations by MC and
others of Louis Aragon's poems which had not
yet appeared in this country (see N3-7).

G190 "Laureate of the Maquis' Campfires." Saturday
Review of Literature XXVIII (November 10,
1945): 7-9.

On Louis Aragon's wartime poetry.
Revised with G187 as "Poet of This War" as
introduction to Aragon: Poet of the French
Resistance (see B4).

G191 "For the Postwar Writers." New Republic CXIII
(December 3, 1945): 751-52.

A comparison of opportunities available to
the postwar writers with those available to
their immediate predecessors.

G192 "A Promise Paid." New Republic CXIII (December
10, 1945): 805.

On Ellen Glasgow.

1946

G193 "Louis Aragon: Poet of the French Resistance."
Salute I (May 1946): 11.

Aragon's poetry symbolizes the French
Resistance.

G194 "Walt Whitman: The Miracle." New Republic CXIV
(March 18, 1946): 185-88.

Toward a reevaluation of Leaves of Grass,
which is "an extraordinary mixture of
greatness, false greatness and mediocrity."
Combined with G195, G207, and G208, this
forms the introduction to The Complete
Poetry and Prose of Walt Whitman (see B7).

Introduction was reprinted as "Whitman: The Poet and the Mask" in A Many-Windowed House, pp. 35-75 (see A12).

G195 "Walt Whitman: The Secret." New Republic CXIV (April 8, 1946): 481-84.

This second of four articles on Whitman discusses his homoeroticism. For subsequent appearances of the four articles, see preceding entry.

G196 "American Books Overseas." New Republic CXV (July 8, 1946): 16-18, 20.

The attitude of the world at large towards American literature has greatly changed during the last forty years.

Like the following entry, G197, this article was taken from a chapter that MC contributed to Literary History of the United States (see D9).

G197 "U.S. Books Abroad." Life XXI (September 16, 1946): 2, 4, 6, 8, 11.

On the reception given American literature in other countries (see D9).

G198 "Magazine Business: 1910-46." New Republic CXV (October 21, 1946): 521-23.

A short history of magazine publishing in this country.

G199 "Limousines on Grub Street." New Republic CXV (November 4, 1946): 588-92.

How writers earned their livings, 1940-46. Reprinted, enlarged, as "How the Writer Lives" in Twentieth Century Unlimited, edited by Bruce Bliven (Philadelphia and New York: Lippincott, 1950), pp. 254-65 (see D11)

and abridged in Writer LXIV (June 1951):
181-83.

1947

G200 "A Note on Publishing." New Republic CXVI
(January 20, 1947): 38-40.
". . . in spite of its various corporate
arrangements [the publishing business]
. . . has been largely a matter of individuals.

G201 "Ten Little Magazines." New Republic CXVI
(March 31, 1947): 30-33.
Ten new "little magazines" enter a field
that has been essential in American letters.

G202 "Naturalism's Terrible McTeague." New Republic
CXVI (May 5, 1947): 31-33.
On Frank Norris and the beginnings of
naturalism in America. Part 1 of a three-
part series.
Reprinted with G205 in "Naturalism in Ameri-
can Literature," in Evolutionary Thought in
America, edited by Stow Persons (see D10).
Collected with G205 as "A Natural History
of American Naturalism" in A Many-Windowed
House, pp. 116-52 (see A12).

G203 "Sister Carrie's Brother." New Republic CXVI
(May 26, 1947): 23-25.
On Dreiser and naturalism in America. Part 2
of a three-part series.
Reprinted with G204 in The Stature of
Theodore Dreiser, edited by Alfred Kazin and
Charles Shapiro (Bloomington: Indiana
University Press, 1955), pp. 171-74.

Collected with G204 as "Sister Carrie's
Brother" in A Many-Windowed House, pp. 153-6
(see A12).

G204 "The Slow Triumph of Sister Carrie." New
Republic CXVI (June 23, 1947): 24-27.
On the beginnings of American naturalism.
Part 3 of a three-part series.
Reprinted with G203 in The Stature of
Theodore Dreiser, edited by Alfred Kazin and
Charles Shapiro (Bloomington: Indiana
University Press, 1955), pp. 174-81.
Collected with G203 as "Sister Carrie's
Brother" in A Many-Windowed House, pp. 153-6
(see A12).

G205 "'Not Men': A Natural History of American
Naturalism." Kenyon Review IX (Summer 1947):
414-35.
Naturalism in American fiction.
Reprinted in Critiques and Essays on Modern
Fiction, 1920-1951 (see D10), and with G202
in Evolutionary Thought in America, edited
by Stow Persons (see D10).
Collected with G202 as " A Natural History
of American Naturalism" in A Many-Windowed
House, pp. 116-52 (see A12).

G206 "The Little Magazines Growing Up." New York
Times Book Review, September 14, 1947, pp. 5,
35.
A comparison between the "little magazines"
in 1947 and those of the 1920s.
Revised for chapter 1, "The New Age of the
Rhetoricians," of The Literary Situation (see
A6).

G207 "Walt Whitman: The Philosopher." New Republic
      CXVII (September 29, 1947): 29-31.
         The third of four articles on Whitman.
         Collected with G194, G195, and G208 as
         "Whitman: The Poet and the Mask" in A Many-
         Windowed House, pp. 35-75 (see A12).
G208 "Whitman: The Poet." New Republic CXVII
      (October 20, 1947): 27-30.
         A tribute to Whitman's greatness as a poet.
         This and the preceding entry form part of
         the introduction to The Complete Poetry and
         Prose of Walt Whitman (see B7, G194, G195).
         Collected with G194, G195, and G207 as
         "Whitman: The Poet and the Mask" in A Many-
         Windowed House, pp. 35-75 (see A12).

      1948
G209 "Desk-Size Dictionaries: A Consumer's Report."
      New Republic CXVIII (February 2, 1948): 26-28.
         On lexicography and the business of selling
         dictionaries.
G210 "The Young Conquerors." New Republic CXVIII
      (June 28, 1948): 22-24.
         What the new writers are saying about the
         war: nine first novels by American veterans.
         Rewritten for chapter 2, "War Novels: After
         Two Wars," of The Literary Situation (see A6).
G211 "Two Wars--And Two Generations." New York
      Times Book Review, July 25, 1948, pp. 1, 20.
         The novelist's climate in the twenties and
         legacy to the novelist of today.
         Rewritten for chapter 2, "War Novels: After
         Two Wars," of The Literary Situation (see A6).

G212 "Hawthorne in Solitude." New Republic CXIX
     (August 2, 1948): 19-23.
     "Out of the self-realization of this lonely
     and prodigious mind came the freshest of the
     American literary streams."
     Included in introduction to The Portable
     Hawthorne (see B6).
     Collected with G213 in A Many-Windowed
     House, pp. 3-34 (see A12).
G213 "Hawthorne in the Looking-Glass." Sewanee
     Review LVI (Autumn 1948): 545-63.
     On Hawthorne's use of mirror images and the
     relation they bear to his personal and
     literary problems.
     Collected with G212 in A Many-Windowed
     House, pp. 3-34 (see A12).

     1949
G214 "A Portrait of Mister Papa." Life XXVI
     (January 10, 1949): 86-90, 93-94, 96-98,
     100-1.
     Ernest Hemingway in 1949.
     Reprinted in Ernest Hemingway: The Man and
     His Work, edited by John K.M. McCaffery
     (Cleveland and New York: World, 1950), pp. 3-
     56.
     A German translation appeared in Monat VII
     (December 1954): 204-10.
G215 "Dos Passos and His Critics." New Republic CXX
     (February 28, 1949): 21-23.
     Reactions to The Grand Design by John Dos
     Passos.
G216 "T.S. Eliot's Ardent Critics--and Mr. Eliot."

New York Herald Tribune Weekly Book Review,
March 13, 1949, pp. 1-2.

". . . the excessive denseness or difficulty
of Eliot's poems has been a challenge to
many of our ablest critics."

G217 "Lafcadio Herun-san." New Republic CXX
(April 18, 1949): 22-24.

On the career of Lafcadio Hearn and his
Japanese ghost and fairy stories.
Included in the introduction to The Selected
Writings of Lafcadio Hearn (see C2).
Collected in A Many-Windowed House, pp. 100-
15 (see A12).

G218 "The Literary Atmosphere of Two Eras." New
York Herald Tribune Weekly Book Review,
September 25, 1949, p. 6.

Characteristics of literary life in the 1920s
and in the 1940s.
Revised for chapter 2, "War Novels: After
Two Wars," of The Literary Situation (see A6).

G219 "A Tabular History of the Literary Life, 1924-
1949." New York Herald Tribune Weekly Book
Review, September 25, 1949, p. 7.

"Fashions among the younger writers: how
they learned, lived and amused themselves"
[in tabular form].

G220 "The Battle over Ezra Pound." New Republic CXXI
(October 3, 1949): 17-20.

"The literary battle of the year is being
fought over Ezra Pound and the Bollingen
Award."
Reprinted in The Case against the Saturday
Review of Literature (Chicago: Poetry, 1949),

pp. 31-38.

G221 "New Tendencies in the Novel: Pure Fiction."
New Republic CXXI (November 28, 1949): 32-35.
The "new" fiction avoids the taint of
journalism by being aggressively nonsocial
and nonpolitical.

1950

G222 "On Writing as a Profession." New Republic
CXXII (April 24, 1950): 15-19.
Part history and part survey of opportunities available to beginning and experienced
writers.

G223 "100 Years Ago: Hawthorne Sets a Great New
Pattern." New York Herald Tribune Book Review,
August 6, 1950, pp. 1, 13.
On The Scarlet Letter as a tragedy in five
acts.
A revised version appeared in College English
(October 1957) (see G268).
Reprinted in a greatly expanded version in
Twelve Original Essays on Great American
Novels, edited by Charles Shapiro (see D13).

G224 "Concerning the Prevalance of Witches." New
Republic CXXIII (October 23, 1950): 18-20.
The possibility that witches were "real" in
the sense of being adherents of a heretical
faith leads to a parallel between the perse-
cution of witches and the loyalty crusade.

1951

G225 "The Scott Fitzgerald Story." New Republic
CXXIV (February 12, 1951): 17-20.

About Fitzgerald, with emphasis on "the
moral atmosphere of the period in which
Fitzgerald flourished and declined."
Used in introduction to The Stories of
F. Scott Fitzgerald (see B8).

G226 "Fitzgerald: The Double Man." Saturday Review
of Literature XXXIV (February 24, 1951): 9-10,
42-44.

F. Scott Fitzgerald's ability to live in his
times while standing apart from them is one
of his distinguishing marks as a writer.
Reprinted in Saturday Review Reader (New
York: Bantam Books, 1951), pp. 69-77.
Used in introduction to The Stories of F.
Scott Fitzgerald (see B8).

G227 "Fox in Flight." Furioso VI (Spring 1951):
7-10.

On Ezra Pound.
Used in revised edition of Exile's Return,
pp. 119-24 (see A3a).

G228 "Twenty-Five Years After: The Lost Generation
Today." Saturday Review of Literature XXXIV
(June 2, 1951): 6-7, 33-34.

Rewritten for "Epilogue: New Year's Eve" of
the revised edition of Exile's Return (see
A3a).
How the "exiles" assimilated as individuals
and as a group.

G229 "Fitzgerald's 'Tender'--The Story of a Novel."
New Republic CXXV (August 20, 1951): 18-20.

Part of the introduction to Tender Is the
Night, by F. Scott Fitzgerald (see B9).

G230 "Notes on the Literary Stock Exchange." New

<u>Republic</u> CXXV (December 10, 1951): 14-16.
How the rise and fall of literary reputa-
tions is quoted as if on the stock market.
Revised for chapter 7, "Hardbacks or Paper-
backs?" of <u>The</u> <u>Literary</u> <u>Situation</u> (see A6).

1952

G231 "Marginalia." <u>New</u> <u>Republic</u> CXXVI (May 26, 1952)
17-18.
Notes on "the paranoid era," Mickey Spillane,
critics, and Mary McCarthy.

G232 "More Marginalia." <u>New</u> <u>Republic</u> CXXVI (June 9,
1952): 17-18.
Notes on Van Wyck Brooks, and on Alan
Condor, translator of Rimbaud's <u>The</u> <u>Drunken</u>
<u>Boat</u>.

G233 "Dewey in an Age of Unreason." <u>New</u> <u>Republic</u>
CXXVI (June 16, 1952): 8.
John Dewey's "is a reasonable and practical
. . . voice, and it is needed now more than
ever."

G234 "Biography with Letters." <u>Wake</u> XI (Summer
1952): 26-31.
Recollections of Conrad Aiken, mostly based
on forty letters written from Aiken to MC
between 1923 and 1952.

1953

G235 "Haven't You Read These Novels?" <u>New</u> <u>Republic</u>
CXXVIII (March 30, 1953): 26, 30.
Six stereotypes most frequently found among
the novels now circulating in manuscript.
Revised for chapter 4, "Critics over

Novelists," of The Literary Situation (see
A6).

G236 "A Tidy Room in Bedlam." Harper's CCVI (April
1953): 27-33.

"Notes on the 'new' fiction."
Revised for chapter 3, "The 'New' Fiction:
A Tidy Room in Bedlam," of The Literary
Situation (see A6).

G237 "F. Scott Fitzgerald: The Romance of Money."
Western Review XVII (Summer 1953): 245-55.

Revised and reprinted as introduction to
The Great Gatsby (see B10).

G238 "The New Critics and the New Fiction." Saturday
Review of Literature XXXVI (July 25, 1953):
7-8, 34-36.

Young writers are too much influenced by
aesthetic catchwords; they have been led
astray by fashionable critical slogans.
Revised for chapter 4, "Critics over
Novelists," of The Literary Situation (see
A6).

Reprinted in the Saturday Review Reader No.
3 (New York: Bantam Books, 1954), pp. 119-27.

G239 "The Literary Situation: 1953." Perspectives
U.S.A. V (Fall 1953): 5-13.

"Introduction," written by MC as guest editor
for this issue, was the starting point of
The Literary Situation (see A6).

G240 "American Novels since the War." New Republic
CXXIX (December 28, 1953): 16-18.

A "topographical" view of postwar American
fiction.

Reprinted in The Arts at Mid Century, edited

by Robert Richman (New York: Horizon Press,
1954), pp. 243-50.

1954

G241 "New Novels: Hardbacks or Paperbacks." New
Republic CXXX (April 26, 1954): 18-19.
    On the economics of paperback publishing.
    Revised for chapter 7, "Hardbacks or Paper-
    backs?" of The Literary Situation (see A6).
G242 "New Novels in Soft Covers." New Republic CXXX
(May 3, 1954): 16-17.
    Why more novels aren't published as soft-
    cover originals.
    Revised for chapter 7, "Hardbacks or Paper-
    backs?" of The Literary Situation (see A6).
G243 "Russian and American Fiction: Two Ideals."
New Republic CXXX (June 14, 1954): 21-23.
    On the movement from public to private in
    the West and from private to public in the
    East.
G244 "New Times, New Values." New Republic CXXXI
(August 16, 1954): 17-18.
    On the word "values" and its abuse by many
    critics.
    Revised for chapter 4, "Critics over
    Novelists," of The Literary Situation (see
    A6).
G245 "Invitation to Innovators." Saturday Review of
Literature XXXVII (August 21, 1954): 7-8,
38-41.
    On the types of serious writing that the
    writers born after 1920 are likely to
    produce.

Revised for chapter 12, "The Next Fifty
Years in American Literature," of The
Literary Situation (see A6).

G246 [Introductory note to "Introduction to the
Nineteen Twenties: An Interior," by Nathan
Asch]. Paris Review VI (Summer 1954): 82.

G247 "In Praise of the Rejected." New Republic CXXXI
(September 20, 1954): 16-17.

A memorial to the American author who, after
publishing several books, loses his audience
(partly based on letters from Nathan Asch).
Revised for chapter 10, "A Natural History,
Still Continued," of The Literary Situation
(see A6).

G248 "American Writers and Where They Come From."
Reporter XI (September 23, 1954): 49-52.

On the racial, economic, and sectional back-
grounds of American writers at midcentury.
Revised for chapter 9, "A Natural History,
Continued," of The Literary Situation (see
A6).

G249 "How Writers Earn Their Livings." Saturday
Review of Literature XXXVII (September 25,
1954): 9-10, 36-37, 40-51.

Revised for chapter 10, "A Natural History,
Still Continued," of The Literary Situation
(see A6).

G250 "Jean-Paul Sartre at Walgreen's." Chicago I
(September 1954): 34-35.

Revised for chapter 6, "Cheap Books for the
Millions," of The Literary Situation (see
A6).

G251 "Psychoanalysts and Writers." Harper's CCIX

(September 1954): 87-93.

The simplistic explanations by some psycho-
analysts--including Dr. Edmund Bergler--of
complicated patterns of behavior.

Revised for chapter 8, "A Natural History of
the American Writer," of The Literary Situation (see A6).

G252 "What Writers Are and Why." New Republic CXXXI
(October 4, 1954): 16-17.

"For me a writer is a man or woman who
writes."

Revised for chapter 8, "A Natural History of
the American Writer," of The Literary Situation (see A6).

G253 "Personalism: A New School of Fiction." New
Republic CXXXI (October 18, 1954): 16-18.

"Each of the novelists [mentioned] seems to
believe that the author himself should be a
personality instead of a recording machine."
Revised for chapter 5, "Naturalism: No
Teacup Tragedies," of The Literary Situation
(see A6).

G254 "Some Dangers to American Writing." New Republic
CXXXI (November 22, 1954): 114-17.

"American authorship is now more precisely
threatened than at any other time in the
century."

G255 "The Time of the Rhetoricians," New World
Writing, 5th Mentor Selection (New York: New
American Library, 1954), pp. 180-92.

On "the new criticism." Includes a comparison of the "little magazines" of the 1920s
with those of the 1950s.

Revised for chapter 1, "The New Age of the
Rhetoricians," of The Literary Situation
(see A6).

G256 "Gammon for Dinner." Interim IV (1954): 21-24.
On the attempt to blacklist MC at the
University of Washington, where he was a
visiting lecturer in 1950.

G257 [Unsigned] "Prophets without Honour? The Public
Status of American Writers," Times Literary
Supplement (London), September 17, 1954,
p. liv.
Revised for chapter 11, "A Natural History,
Concluded," of The Literary Situation
(see A6). For a review of this issue,
see F504.

1955

G258 "The Function of an Academy." Proceedings of
the American Academy of Arts and Letters and
the National Institute of Arts and Letters,
2nd series, no. 5 (1955), pp. 51-62.
Address at a dinner meeting of the Academy,
December 20, 1954.

G259 "Brooks' Mark Twain: Thirty-Five Years After."
New Republic CXXXII (June 20, 1955): 17-18.
A reassessment of The Ordeal of Mark Twain,
by Van Wyck Brooks.
Reprinted as the introduction to the 1955
edition of The Ordeal of Mark Twain (see C4).

G260 "Whitman: A Little Anthology." New Republic
CXXXIII (July 25, 1955): 16-21.
Lyrical passages from Leaves of Grass,
selected and with notes by MC.

1956

G261 "The Limits of the Novel." New Republic CXXXV
     (July 9, 1956): 16-18.

     The novel "keeps moving toward limits, as if
     by decree, yet the more it approaches them,
     the less hold it may have on the great body
     of literate persons who make the novel pos-
     sible."
     Reprinted as introduction to Great Scenes
     from Great Novels, edited by Robert Terrall
     (see C6).

G262 "Sociological Habit Patterns in Linguistic
     Transmogrification." Reporter XV (September 20,
     1956): 41-43.

     Criticism of the jargon of sociologists.
     Reprinted in Modern Prose Form and Style,
     edited by William Van O'Connor (New York:
     Thomas Y. Crowell, 1959), pp. 257-61. Also
     reprinted in many other classroom antholo-
     gies.

G263 "The Man Who Abolished Time: Thornton Wilder
     and the Spirit of Anti-History." Saturday
     Review of Literature XXXIX (October 6, 1956):
     13-14, 50-52.

     Adapted and shortened by MC for prior
     magazine publication from the introduction
     he had written for A Thornton Wilder Trio
     (see C5).

1957

G264 "Presentation of Arts and Letters Grants and
     American Academy in Rome Fellowship." Pro-
     ceedings of the American Academy of Arts and

Letters and the National Institute of Arts and
Letters, 2nd series, no. 7 (1957), pp. 94-97.
Made at the Joint Ceremonial, May 23, 1956.

G265 "The Miserly Millionaire of Words." Reporter
XVI (February 7, 1957): 38-40.
Thomas Wolfe's voracious passion for words is
a clue to his character.
Part 2 of a long essay on Wolfe first
published integrally in A Second Flowering,
pp. 156-90 (see A13).

G266 "Who Are the Intellectuals?" New Republic
CXXXVI (February 25, 1957): 14-16.
What we mean by "the intellectuals" and what
part they play in American society.
Reprinted in Cross Currents, edited by H.P.
Simonson (New York: Harper & Bros., 1959),
pp. 315-22.

G267 "A Weekend with Eugene O'Neill." Reporter XVII
(September 5, 1957): 33-36.
Memories of a bizarre weekend at Brook Farm
with the O'Neills and Hart Crane in November
1923.
Reprinted in O'Neill and His Plays, by Oscar
Cargill, N. Bryllion Fagin, and William J.
Fisher (New York: New York University Press,
1961), pp. 41-49; collected as "A Weekend
with Eugene O'Neill" in A Many-Windowed
House, pp. 191-200 (see A12).

G268 "Five Acts of The Scarlet Letter." College
English XIX (October 1957): 11-16.
A consideration of Hawthorne's The Scarlet
Letter as a Racinian drama.
Appeared in an early short version and also

in a greatly expanded version (see G223 and
D13).

G269 "How Writers Write." Saturday Review XL
(November 30, 1957): 11-13, 35-36.

On The Paris Review interviews (see B11).

G270 "Thomas Wolfe: The Professional Deformation."
Atlantic Monthly CC (November 1957): 202-4,
206, 208, 210, 212.

Wolfe paid an even heavier price for his
virtues than he did for his vices.

Parts 3 and 4 of a long essay on Wolfe first
published integrally in A Second Flowering,
pp. 156-90 (see A13).

Reprinted in American Critical Essays,
Twentieth Century, edited by Harold Beaver,
pp. 89-105 (see D14); in The World of
Thomas Wolfe, edited by Clarence Hugh Holman
(New York: Charles Scribner's Sons, 1962),
pp. 167-74; and in This Is My Rest, edited
by Whit Burnett (New York: Doubleday &
Company, 1970), pp. 636-48.

G271 "The Story Tellers' Story." New Republic
CXXXVII (December 9, 1957): 20-23.

Distinctions between the novel and the short
story as revealed in The Paris Review interviews.

Part of the introduction to The Paris Review
Interviews (see B11).

G272 "The Beginning Writer in the University."
Michigan Alumnus Quarterly Review LXIV (1957):
65-74.

Suggestions for university preparation of
would-be writers.

Reprinted in To the Young Writer: Hopwood
Lectures, Second Series, edited by A.L. Bader
(see D16).

1958

G273 "Presentation of Awards." Proceedings of the
American Academy of Arts and Letters and the
National Institute of Arts and Letters, 2nd
series, no. 8 (1958), pp. 176-79.
   Made at the Joint Ceremonial, May 22, 1957.
G274 "The Leopard in Hart Crane's Brow." Esquire L
(August 1958): 264-71.
   Dissipation, Crane's method for achieving the
   poetic vision, ended in suicide.
   Revised and collected in A Second Flowering,
   pp. 191-215 (see A13).
G275 "The Hawthornes in Paradise." American Heritage
X (December 1958): 30-35.
   Nathaniel Hawthorne's courtship and conquest
   of Sophia Peabody.

1959

G276 "Presentation of Grants and Awards." Proceedings
of the American Academy of Arts and Letters and
the National Institute of Arts and Letters, 2nd
series, no. 9 (1959), pp. 257-61.
   Made at the Joint Ceremonial, May 21, 1958.
G277 "A Ten-Dollar Shelf: 20th Century American
Literature," New York Herald Tribune Book
Review (Paperback Section), January 18, 1959,
p. 2.
   MC lists fifteen paperbacks one can buy for
   a total of $10.15.

G278 "Speaking of Books," New York Times Book
     Review, June 28, 1959, p. 2.
     Obscene or blasphemous words have lost their
     prestige and power from overuse.
G279 "The Guru, the Beatnik and the Good Gray Poet,"
     New Republic CXLI (October 26, 1959): 17-19.
     Six years of Whitman's life from 1855 to
     1861 have not been properly interpreted.
     Used in introduction to Leaves of Grass: The
     First (1855) Edition (see B12, G280).
G280 "Walt Whitman's Buried Masterpieces." Saturday
     Review XLII (October 31, 1959): 11-13, 32-34.
     The first edition of Leaves of Grass is
     a great mystical work too little known
     today.
     Combined with G279 as introduction to
     Leaves of Grass: The First (1855) Edition,
     by Walt Whitman (see B12). Reprinted in
     Sunrise XVIII (October 1968): 9-20.
G280a "Two Winters with Hart Crane." Sewanee Review
     LXVII (Autumn 1959): 547-56.
     Reminiscences of Hart Crane and Allen Tate.
     Reprinted as "Two Winters with Allen Tate
     and Hart Crane" in Allen Tate and His Work,
     edited by Radcliffe Squires (Minneapolis:
     University of Minnesota Press, 1972),
     pp. 26-33.

1960
G281 "Presentation to Aldous Huxley of the Award of
     Merit Medal for the Novel." Proceedings of the
     American Academy of Arts and Letters and the
     National Institute of Arts and Letters, 2nd

series, no. 10 (1960), pp. 333-34.

Made at the Joint Ceremonial, May 20, 1959.

G282 "Anderson's Lost Days of Innocence." New
Republic CXLII (February 15, 1960): 16-18.

Sherwood Anderson's influence on the style
and vision of the generation that followed.
Expanded as introduction to Winesburg, Ohio,
by Sherwood Anderson (see B13).
Reprinted in London Magazine VII (July 1960):
61-66, as "The Living Dead--IX: Sherwood
Anderson's Epiphanies"; and in The Achievement of Sherwood Anderson, edited by Ray
Lewis White, pp. 224-30 (see D17); collected
as "Sherwood Anderson's Book of Moments" in
A Many-Windowed House, pp. 166-77 (see A12).

G283 "The Paperback Title Fight." Reporter XXIII
(July 7, 1960): 44-47.

The dilemmas that paperback publishers face
in their efforts to find titles that will
sell.

G284 "The Big Change in Publishing." Esquire LIV
(December 1960): 309-15.

Publishing business today is in a state of
healthy confusion.

1961

G285 "Van Wyck Brooks at 75." Saturday Review XLIV
(February 18, 1961): 15-73.

Brooks's interests have remained constant.
Printed with G298 as introduction to An
Autobiography, by Van Wyck Brooks (see C14).
Collected with G298 as "Van Wyck Brooks's
'Usable Past'" in A Many-Windowed House,

pp. 213-28 (see A12).

G286 "Pound Reweighed." Reporter XXIV (March 2,
1961): 35-36, 38-40.
On Ezra Pound's Cantos, mostly in dispraise.
Collected in A Many-Windowed House, pp. 178-
90 (see A12).

G287 "One Man's Hemingway." New York Herald Tribune
Books, July 9, 1961, pp. 3, 15.
Recollections of Hemingway in Paris in the
early 1920s.

G288 "Criticism: A Many-Windowed House." Saturday
Review XLIV (August 12, 1961): 10-11, 46-47.
The pitfalls of "scientific" or impersonal
criticism.
Reprinted in An English Teacher's Reader--
Grades 7-12, edited by M. Jerry Weiss (New
York: Odyssey Press, 1962), pp. 452-58; col-
lected in A Many-Windowed House, pp. 244-52
(see A12).

G289 "A Job To Do." Saturday Review XLIV (November
25, 1961): 14-15.
A salute to James Thurber by MC and others.

G290 "Presentation to James Gould Cozzens of the
Howells Medal for Fiction." Proceedings of the
American Academy of Arts and Letters and the
National Institute of Arts and Letters, 2nd
series, no. 11 (1961), pp. 38-39.
Made at the Joint Ceremonial, May 25, 1960,
for Cozzens's By Love Possessed.

1962
G291 (With Daniel P. Mannix) "Middle Passage."
American Heritage XIII (February 1962): 22-25,
103-7.

An excerpt from Black Cargoes (see A7)
printed before the book was published.

G292 "The Unsettled Literary Future of the U.S."
Saturday Review XLV (June 9, 1962): 15-17, 61.
Some literary predictions with emphasis on
the novel as the dominant form.

G293 "Artists, Conscience, and Censors." Saturday
Review XLV (July 7, 1962): 8-10, 47.
A shorter version of the essay "Ethics in
the Arts," in Ethical Problems for the
Sixties (see D15).

G294 "American Myths, Old and New." Saturday Review
XLV (September 1, 1962): 6-8, 47.
Early American myths were based on the
countryside and the frontier; later ones were
based on the great cities; now we begin to
see the outlines of a new series of myths
based on the suburbs.
Reprinted in St. Thomas More Series: Prose
and Poetry in America, Volume 4, edited by
Julian L. Maline (New York: L.W. Singer Co.,
1965), pp. 238-48; collected as "Three
Cycles of Myth in American Writing" in A
Many-Windowed House, pp. 229-43 (see A12).

G295 "A Farewell to the Last Harvard 'Dandy'." New
York Herald Tribune Books, September 9, 1962,
p. 5.
The rebellious spirit of E.E. Cummings can
be traced back to his college years.

1963

G296 "Presentation of Grants and Awards." Proceedings of the American Academy of Arts and Letters and the National Institute of Arts and

Letters, 2nd series, no. 13 (1963), pp. 238-45.

Made at the Joint Ceremonial, May 24, 1962.

G297 [Remarks included in] "Homage to Marianne Moore on Her Seventy-Fifth Birthday." Proceedings of the American Academy of Arts and Letters and the National Institute of Arts and Letters, 2nd series, no. 13 (1963), pp. 273-82.

Made at a dinner meeting, November 15, 1962. Reprinted in Festschrift for Marianne Moore's Seventy-Seventh Birthday, by various hands, edited by Tambimuttu (New York, Tambimuttu and Mass, 1964), pp. 120-21.

G298 "Van Wyck Brooks: A Career in Retrospect." Saturday Review XLVI (May 25, 1963): 17-18, 38.

Brooks constantly emphasized changing the creative climate in America.

Printed with G285 as introduction to An Autobiography, by Van Wyck Brooks (see C14).

Collected with G285 as "Van Wyck Brooks's 'Usable Past'," in A Many-Windowed House, pp. 213-28 (see A12).

G299 "The Last of the Lost Generation." Esquire LX (July 1963): 77-79.

The name for this generation seems particularly inept; it was a lucky generation.

G300 "When a Young American . . ." Mercure de France CCCXLIX (August-September 1963): 57-59.

A tribute to Sylvia Beach.

G301 "Laforgue in America: A Testimony." Sewanee Review LXXI (Winter 1963): 62-74.

The influence of Jules Laforgue on the young writers of 1920. Includes the first appearance of "Variations on a Cosmical Air," a

poem by MC (see M123).
Reprinted in Jules Laforgue: Essays on a
Poet's Life and Work, edited by Warren
Ramsey (Carbondale: Southern Illinois Uni-
versity Press, 1969), pp. 3-15.

1964

G302 "A Ghost Story of the Jazz Age. Reminiscences
of Twenty-four Hours with F. Scott Fitzgerald."
Saturday Review XLVII (January 25, 1964): 20-
21.
MC visited the Fitzgeralds in May 1933, at
La Paix.
Reprinted in The Saturday Review Sampler of
Wit and Wisdom, edited by Martin Levin (New
York: Simon and Schuster, 1966), pp. 59-63.

G303 "A Remembrance of the Red Romance." Esquire
LXI (March 1964): 124, 126-31.
Writers and Communism in the 1930s. Part 1
of two parts.

G304 "A Remembrance of the Red Romance." Esquire
LXI (April 1964): 78-81.
Part 2 of two parts.

G305 "While They Waited for Lefty." Saturday Review
XLVII (June 6, 1964): 16-19, 61.
Reflections on proletarian literature.

G306 "The Writer as Craftsman." Saturday Review
XLVII (June 27, 1964): 17-18.
On the literary heroism of Hamilton Basso.

G307 "Dr. Canby and His Team." Saturday Review
XLVII (August 29, 1964): 54-55, 177.
On Henry Seidel Canby, the first editor of
the Saturday Review of Literature.

G308 "The 1930's Were an Age of Faith." New York
      Times Book Review, December 13, 1964, pp. 4-5,
      14-17.
      "The distinguishing mark of [this] literary
      age was its absorbed interest in social
      ideas."

G309 "Presentation of Grants and Awards." Proceed-
      ings of the American Academy of Arts and Let-
      ters and the National Institute of Arts and
      Letters, 2nd series, no. 14 (1964), pp. 342-47.
      Made at the Joint Ceremonial, May 22, 1963.

      1965
G310 "Presentation of Grants and Awards." Proceed-
      ings of the American Academy of Arts and Let-
      ters and the National Institute of Arts and
      Letters, 2nd series, no. 15 (1965), pp. 419-24.
      Made at the Joint Ceremonial, May 20, 1964.

G311 "To Greet New Members." Proceedings of the
      American Academy of Arts and Letters and the
      National Institute of Arts and Letters, 2nd
      series, no. 15 (1965), pp. 447-59.
      MC greets new members, April 1, 1964: Leon
      Edel, John Updike, Hannah Arendt, James
      Baldwin, Chaim Gross, Ralph Ellison,
      Theodore Roszak.

G312 "A Bow to the Institute." Proceedings of the
      American Academy of Arts and Letters and the
      National Institute of Arts and Letters, 2nd
      series, no. 15 (1965), pp. 460-66.
      As retiring president, MC appraises the
      three years during which he led the Insti-
      tute. Read at a dinner meeting, November 17,
      1964.

G313 "Hamilton Basso, 1904-1964." Proceedings of the
      American Academy of Arts and Letters and the
      National Institute of Arts and Letters, 2nd
      series, no. 15 (1965), pp. 476-78.
      A tribute to an old friend.
G314 "The Old House in Chelsea . . ." Carleton
      Miscellany VI (Winter 1965): 40-49.
      The New Republic in the early 1930s.
G315 "The Meriwether Connection." Southern Review I
      (Winter 1965): 46-56.
      Account of ten weeks at Cloverlands (near
      Clarksville, Tennessee) and of a reunion of
      the Fugitive poets, in Nashville, May 1933,
      to which MC was taken by Allen Tate.
G316 "The Sense of Guilt." Kenyon Review XXVII
      (Spring 1965): 260-78.
      The former radicals of the 1930s feel a sense
      of guilt.
G317 "The Literary Situation, 1965." University of
      Mississippi Studies in English VI (1965):
      91-98.
      Literary fashions fluctuate like the stock
      market; southern writers are high at present.
      Transcript of a seminar conducted by MC at
      the Southern Literary Festival, April 23,
      1965.
G318 (With Robert Cowley) "Memoranda of a Decade."
      American Heritage XVI (August 1965): 33-40.
      Selections, with commentary, of typical
      writing from the 1920s. Excerpt from Fitz-
      gerald and the Jazz Age (see B15), printed
      before the book appeared.
G319 "Cowley on Sholokhov: One Great Book." New York
      Herald Tribune, October 17, 1965, p. 23.

The significance of awarding the Novel Prize
to Mikhail Sholokhov.

1966

G319a"The Solitude of William Faulkner." Atlantic
Monthly CCXVII (June 1966): 97-115.
Selections, printed in advance of book
publication, from The Faulkner-Cowley
File (see A9).

G320 "A Fresh Look at Faulkner." Saturday Review
XLIX (June 11, 1966): 22-26.
Part of the last chapter of The Faulkner-
Cowley File (see A9).

G321 "Afterthoughts on William Faulkner." Critic
XXV (October-November 1966): 90-92.
MC reevaluates his introduction to The
Portable Faulkner (see B5) twenty years after
writing it. With a few changes, this article
serves as an "Afterword" to the introduction
in the revised (1967) edition of the Portable
(see B5a).

1967

G322 "The Twenties in Montparnasse." Saturday
Review L (March 11, 1967): 51, 55, 98-101.
"Recollections of the Paris milieu."
Revised and collected in A Second Flowering,
pp. 53-58 (see A13).

G323 "Papa and the Parricides." Esquire LXVII
(June 1967): 100-1.
MC deplores recent attacks on Ernest
Hemingway's reputation.

1968

G324 "Aprés la guerre finie." Horizon X (Winter
      1968): 112-19.
         Some effects of World War I on the wartime
         generation of American writers; a slightly
         different version of G325.
         Revised and collected in A Second Flowering,
         pp. 3-18 (see A13).

G325 "American Writers and the First World War."
      Proceedings of the American Academy of Arts
      and Letters and the National Institute of Arts
      and Letters, 2nd series, no. 18 (1968), pp. 25-
      46.
         Address at a dinner meeting, March 29, 1967,
         in observance of the fiftieth anniversary of
         the entrance of the United States into World
         War I. For an earlier version, see G324.

G326 "The Self-Obliterated Author: S. Foster Damon."
      Southern Review n.s. IV (Winter 1968): 20-32.
         Reprinted, slightly enlarged, as "S. Foster
         Damon: The New England Voice," in William
         Blake: Essays for S. Foster Damon, edited by
         Alvin H. Rosenfeld (see D19).

1969

G327 "Five Tributes." Shenandoah XX (Spring 1969):
      36-39.
         Brief tribute to Eudora Welty.

1970

G328 "Horatio Alger: Failure." Horizon XII (Summer
      1970): 62-65.

Includes material from an earlier Alger
article (see F437).
Collected with F437 and G188 as "The Real
Horatio Alger Story" in A Many-Windowed
House, pp. 76-87 (see A12).

1971

G329 "Holding the Fort on Audubon Terrace." Saturda
Review LIV (April 3, 1971): 17, 41-42.
    On the National Institute of Arts and Letter
    and the American Academy of Arts and Letters

G330 "The Last Years of Ernest Hemingway." Academy
(University of Minnesota) VI (Spring 1971):
8-15.
    An early draft of chapter 10, section 2, of
    A Second Flowering.

G330a"John Dos Passos, 1896-1970." Proceedings of
the American Academy of Arts and Letters and
the National Institute of Arts and Letters,
2nd series, no. 21 (1971), pp. 68-73.
    A tribute to Dos Passos that was revised
    and greatly expanded for G336.

1972

G330b"Sir, I Have the Honor." Southern Review
n.s. VIII (Winter 1972): 1-14.
    Notes on the history of the National
    Institute and the American Academy of
    Arts and Letters.

G331 "A Reminiscence: Edmund Wilson on The New
Republic." New Republic CLXVII (July 1, 1972):
25-28.

G332 "The Lucky Generation." Atlantic Monthly

CCXXX (December 1972), 55-61.

Expanded and collected in A Second Flowering,
pp. 233-55 (see A13).

1973

G333 "Hemingway: Image and Shadow." Horizon XV
     (Winter 1973): 112-17.

     Combined with F535 and collected in A Second
     Flowering as chapter 10 (see A13).

G334 "Dos Passos." Southern Review n.s. IX (Winter
     1973): 3-17.

     Revised and collected in A Second Flowering,
     pp. 74-89 (see A13).

G335 "Cummings: One Man Alone." Yale Review LXII
     (April 1973): 332-54.

     Collected in A Second Flowering, pp. 90-113
     (see A13).

G336 "The Greene-ing of the Portables." Book World
     (Washington Post) VII (April 29, 1973): 13.

     An inside story of the Viking Portable
     Library from its inception in 1943 to The
     Portable Graham Greene, edited by Philip
     Stratford, published in February 1973.

G337 "A Lake Is Backdrop for Debate on Suburban
     Integration Plan." Pro, by Paul Davidoff; Con,
     by Malcolm Cowley. New York Times, Sunday,
     November 4, 1973, section 8, pp. 1, 12, 16.

     Answering Davidoff, MC ridicules the notion
     of building a new town of 8000 people on an
     inaccessible lakeside.

H.   SHORT FICTION

H1   "Then Fear Crept in at the Window." Harvard
     Advocate CII (October 10, 1916): 4.
H2   "The Wages of Death." Harvard Advocate CII
     (January 10, 1917): 105-6.
H3   "A Broken Axle." Harvard Advocate CIII (Febru-
     ary 20, 1917): 13.
H4   "The Author of His Being." Sansculotte I
     (April 1917): 2.
H5   "The Journey to Paris." Gargoyle I (October
     1921): 8-12.
H6   "Young Man with Spectacles." Broom III (Octobe
     1922): 199-203.
     A humorous portrait of a young man befuddled
     by aesthetic questions.
H7   "Young Mr. Elkins." Broom IV (December 1922):
     52-56.
     A satirical handling of the general reaction
     against Puritanism in America. (The young
     Mr. Elkins was Harold Stearns.)
H8   "Snapshot of a Young Lady." Broom V (August
     1923): 3-10.
H9   "Race between a Subway Local and a Subway Ex-
     press." Transition X (January 1928): 51-54.

I.   PROSE TRANSLATED

I1   "On Board the Morning Star," by Pierre MacOrla
     [pseud. of Pierre Dumarchey]. Broom V (August
     1923): 17-28.
     Fifth, eighth, twelfth, and sixteenth
     episodes (see E1).

I2   "The Extra," by Louis Aragon. <u>Broom</u> V (November
     1923): 211-16.
I3   "Poison," by Roger Vitrac. <u>Broom</u> V (November
     1923): 226-28.
I4   "My Dear Jean," by Philippe Soupault. <u>Broom</u> VI
     (January 1924): 6-9.
I5   "Joan Miró," by Michel Leiris. <u>Little</u> <u>Review</u>
     XII (Spring-Summer 1926): 8-9.
I6   "The Cultural Heritage," by André Malraux.
     <u>New</u> <u>Republic</u> LXXXVIII (October 21, 1936): 315-
     17.
     Malraux's address to the Writers' Interna-
     tional Association for the Defense of Culture,
     London, 1936.
I7   "They Die for France," by Louis Aragon. <u>Life</u>
     XII (May 25, 1942): 12, 14, 16.
     MC did this unsigned translation from an
     anonymous manuscript without knowing that
     Aragon was the author. It is an abbreviated
     version of "The Martyrs, by Their Witness"
     in <u>Aragon</u>, <u>Poet</u> <u>of</u> <u>the</u> <u>French</u> <u>Resistance</u>
     (see B4).
I8   "The War Is Only the Beginning," by Heinrich
     Mann. <u>New</u> <u>Republic</u> CVI (June 8, 1942): 804-5.
     Review of the <u>Edge</u> <u>of</u> <u>the</u> <u>Sword</u>, by Vladimir
     Pozner.
I9   "The Things I Stand For," by Ignazio Silone.
     <u>New</u> <u>Republic</u> CVII (November 2, 1942): 582-83.
I10 "Eisenhower Africanus," by "Gallicus." <u>New</u>
     <u>Republic</u> CIX (November 1, 1943): 609-12.
     "Gallicus" was Pierre Soupault.
I11 "The Rebirth of French Poetry: An Imaginary
     Interview," by André Gide. <u>Saturday</u> <u>Review</u> <u>of</u>
     <u>Literature</u> XXVII (April 29, 1944): 5-7.

From Gide's _Imaginary Interviews_ (see E9).

I12   "St. Mallarme the Esoteric," by André Gide.
Partisan Review XI (Summer 1944): 288-93.
Another passage from Gide's _Imaginary_
Interviews (see E9).

I12a   "Jean-Paul Sartre: Strictly Personal," by
Simone de Beauvoir. _Harper's Bazaar_ LXXX
(January 1946): 113, 158, 160.
Reprinted in _The Writings of Jean-Paul_
Sartre, edited by Michel Contat and
Michel Rybalka, 1974.

I13   "The Existence of Symbolism," by Paul Valéry.
Kenyon Review XIX (Summer 1957): 425-47.
Collected in _Leonardo_, _Poe_, _Mallarmé_,
pp. 215-39 (see E11).

I14   "Leonardo da Vinci," by Paul Valéry. _New_
Republic CXXXVIII (March 3, 1958): 17-19.
Also from _Leonardo_, _Poe_, _Mallarmé_ (see E11).

I15   "I Sometimes Said to Stéphane Mallarmé . . .,"
by Paul Valéry. _Kenyon Review_ XXVII (Winter
1965): 94-112.
Collected in _Leonardo_, _Poe_, _Mallarmé_,
pp. 272-93 (see E11).

I16   _Leonardo_, _Poe_, _Mallarmé_, by Paul Valéry (see
E11).

J.   INTERVIEWS; QUESTIONNAIRES; SYMPOSIA

J1   "Whither the American Writer." _Modern Quarterl_
VI (Summer 1932): 15, 16.

J2   "Inquiry about the Malady of Language." _Transi_
tion XXIII (July 1935): 148.

Statements by MC, Gottfried Benn, Joe
Bousquet, Marcel Brion, Henry S. Canby,
Luc Durtain, and others.

J3   "Inquiry into the Spirit and Language of Night."
      Transition XXVII (April-May 1938): 148.
      Statements by MC, Sherwood Anderson, Kenneth
      Burke, George Dillon, T.S. Eliot, Waldo
      Frank, and others.

J4   "The Teaching and Study of Writing." Western
      Review XIV (Spring 1950): 174-75.
      Entire symposium (pp. 105-79) includes state-
      ments by MC, Allen Tate, Eudora Welty, Lionel
      Trilling, Walter Van Tilburg Clark, and
      Wallace Stegner.

J5   "American Scholar Forum: The New Criticism."
      American Scholar XX (1950-51): 86-104, 218-31.
      A stenographic record of a discussion held at
      William Barrett's home, attended by MC, Allen
      Tate, Kenneth Burke, Robert Gorham Davis,
      and Hiram Haydn.

J6   "On the Books, On an Author." New York Herald
      Tribune Book Review, June 24, 1951, pp. 2, 14.
      Interview by John K. Hutchens.

J7   "Talk with Malcolm Cowley." New York Times Book
      Review, July 8, 1951, p. 13.
      Interview by Harvey Breit.

J8   "Authors Speak for Themselves." New York
      Herald Tribune Book Review, October 7, 1951,
      p. 8.
      A brief autobiography.

J9   "Who the Hell Is Hemingway?" True XXXVI
      (February 1956): 19.

J10   "A Final View." Four Quarters V (March 1956):

18.

"Why do not the Catholic colleges and universities in the United States produce an ade-
quate supply of Catholic writers?"

J11   "Creative Writing Symposium." Four Quarters X
(November 1960): 16.

J12   "Who's To Take the Place of Hemingway and
Faulkner?" New York Times Book Review, October
7, 1962, pp. 4, 26.

J13   "An Interview with Malcolm Cowley." Dalhousie
Review XLIV (Autumn 1964): 290-93.
      Interview by L.L. Graelle.

J14   "Critic Malcolm Cowley Appraises America's
Literary Situation." Literary Times (Chicago)
IV (April 1965): 8, 9.

J15   "American Fiction: The Postwar Years, 1945-
1965." New York Herald Tribune Book Week,
September 26, 1965, p. 6.

J16   "Thirty Years Later: Memories of the First
American Writers' Congress," The American
Scholar (Summer 1966), pp. 495-516.
      The stenographic record of a discussion held
      on December 8, 1965, by MC, Kenneth Burke,
      Granville Hicks, and William Phillips, with
      Daniel Aaron as moderator.

J17   "Books To Send to a Distant Planet." New York
Times Book Review, December 3, 1967, p. 2.

J18   "An Interview with Malcolm Cowley." Per/Se II
(Winter 1967-68); 34-39.
      Interview by Page Stegner and Robert
      Canzoneri at Denison University, November
      1966.

J19   "A Question of Commitment." New York Times Book
Review, June 2, 1968, p. 2.

J20   "Making It: Gossip of the Literary Marketplace
       Reported by Alice Glaser." Book World (Washing-
       ton Post) II (October 6, 1968): 8.
          On the publication of Blue Juniata: Collected
       Poems (see L4).
J21   "Critics of Two Generations: Malcolm Cowley
       and Theodore Solotaroff." Chicago Daily News,
       Panorama, April 24-25, 1971, pp. 4, 5, 10.
          Interview by Joseph Haas.
J22   "Importance of Knowing Ernest." Esquire LXXII
       (February 1972): 98-101, 164-70.
          Interviews with people who knew Hemingway by
       Denis Brian. MC's comments are on pp. 100-1.
       Reprinted in Murderers and Other Friendly
       People, edited by Denis Brian (New York:
       McGraw-Hill, 1973), pp. 15-24.
J23   "How Has the Most Famous Third-Rate Burglary
       Affected Your Life?" New York VI (October 22,
       1973): 36-37.
          On the Watergate scandal.

K.   LETTERS

K1   "Praise for the S4N." S4N IV, no. 26-29 (May-
       August 1923): [87].
K2   "On Issue 25." S4N IV, no. 26-29 (May-August
       1923): [100].
K3   "Letter: John Carter." S4N IV, no. 26-29 (May-
       August 1923): [109].
K4   "Munsoniana." Contempo I (January 1, 1932): 1,
       4.
          MC defends his account of the Munson-
       Josephson battle as given in "Coffee

and Pistols for Two" (see G76). For
Munson's side, see "The Fledgeling Years"
(see O2).

K5   "World Congress against War." New Republic LXXI
(August 10, 1932): 346.

A request for contributions to send an
American delegation to the Congress.

K6   "The Dead of the Next War." New Republic LXXVI
(October 4, 1933): 214-16.

Exchange between Archibald MacLeish and MC
about MacLeish's review of The First World
War, edited by Laurence Stallings (see G89).
Cowley's reply is on pp. 215-16.
Collected with G89 as "A Debate Continued:
The Dead of the Next War" in Think Back on
Us, pp. 35-47 (see A10).

K7   "To Save Ernst Torgler's Life." New Republic
LXXVII (January 10, 1934): 255-56.

Includes a letter to MC from Romain Rolland.

K8   "Marx and David Markand." New Republic LXXXI
(November 21, 1934): 47-48.

Includes a letter to MC from Waldo Frank.

K9   "The Paris Congress of Writers." New Republic
LXXXIII (June 19, 1935): 169.

Collected in Think Back on Us, p. 97 (see
A10).

K10   "Correspondence." Southern Review III (Summer
1937): 199.

MC's reaction to Frederick L. Schuman's
article, "Leon Trotsky: Martyr or Renegade."

K11   "Red Ivory Tower." New Republic XCVII (November 9, 1938): 22-23.

A response to accusations by the editors of
the Partisan Review.

Collected with K12 in *Years of Protest: A Collection of American Writings of the 1930's*, edited by Jack Salzman (New York: Pegasus, 1967), pp. 304-7.

K12   "Partisan Review Finale." *New Republic* XCVII (December 21, 1938): 203.

A further response to accusations by the editors of the *Partisan Review*.

Collected with K11 in *Years of Protest: A Collection of American Writings of the 1930's*, edited by Jack Salzman (New York: Pegasus, 1967), pp. 304-7.

K13   "More Fighting Words." *New Republic* CIII (August 26, 1940): 280.

MC's reply to the League of American Writers concerning his resignation.

K14   "Defense of the Hemisphere." *New Republic* CIV (June 30, 1941): 889-90.

MC responds to letter from Hanson W. Baldwin concerning Baldwin's *United We Stand!*

K15   "Justice for Federal Workers." *New Republic* CVI (May 4, 1942): 592-93.

Excerpt from MC's letter of resignation to the Office of Facts and Figures upon his investigation by the Dies Committee.

K16   "The Happiness Boys." *New Republic* CX (January 3, 1944): 25-26.

MC's reaction to an article about him in *The New Masses*, December 14, 1943.

K17   [Three letters from MC to Harold Loeb, September 15, 1924, September 17, 1924, November 23, 1924] in *The Way It Was*, by Harold Loeb (New York: Criterion Books, 1959), pp. 221-25, 229-30.

K18   [Three letters from MC to Hart Crane, May 20,
      1923, November 28, 1923, October 8, 1926, and
      a note by MC] in Robber Rocks: Letters and
      Memories of Hart Crane, 1923-1932, by Susan
      Jenkins Brown (Middletown, Connecticut:
      Wesleyan University Press, 1969), pp. 10, 19,
      65-66, 102-7 (see D20).

K19   [Letter from MC to Matthew J. Bruccoli,
      October 13, 1970] in Fitzgerald/Hemingway
      Annual, 1971, edited by Matthew J. Bruccoli
      (Dayton, Ohio; Washington: NCR Microcard Edi-
      tions Books, National Cash Register Company,
      1971), pp. 317-18.

      Discusses The Portable Hemingway and The
      Portable Faulkner published by Viking.

PART 3: POETRY
_____

L.   COLLECTIONS OF POEMS

L1   (With others) Eight More Harvard Poets, edited
     by S. Foster Damon and Robert Silliman Hillyer.
     New York: Brentano's, 1923. 130 pp.
        11 poems by MC, pp. 25-42 (see M26, M32, M40,
        M41, M43-46, M48, M51, M72).
L2   Blue Juniata. New York: Jonathan Cape and
     Harrison Smith, 1929. 115 pp.
        56 poems in five parts: 1. Blue Juniata;
        2. The Adolescent; 3. Valuta; 4. The City of
        Anger; 5. Old Melodies: Love and Death (see
        M31, M35, M38, M40, M41, M43-47, M50, M51,
        M53, M57-59, M61-70, M72, M74, M75, M77,
        M78, M80, M82-92, M95-98 [reprints]; M99-102
        [new poems]). See Introduction.
L3   The Dry Season. Norfolk, Connecticut: New
     Directions, 1941. [32] pp.
        17 poems, most of them written from 1935 to
        1941 (see M76, M94, M103-17). "The Poet of
        the Month" for December 1941.
L4   Blue Juniata: Collected Poems. New York: The
     Viking Press, 1968. x, 149 pp.
        86 poems, including 50 from the first Blue

Juniata (excluding M47, M58, M59, M80, M99,
M100), most of them revised; all 17 from The
Dry Season; and 19 hitherto uncollected (see
M52, M93, M118-33, N4) arranged in seven
parts: 1. Blue Juniata; 2. The Crooked
Streets; 3. Valuta; 4. The City of Anger;
5. The Dry Season; 6. The Unsaved World;
7. Another Country.

M.   INDIVIDUAL POEMS

M1   "To Certain Imagist Poets." Harvard Advocate
      CI (March 31, 1916): 42.

M2   "On Rereading Wordsworth." Harvard Advocate CI
      (June 5, 1916): 109.

M3   "Execution." Harvard Advocate CI (June 5, 1916)
      114.

M4   "To a Girl I Dislike." Harvard Advocate CII
      (November 8, 1916): 42.

      Reprinted in The Harvard Advocate Anthology,
      edited by Donald Hall (New York: Twayne
      Publishers, 1950), pp. 151-52.

M5   "To a Chance Acquaintance." Harvard Advocate
      CII (December 6, 1916): 69.

M6   "A Letter to Jim." Harvard Advocate CII
      (December 20, 1916): 82.

M7   "Smiles." Sansculotte I (January 1917): 5.

M8   "The Harbor at Night." Slate I (January 1917):
      14.

M9   "Ante Mortem." Harvard Advocate CII (February
      7, 1917): 152.

M10   "Ragtime." Harvard Advocate CII (February 7,
      1917): 152.

M11 "An Old Fellow to His Friends." Harvard Advo-
     cate CIII (February 28, 1917): 3.
        Reprinted in The Harvard Advocate Anthology,
        edited by Donald Hall (New York: Twayne
        Publishers, 1950), pp. 152-53.
M12 "From the Diary of a Restoration Gentleman."
     Harvard Advocate CIII (February 28, 1917): 5.
M13 "The Oldest Inhabitant." Sansculotte I
     (February 1917): 7.
M14 "Before Closing." Sansculotte I (February 1917):
     9.
M15 "The Adventurer." Harvard Advocate CIII (March
     28, 1917): 40.
M16 "On Visiting the Revere." Harvard Advocate CIII
     (April 4, 1917): 64.
M17 "The Veteran." Sansculotte I (April 1917): 7.
M18 "Wistfulness." Slate I (April 1917): 87.
M19 "Ballade of French Service." Harvard Advocate
     CIII (May 14, 1917): 7.
M20 "Poetic Love." Harvard Advocate CIV (October
     19, 1917): 20.
M21 "Last Night We Held Great Argument." Harvard
     Advocate CIV (February 1918): 280.
M22 "To a Dilettante Killed at Vimy." Harvard
     Advocate CIV (February 1918): 280.
        Reprinted in The Harvard Advocate Anthology,
        edited by Donald Hall (New York: Twayne
        Publishers, 1950), p. 153, and in Harvard
        Advocate Centennial Anthology, edited by
        Jonathan D. Culler (Cambridge: Schenkman
        Publishing Co., 1966), p. 111.
M23 "Louisburg Square." Harvard Advocate CIV (March
     1918): 308.
M24 "Sentimental." Harvard Advocate CIV (March

1918): 324.

M25 "A Theme with Variations." Harvard Advocate
CIV (April 1918): 337-38.

Reprinted in Harvard Advocate Centennial
Anthology, edited by Jonathan D. Culler
(Cambridge: Schenkman Publishing Co., 1966),
p. 109.

M26 "Runaway." Harvard Advocate CIV (Class Day,
1918): 421.

Reprinted in Eight More Harvard Poets,
pp. 35-38 (see L1).

M27 "Two French Towns, I: Ostel, II: Nouvron-
Vingré." Youth: Poetry of Today I (October
1918): 5.

M28 "Bayonet Drill: Two Sonnets." Harvard Advocate
CIV (November 1918): 18.

Sonnet 1 is by MC; sonnet 2 by S. Foster
Damon.

M29 "Parting--Gare du Nord." Youth: Poetry of
Today I (June 1919): 92-93.

M30 "Sunday Afternoon (After Jules Laforgue)."
Little Review VI (July-August 1919): 61-62.

Reprinted in The Little Review Anthology,
edited by Margaret Anderson (New York:
Hermitage House, 1953), pp. 295-97.

M31 "Nantasket." Harvard Advocate CVI (November
1919): 51.

Collected as "Young Kuppenheimer Gods" in
Blue Juniata, p. 36 (see L2), and in Blue
Juniata: Collected Poems, p. 36 (see L4);
reprinted in Harvard Advocate Centennial
Anthology, edited by Jonathan D. Culler
(Cambridge: Schenkman Publishing Co., 1966),
p. 113.

M32   "Moonrise." Poetry XV (November 1919) 76-77.
      Reprinted as "For a Georgian Anthology" in
      Eight More Harvard Poets, pp. 33-34 (see L1).
M33   "Barn Dance." Poetry XV (November 1919): 77-78.
      Reprinted in New York Sunday Tribune, Novem-
      ber 6, 1919, section 3, p. 1.
M34   "Danny." Poetry, XV (November 1919): 78-79.
      Reprinted in New York Sunday Tribune, Novem-
      ber 6, 1919, section 3, p. 1.
M35   "One O'Clock at O'Connors." Pagan IV (January
      1920): 52.
      Reprinted as "Kelly's Barroom" in Hound &
      Horn II (Summer 1929): 373; revised and
      collected in Blue Juniata, p. 35 (see L2),
      and in Blue Juniata: Collected Poems, p. 33
      (see L4).
M36   "Colloquy with Himself." Pagan IV (February
      1920): 17.
M37   "Eighteenth-Century Sonnet." Harvard Advocate
      CVI (April 1, 1920): 254.
M38   "Clinic." Little Review VI (April 1920): 23-25.
      Revised and collected as "Free Clinic" in
      Blue Juniata, pp. 41-43 (see L2), and in
      Blue Juniata: Collected Poems, pp. 41-42
      (see L4).
M39   "From a Young Wife." Pagan IV (April-May 1920):
      8.
M40   "Four Horological Poems." Little Review VII
      (July-August 1920): 18-21.
      1. "If I should go out of this room to
      walk . . ."
      2. "And observe if you please the action . . ."
      3. "There is nothing at all that lives in this
      room by day . . ."

Reprinted as "Fifteen Minutes" in Eight More
Harvard Poets, pp. 30-31 (see L1); revised
and collected as "Time" in Blue Juniata,
pp. 93-96 (see L2), and, as "So Perish Time,"
in Blue Juniata: Collected Poems, pp. 44-45
(see L4).

4. "These skeletons which I discuss, said the
philosopher, . . ."

M41   "About Seven O'Clock." Literary Review of the
New York Evening Post I (January 22, 1921): 7.
Reprinted in Eight More Harvard Poets, p. 40
(see L1); reprinted as "Seven O'Clock," in
Transition XIII (Summer 1928): 54; collected
in Blue Juniata, p. 12 (see L2), and, revised
as "The Rocking Chairs," in Blue Juniata:
Collected Poems, p. 6 (see L4); reprinted in
Poetry CXII (June 1968): 151.

M42   (With Ronald Levinson) "Wells' Springs of
History." Literary Review of the New York
Evening Post I (March 19, 1921): 7.

M43   "Mountain Valley." Dial LXXI (December 1921):
670.
Reprinted in Current Opinion LXXII (May
1922): 679-80, and Eight More Harvard Poets,
p. 41 (see L1); collected as "Hickory Cove"
in Blue Juniata, p. 16 (see L2); revised and
collected as "Poverty Hollow" in Blue Juniata
Collected Poems, p. 12 (see L4); reprinted
in Poetry CXII (June 1968): 152.

M44   "Château de Soupir: 1917." Broom I (January
1922): 226.
Reprinted in Eight More Harvard Poets,
pp. 25-26 (see L1); collected in Blue Juniata

pp. 63-64 (see L2), and (revised) in Blue
Juniata: Collected Poems, pp. 57-58 (see L4).

M45 "Mountain Farm." Broom II (May 1922): 134.
Reprinted in Eight More Harvard Poets, p. 32
(see L1); collected as "The Farm Died" in
Blue Juniata, p. 17 (see L2); revised and
collected as "The Blown Door" in Blue Juniata:
Collected Poems, p. 25 (see L4); reprinted in
Poetry CXII (June 1968): 152-53.

M46 "Day Coach." Secession I (Spring 1922): 1-3.
Reprinted in Eight More Harvard Poets,
pp. 42-47 (see L1); collected in Blue
Juniata, pp. 25-29 (see L2), and revised in
Blue Juniata: Collected Poems, pp. 21-24
(see L4).

M47 ("Play It for Me Again: The Theme Repeated").
Secession II (July 1922): 5.
Collected as "A Solemn Music" in Blue
Juniata, pp. 97-98 (see L2).

M48 "Poem" ("One morning during carnival").
Secession II (July 1922): 6.
Reprinted as "Two Swans" in Eight More
Harvard Poets, p. 27 (see L1); collected in
Blue Juniata, p. 67 (see L2); revised and
collected in Blue Juniata: Collected Poems,
p. 65 (see L4).

M49 "Poem" ("Meanwhile, I observed him from a
gable"). Secession III (August 1922): 13.

M50 "Mediterranean Beach." Gargoyle III (August
1922): 12.
Collected in Blue Juniata, pp. 57-58 (see L2),
and as "The Beach at Palavas," in Blue
Juniata: Collected Poems, p. 60 (see L4).

M51 "Coal Town." North American Review CCXVI
     (August 1922): 207.

     Reprinted in Eight More Harvard Poets, p. 39
     (see L1); collected as "Mine No. 6" in Blue
     Juniata, p. 9 (see L2), and in Blue Juniata:
     Collected Poems, p. 9 (see L4).

M52 "Three Americans in Paris." Literary Review of
     the New York Evening Post II (November 14,
     1922): 351.

     1. "Harold Stearns."

     2. "Ezra Pound."

     Revised and collected as "Ezra Pound at the
     Hotel Jacob" in Blue Juniata: Collected
     Poems, p. 59 (see L4).

     3. "Sinclair Lewis Imitates a Member of the
     Gopher City Rotary Club."

M53 "Valuta." Broom III (November 1922): 250-51.

     Collected in Blue Juniata, pp. 51-52 (see L2)
     and in Blue Juniata: Collected Poems, pp. 49-
     50 (see L4).

M54 "For a New Hymnal." Literary Review of the New
     York Evening Post III (January 20, 1923): 393.

M55 "Mortuary." Broom IV (February 1923): 170.

     Collected as "Death" in Blue Juniata, p. 94
     (see L2), and, as "Mortality," in Blue
     Juniata: Collected Poems, p. 43 (see L4).

M56 "History." Double Dealer V (February 1923): 52.

M57 "Poem for Two Voices." Poetry XXI (February
     1923): 233-34.

     Reprinted as "The Chestnut Trees Are Dead" in
     Transition X (January 1928): 89; collected in
     Blue Juniata, p. 30 (see L2); reprinted in
     Between Worlds I (Summer 1960): 62; revised

and collected as "The Chestnut Woods" in
Blue Juniata: Collected Poems, p. 26 (see
L4).

M58 "Nocturnal Landscape." Poetry XXI (February
1923): 234-35.
Collected as "The Cast-Iron Panthers" in Blue
Juniata, pp. 61-62 (see L2).

M59 "Interment." Poetry XXI (February 1923): 235-36.
Collected in Blue Juniata, p. 45 (see L2).

M60 "Sudden Encounter." Poetry XXI (February 1923):
236-37.

M61 "Prophetic." Poetry XXI (February 1923): 237.
Collected as "Ten Good Farms (To W.S.B.)" in
Blue Juniata, p. 90 (see L2); revised and
collected as "Ten Good Farms (For Slater
Brown)" in Blue Juniata: Collected Poems,
p. 86 (see L4).

M62 "Three Hills." Poetry XXI (February 1923):
237-39.
Reprinted in the Bookman LVII (May 1923):
301-2; collected in Blue Juniata, pp. 69-70
(see L2); revised and collected as "The
Peppermint Gardens" in Blue Juniata: Collected Poems, pp. 66-67 (see L4).

M63 "The Fishes." Dial LXXIV (May 1923): 494.
Collected as "The Willow Branch" in Blue
Juniata, p. 13 (see L2); reprinted in the
Roanoke Review I (Fall 1967): 19; revised
and collected as "The Silvery Fishes" in
Blue Juniata: Collected Poems, pp. 133-34
(see L4).

M64 "The Starlings." Dial LXXIV (May 1923): 494.
Collected in Blue Juniata, p. 68 (see L2);

revised and reprinted as "A Smoke of Birds"
in the Roanoke Review I (Fall 1967): 19;
collected in Blue Juniata: Collected Poems,
p. 62 (see L4).

M65 "Processional of the Third Season." Chapbook
XXXVIII (June 1923): 10.

Collected in Blue Juniata, pp. 14-15 (see L2)
revised and collected in Blue Juniata: Collected Poems, pp. 19-20 (see L4).

M66 "Love and Death, I" ("There Is a Moment").
Secession V (July 1923): 18.

Collected as "There Is a Moment" in Blue
Juniata, p. 93 (see L2), and in Blue Juniata:
Collected Poems, p. 127 (see L4).

M67 "They Carry Him Off in a One-Horse Hack . . ."
Secession V (July 1923): 19.

Reprinted as "Memphis Johnny" in Broom V
(September 1923): 97-98; collected as "Mem-
phis Johnny (To N.A.)" in Blue Juniata,
pp. 85-86 (see L2); reprinted as "Memphis
Johnny (For Nathan Asch)" in Blue Juniata:
Collected Poems, pp. 79-80 (see L4).

M68 "Carnaval in Provence." S4N IV (Summer 1923):
[7-8].

Collected in Blue Juniata, pp. 65-66 (see L2)
revised and collected as "Carnaval in the
Midi" in Blue Juniata: Collected Poems,
pp. 63-64 (see L4).

M69 "The Strange Companion." Bookman LVII (August
1923): 617.

Revised and collected as "William Wilson" in
Blue Juniata, pp. 99-100 (see L2); reprinted
in Lyric America: An Anthology (1630-1930),

edited by Alfred Kreymborg (New York:
Coward-McCann, 1930), p. 570, and in Modern
Verse in English (1900-1950), edited by
David Cecil and Allen Tate (New York: Macmillan Co., 1958), p. 426; revised and collected in Blue Juniata: Collected Poems,
p. 130 (see L4).

M70 "Into That Rarer Ether . . ." Secession VI
(September 1923): 5-6.
    Revised and collected as "Sunrise over the
    Heiterwand" in Blue Juniata, pp. 53-55
    (see L2); collected in Blue Juniata: Collected
    Poems, pp. 51-53 (see L4).

M71 "Towards a More Passionate Apprehension of Life
and Dedicated to Gorham B. Munson." Broom V
(November 1923): 217.
    Reprinted as "Gorham B. Munson" in the Little
    Review XII (Spring-Summer 1926): 35.

M72 "Transluscent Fingers," Eight More Harvard
Poets, pp. 28-29 (see L1).
    Revised and collected as "Angelica" in Blue
    Juniata, pp. 59-60 (see L2), and in Blue
    Juniata: Collected Poems, pp. 55-56 (see L4).

M73 "Madrigals." Mécano (Leiden), numbers 4 and 5
(1923), n.p.
    Three short, rather scabrous poems printed in
    a Dutch Dadaist magazine edited by Theo van
    Doesburg. Never reprinted (see Introduction).

M74 "Those of Lucifer." Dial LXXIX (July 1925): 46.
    Reprinted in Poetry XXXI (November 1927):
    109; collected as "Towers of Song (To A.T.)"
    in Blue Juniata, p. 88 (see L2), and, as
    "Those of Lucifer (For Allen Tate)," in Blue

Juniata: Collected Poems, p. 85 (see L4).

M75   "Kenneth Burke." *Little Review* XII (Spring-
      Summer 1926): 33.

      Collected as "The Narrow House (To K.B.)" in
      Blue Juniata, pp. 75-76 (see L2); revised and
      collected as "The Narrow House (For Kenneth
      Burke)" in *Blue Juniata: Collected Poems*,
      p. 77 (see L4).

M76   "Robert M. Coates." *Little Review* XII (Spring-
      Summer 1926): 33-34.

      Revised and collected as "The Eater of Dark-
      ness (To R.M.C.)" in *The Dry Season*, p. 13
      (see L3); reprinted in *Poetry* LIX (December
      1941): 117; collected as "The Eater of Dark-
      ness (For Robert M. Coates)," in *Blue Juniata
      Collected Poems*, p. 75 (see L4).

M77   "Hart Crane." *Little Review* XII (Spring-Summer
      1926): 34.

      Collected as "The Flower in the Sea (To
      H.H.C.)" in *Blue Juniata*, p. 82 (see L2),
      and, as "The Flower in the Sea (For Hart
      Crane)," in *Blue Juniata: Collected Poems*,
      p. 76 (see L4).

M78   "Matthew Josephson." *Little Review* XII (Spring-
      Summer 1926): 34-35.

      Collected as "Buy 300 Steel (To M.J.)" in
      Blue Juniata, pp. 80-81 (see L2), and, as
      "Buy 300 Steel (For Matthew Josephson)," in
      Blue Juniata: Collected Poems, p. 74 (see
      L4).

M79   "Malcolm Cowley." *Little Review* XII (Spring-
      Summer 1926): 35-36.

M80   "Walter S. Hankel." *Little Review* XII (Spring-

Summer 1926): 36.

>Collected as "The Death of Crowds (To P.B.)
[Peter Blume]" in Blue Juniata, p. 89 (see
L2).

M81 "Several." Little Review XII (Spring-Summer
1926): 36.

M82 "Romance in a Major Key." Modern S4N Review I
(August 1926): 11-12.

>Revised as "Nocturne" in Hound & Horn II
(Summer 1929): 374-76; collected in Blue
Juniata, pp. 37-39 (see L2); collected in
Blue Juniata: Collected Poems, pp. 37-39
(see L4).

M83 "Bones of a House." Poetry XXIX (November
1926): 61-62.

>Reprinted in Poetry XXXI (November 1927): 108;
collected as "Blue Juniata" in Blue Juniata,
pp. 7-8 (see L2); reprinted in Prize Poems,
1913-1929, edited by Charles A. Wagner (New
York: A. and C. Boni, 1930), pp. 193-94;
collected in Blue Juniata: Collected Poems,
p. 5 (see L4).

M84 "Chestnut Ridge." Poetry XXIX (November 1926):
62-63.

>Collected in Blue Juniata, pp. 5-6 (see L2);
reprinted in Prize Poems, 1913-1929, edited
by Charles A. Wagner (New York: A. and C.
Boni, 1930), pp. 194-95.

M85 "Laurel Mountain." Poetry XXIX (November 1926):
63-64.

>Collected in Blue Juniata, pp. 10-11 (see
L2); reprinted in Prize Poems, 1913-1929,
edited by Charles A. Wagner (New York:

A. and C. Boni, 1930), pp. 195-96; collected
in <u>Blue</u> <u>Juniata</u>: <u>Collected</u> <u>Poems</u>, pp. 13-14
(see L4).

M86   "Empty Barn, Dead Farm." <u>Poetry</u> XXIX (November
      1926): 65-68.

      Collected in <u>Blue</u> <u>Juniata</u>, pp. 20-23 (see
      L2); reprinted in <u>Prize</u> <u>Poems</u>, <u>1913-1929</u>,
      edited by Charles A. Wagner (New York: A.
      and C. Boni, 1930), pp. 196-200; revised and
      collected as "Overbeck's Barn" in <u>Blue</u>
      <u>Juniata</u>: <u>Collected</u> <u>Poems</u>, pp. 15-18 (see L4).

M87   "Bill George." <u>Poetry</u> XXIX (November 1926):
      68-70.

      Collected as "Dan George" in <u>Blue</u> <u>Juniata</u>,
      pp. 18-19 (see L2); reprinted as "Bill
      George" in <u>Prize</u> <u>Poems</u>, <u>1913-1929</u>, edited
      by Charles A. Wagner (New York: A. and C.
      Boni, 1930), pp. 200-201; revised and col-
      lected as "Dan George" in <u>Blue</u> <u>Juniata</u>:
      <u>Collected</u> <u>Poems</u>, pp. 7-8 (see L4).

M88   "The Urn." <u>Poetry</u> XXIX (November 1926): 70.
      Reprinted in <u>Poetry</u> XXXI (November 1927):
      109; collected in <u>Blue</u> <u>Juniata</u>, p. 109 (see
      L2); reprinted in <u>Lyric</u> <u>America</u>: <u>An</u> <u>Anthology</u>
      <u>(1630-1930)</u>, edited by Alfred Kreymborg (New
      York: Coward-McCann, 1930), p. 571, in <u>Prize</u>
      <u>Poems</u>, <u>1913-1929</u>, edited by Charles A.
      Wagner (New York: A. and C. Boni, 1930),
      pp. 201-2, in <u>Modern</u> <u>Verse</u> <u>in</u> <u>English</u> <u>(1900-</u>
      <u>1950)</u>, edited by David Cecil and Allen Tate
      (New York: Macmillan, 1958), p. 426, and in
      <u>Poetry</u> <u>II</u>, edited by R. Stanley Peterson
      (New York: Macmillan, 1962), p. 127;

collected in Blue Juniata: Collected Poems,
p. 142 (see L4).

M89 "The Streets of Air." Poetry XXIX (November
1926): 71.
   Collected in Blue Juniata, p. 108 (see L2);
   reprinted in Prize Poems, 1913-1929, edited
   by Charles A. Wagner (New York: A. and C.
   Boni, 1930), p. 202; revised and collected
   as "John Fenstermaker" in Blue Juniata:
   Collected Poems, p. 136 (see L4).

M90 "Leander." Dial LXXXIII (September 1927):
199-200.
   Collected in Blue Juniata, pp. 106-7 (see
   L2), and in Blue Juniata: Collected Poems,
   pp. 128-29 (see L4).

M91 "Biography." The American Caravan, New York:
Macaulay Co., 1927, p. 52.
   Collected as "Leonora (To P.B.C.)" in Blue
   Juniata, pp. 77-79 (see L2), and, as "Three
   Songs for Leonora (And for Peggy Baird)," in
   Blue Juniata: Collected Poems, pp. 71-73
   (see L4).
   1. "Circus in Town," pp. 71-72.
   2. "Dumbwaiter Song," p. 72.
   3. "Tennessee Blues," pp. 72-73.

M92 "The Hill above the Mine." Transition X
(January 1928): 90-91.
   Collected in Blue Juniata, pp. 3-4 (see L2);
   reprinted in A New Anthology of Modern Poetry,
   edited by Selden Rodman (New York: Random
   House, 1946), pp. 110-11; revised and collected in Blue Juniata: Collected Poems,
   pp. 10-11 (see L4).

M93   "Tablet." Transition XIII (Summer 1928): 85.
      Revised and collected as "Commemorative
      Bronze--1928" in Blue Juniata: Collected
      Poems, p. 84 (see L4).

M94   "Tar Babies." Transition XIII (Summer 1928):
      96-97.
      Collected in The Dry Season, p. 9 (see L3),
      and in Blue Juniata: Collected Poems, p. 95
      (see L4).

M95   "For St. Bartholomew's Eve." Nation XCCVII
      (August 22, 1928): 175.
      Collected in Blue Juniata, pp. 104-5 (see L2)
      reprinted in A New Anthology of Modern
      Poetry, edited by Selden Rodman (New York:
      Random House, 1946), pp. 108-9; collected
      in Blue Juniata: Collected Poems, pp. 103-4
      (see L4).

M96   "In Memory of Florence Mills." Transition XV
      (February 1929): 121.
      Collected as "The Lady from Harlem (In
      Memory of Florence Mills)" in Blue Juniata,
      p. 87 (see L2), and in Blue Juniata: Col-
      lected Poems, p. 82 (see L4).

M97   "Tumbling Mustard." Nation CXXVIII (March 13,
      1929): 309.
      Collected as "Tumbling Mustard (To H.A.L.)"
      in Blue Juniata, pp. 83-84 (see L2); reprin-
      ted in the Literary Digest CI (April 6, 1929)
      31, and in America Forever New: A Book of
      Poems, compiled by Sara and John E. Branton
      (New York: Thomas Y. Crowell, 1968), p. 102;
      collected as "Tumbling Mustard (For Harold
      Loeb)" in Blue Juniata: Collected Poems,
      p. 81 (see L4).

M98 "The Rubber Plant." Hound & Horn II (July-
     September 1929): 374.
          Collected in Blue Juniata, p. 40 (see L2),
          and in Blue Juniata: Collected Poems, p. 40
          (see L4).
M99 "Epitaph." Blue Juniata, p. 24 (see L2).
M100 "Deathbed." Blue Juniata, p. 44 (see L2).
M101 "Still Life." Blue Juniata, p. 101 (see L2).
          Revised and collected in Blue Juniata:
          Collected Poems, p. 61 (see L4).
M102 "Winter: Two Sonnets." Blue Juniata, pp. 102-3
     (see L2).
          Sonnet 1 collected as "The Turning of the
          Year (For Peter Blume)" in Blue Juniata:
          Collected Poems, p. 78 (see L4), and Sonnet
          2 collected as "The Dog Fox" in Blue Juniata:
          Collected Poems, p. 135 (see L4).
M103 "Hunter." New Republic LXXXV (December 11,
     1935): 136.
          Collected as "Ernest" in The Dry Season,
          p. 10 (see L3) and in Blue Juniata: Collected
          Poems, p. 96 (see L4).
M104 "The Last International." New Republic LXXXVI
     (May 6, 1936): 362.
          Collected in The Dry Season, pp. 19-20 (see
          L3), and in Blue Juniata: Collected Poems,
          pp. 105-7 (see L4).
M105 "Yesterday Snow." New Republic LXXXVII (May 13,
     1936): 15.
          Collected as "This Morning Robins" in The
          Dry Season, p. 1 (see L3), and in Blue
          Juniata: Collected Poems, p. 89 (see L4).
M106 "Eight Melons." New Republic XCII (September 8,
     1937): 121.

Collected in The Dry Season, p. 23 (see L3);
reprinted in Twentieth Century American
Poetry, edited by Conrad Aiken (New York:
Random House, 1944), p. 306; collected in
Blue Juniata: Collected Poems, p. 110 (see
L4).

M107 "Tomorrow Morning." New Republic XCIV (February
23, 1938): 79.

Collected in The Dry Season, pp. 21-22 (see
L3), and in Blue Juniata: Collected Poems,
pp. 108-9 (see L4).

M108 "The Dry Season." Poetry LIII (October 1938):
24-25.

Collected in The Dry Season, p. 4 (see L3),
and in Blue Juniata: Collected Poems, p. 90
(see L4).

M109 "The Mother." Poetry LIII (October 1938):
25-26.

Collected in The Dry Season, p. 2 (see L3),
and in Blue Juniata: Collected Poems, p. 91
(see L4).

M110 "The Firstborn." Poetry LIII (October 1938):
26.

Collected in The Dry Season, p. 3 (see L3),
and in Blue Juniata: Collected Poems, p. 92
(see L4).

M111 "The Long Voyage." Poetry LIII (October 1938):
27.

Reprinted in Compass VII (April 1941): 14;
collected in The Dry Season, p. 5 (see L3);
reprinted in A Comprehensive Anthology of
American Poetry, edited by Conrad Aiken (New
York: Random House, 1944), p. 428, in

Twentieth Century American Poetry, edited by
Conrad Aiken (New York: Random House, 1944),
p. 308, in Time XLVI (August 27, 1945): 100,
in A New Anthology of Modern Poetry, edited
by Selden Rodman (New York: Random House,
1946), p. 112, and in Counterpoint in
Literature, edited by Robert C. Pooley (and
others) (Glenview, Illinois: Scott, Foresman,
1967), p. 351; collected in Blue Juniata:
Collected Poems, p. 93 (see L4).

M112 "Stone Horse Shoals." New Yorker XVII (July 5,
1941): 16.

Collected in The Dry Season, p. 25 (see L3);
reprinted in Twentieth Century American
Poetry, edited by Conrad Aiken (New York:
Random House, 1944), p. 304; collected in
Blue Juniata: Collected Poems, pp. 125-26
(see L4).

M113 "The End of the World." New Yorker XVII
(November 22, 1941): 27.

Collected in The Dry Season, p. 24 (see L3),
and in Blue Juniata: Collected Poems, p. 111
(see L4).

M114 "The Lost People." Poetry LIX (December 1941):
117-19.

Collected in The Dry Season, pp. 14-15 (see
L3), and in Blue Juniata: Collected Poems,
pp. 98-99 (see L4).

M115 "Roxane." Poetry LIX (December 1941): 115-16.

Collected in The Dry Season, p. 11 (see L3),
and in Blue Juniata: Collected Poems, p. 97
(see L4).

M116 "Restaurateur with Music." Poetry LIX (December

1941): 116.

Collected in The Dry Season, p. 12 (see L3),
and in Blue Juniata: Collected Poems, p. 83
(see L4).

M117 "Seven." Poetry LIX (December 1941): 120.
Collected in The Dry Season, p. 16 (see L3),
and in Blue Juniata: Collected Poems, p. 100
(see L4).

M118 "The Red Branch." New Yorker XXIII (September
6, 1947): 67.

Collected in Blue Juniata: Collected Poems,
pp. 134-35 (see L4).

M119 "The Man of Promise." '48 II (February 1948):
51.

Collected in Blue Juniata: Collected Poems,
p. 94 (see L4).

M120 "The Source." Poetry LXXII (April 1948): 18-19.
Revised and collected as "The Living Water"
in Blue Juniata: Collected Poems, pp. 131-32
(see L4).

M121 "Passport Blues." Poetry LXXVI (April 1950):
18-19.

Collected in Blue Juniata: Collected Poems,
pp. 114-15 (see L4).

M122 "Piney Woods." New Yorker XXVII (September 15,
1951): 30.

Collected in Blue Juniata: Collected Poems,
p. 133 (see L4).

M123 "Variations on a Cosmical Air." Sewanee Review
LXXI (Winter 1963): 34-35.

Collected in Blue Juniata: Collected Poems,
pp. 71-72 (see L4).

M124 "Winter Tenement: 1920." Saturday Review of
Literature LXIX (July 30, 1966): 47.

Collected as "Winter Tenement" in Blue
Juniata: Collected Poems, p. 46 (see L4).

M125 "Voices from Home: 1923." Saturday Review of
Literature XLIX (July 30, 1966): 47.
Collected in Blue Juniata: Collected Poems,
p. 68 (see L4).

M126 "Rabbit by Day." Roanoke Review I (Fall 1967):
20.
Collected as "A Resentment of Rabbits" in
Blue Juniata: Collected Poems, p. 134 (see
L4).

M127 "Boy in Sunlight." Poetry CXII (June 1968):
149-50.
Collected in Blue Juniata: Collected Poems,
pp. 3-4 (see L4).

M128 "The Pyre." Poetry CXII (June 1968): 153-55.
Collected in Blue Juniata: Collected Poems,
pp. 27-29 (see L4).

M129 "Ode in a Time of Crisis." Nation CCVII
(August 5, 1968): 85.
Collected in Blue Juniata: Collected Poems,
p. 116 (see L4).

M130 "The Enemy Within." Nation CCVII (August 5,
1968): 85.
Collected in Blue Juniata: Collected Poems,
pp. 117-18 (see L4).

M131 "Here with the Long Grass Rippling." Saturday
Review of Literature LI (August 24, 1968): 23.
Collected in Blue Juniata: Collected Poems,
pp. 119-22 (see L4).

M132 "Off Campus." Harper's CCXXXVII (September
1968): 60.
Collected in Blue Juniata: Collected Poems,
pp. 137-38 (see L4).

M133 "The Flower and the Leaf." Southern Review
     n.s. IV (October 1968): 1015-18.
         Collected in Blue Juniata: Collected Poems,
         pp. 139-41 (see L4).

N.   POEMS TRANSLATED

N1   "Marizibill," by Guillaume Apollinaire. Blue
     Juniata, p. 56 (see L2).
         Revised and collected in Blue Juniata:
         Collected Poems, p. 54 (see L4).
N2   (With Rolfe Humphries) "The Waltz of the
     Twenty-Year Olds," by Louis Aragon. New
     Republic CIX (July 5, 1943): 25-26.
         Collected in Aragon, Poet of the French
         Resistance, pp. 26-27 (see B4).
N3   "Twenty Years After," by Louis Aragon. Sewanee
     Review LIII (Autumn 1945): 611-12.
         Collected in Aragon, Poet of the French
         Resistance, pp. 19-20 (see B4).
N4   "The Time of Crossword Puzzles," by Louis
     Aragon. Sewanee Review LIII (Autumn 1945):
     613-14.
         Collected in Aragon, Poet of the French
         Resistance, pp. 22-23 (see B4), and in Blue
         Juniata: Collected Poems, pp. 112-13
         (see L4).
N5   (With Rolfe Humphries) "The Interrupted Poem,"
     by Louis Aragon. Sewanee Review LIII (Autumn
     1945): 616-17.
         Collected in Aragon, Poet of the French
         Resistance, pp. 32-33 (see B4).

N6   (With Rolfe Humphries) "Richard II Forty," by
       Louis Aragon. Sewanee Review LIII (Autumn
       1945): 622-23.
           Collected in Aragon, Poet of the French
           Resistance, pp. 39-40 (see B4).
N7   (With Rolfe Humphries) "Elsa, I Love You," by
       Louis Aragon. Sewanee Review LIII (Autumn
       1945): 624-26.
           Collected in Aragon, Poet of the French
           Resistance, pp. 42-43 (see B4).
N8   (With Rolfe Humphries) "I Wait for Her Letter
       at Sunset," by Louis Aragon. Aragon, Poet of
       the French Resistance, p. 21 (see B4).
N9   (With Rolfe Humphries) "Little Suite for Loud-
       speaker, II," by Louis Aragon. Aragon, Poet of
       the French Resistance, pp. 24-25 (see B4).
N10   "Tapestry of the Great Fear," by Louis Aragon.
       Aragon, Poet of the French Resistance, p. 35
       (see B4).
N11   (With Rolfe Humphries) "Nights," by Louis
       Aragon. Aragon, Poet of the French Resistance,
       pp. 44-48 (see B4).
N12   (With Rolfe Humphries) "Tears Are Alike," by
       Louis Aragon. Aragon, Poet of the French Resis-
       tance, p. 51 (see B4).
N13   (With Helen Burlin) "Christmas Roses," by
       Louis Aragon. Aragon, Poet of the French
       Resistance, pp. 70-71 (see B4).

PART 4: WRITINGS ABOUT MALCOLM COWLEY

O.   PRAISE AND DISPRAISE--A BRIEF SELECTION

O1   "A Regional Poet." New Republic LX (August 28,
      1929): 51-52.
         Allen Tate perceptively defines Blue Juniata
         and its author.
O2   "The Fledgeling Years, 1916-1924," by Gorham
      Munson. Sewanee Review XL (January 1932):
      24-54.
         MC had ridiculed Munson in "Coffee and Pis-
         tols for Two" (G76). Now he gets his forty
         whacks as Munson gives his version of how a
         little magazine was born and departed this
         life. For another reading of the Secession
         story, see "Munsoniana" (K4).
O3   The Double Agent, by Richard P. Blackmur (New
      York: Arrow Editions, 1935).
         See "The Dangers of Authorship," pp. 172-83.
O4   "Malcolm Cowley: Portrait of a Stalinist Intel-
      lectual." New Militant II (April 18, 1936): 2-3
         Felix Morrow makes a sulphurous attack on MC
         from the Trotskyist point of view.
O5   Forays and Rebuttals, by Bernard DeVoto
      (Boston: Little, Brown, 1936).

194

Another excoriation of Exile's Return and its
author, this time from a Freudian point of
view, is reprinted on pp. 315-23. It had
first appeared in Saturday Review of Literature X (June 2, 1934): 721.

O6   A Note on Literary Criticism, by James T.
Farrell (New York: Vanguard Press, 1936).
On pp. 157-74, Farrell analyzes and attacks
at length the notions about art and propa-
ganda put forward in the original epilogue
to Exile's Return.

O7   Twentieth Century Authors, edited by Stanley J.
Kunitz and Howard Haycraft (1942); also
Twentieth Century Authors: First Supplement,
edited by Stanley J. Kunitz (1955).
For this double item, see D6a and D12a.

O8   "Most Vivacious Account of Literary Life in the
Twenties." New York Herald Tribune Books,
July 8, 1951, pp. 1, 10.
Lloyd Morris's long eulogy of the reissued
Exile's Return.

O9   In Search of Heresy, by John W. Aldridge (New
York: McGraw-Hill, 1956).
On pp. 166-76, Aldridge compares The
Literary Situation at length and unfavorably
with Exile's Return. The piece originally
appeared as a review in the Nation CLXXX
(February 19, 1955): 162.

O10 Part of Our Time: Some Monuments and Ruins of
the Thirties, by Murray Kempton (New York:
Simon & Schuster, 1955).
Chapter 4, "The Social Muse," discusses MC
with other left-wing writers of the 1930s.

O11 The Way It Was, by Harold Loeb (New York:
      Criterion Books, 1959).
          Memoirs of Paris in the 1920s, with MC
          figuring in several episodes (see also K17).

O12 "Malcolm Cowley's Criticism on the Work of Art
      and on the Function of Criticism," by Betty
      Cox, 1960.
          An unpublished master's thesis for the
          University of Pittsburgh.

O13 "The Long Debauch." New Statesman LXII (Septem-
      ber 29, 1961), 433-34.
          Arthur Mizener reconsiders the two editions
          of Exile's Return on the belated appearance
          of the revised edition in England.

O14 Writers on the Left, by Daniel Aaron (New York:
      Harcourt, Brace and World, 1961).
          "Cowley's Return," pp. 334-42; also briefer
          passages about MC listed in the book's index.

O15 Starting Out in the Thirties, by Alfred Kazin
      (Boston: Little, Brown, 1965).
          Contains a portrait of MC at the New Republic
          pp. 15-20.

O16 "Art and the Book Reviewer." Nation CCIV (June
      5, 1967): 732.
          A review of Think Back on Us by Leonard
          Kriegel, who also reviews the author's
          career in comparison with that of Edmund
          Wilson.

O17 "The Long Voyage: A Study of the Poetry of
      Malcolm Cowley," by Margaret Binney Smith,
      1968.
          An unpublished master's thesis for
          Indiana University of Pennsylvania,
          Indiana, Pa.

O18 "'I dipped my finger in the lake and wrote'."
New York Times Book Review (November 17, 1968),
pp. 8, 76.
     Kenneth Burke's judgment and retrospect of
     Blue Juniata: Collected Poems.
O19 "That extraordinary company of writers
     ironically known as the Lost Generation." New
     York Times Book Review, May 6, 1973, pp. 8,
     10-12.
     William Styron's long review of A Second
     Flowering and his tribute to the author at
     75.
O20 "Malcolm Cowley." Publishers' Weekly CCIX
     (September 17, 1973): 20-21.
     A profile and appreciation by Roy Bongartz.
O21 American Literature: The Makers and the Making,
     edited by Cleanth Brooks, R.W.B. Lewis, and
     Robert Penn Warren (New York: St. Martin's
     Press, 1973).
     "Malcolm Cowley (1898-)," in Vol. II,
     pp. 2785-97, consists of well-chosen extracts
     with commentary.
O22 "For Malcolm Cowley: Critic, Poet, 1898--."
     Southern Review n.s. IX (Autumn 1973): 778-95.
     Philip Young's informative but curiously
     niggling tribute.
O23 "Malcolm Cowley: A Study of His Literary,
     Social, and Political Thought to 1940," by
     Eleanor Bulkin, 1973.
     An unpublished doctoral dissertation for New
     York University, well-researched and fair-
     minded.
O24 Memoirs by various authors.
     There is a mention of MC, often passim, but

sometimes at greater length, in various memoirs of the 1920s and 1930s. Besides those already mentioned--Munson (O2) and Loeb (O11)--the following might be listed: Samuel Putnam, Paris Was Our Mistress (New York: Viking, 1947); James A. Wechsler, The Age of Suspicion (New York: Random House, 1953); Matthew Josephson, Life among the Surrealists (New York: Holt, Rinehart & Winston, 1962) and Infidel in the Temple (New York: Knopf, 1967); Granville Hicks, Part of the Truth (New York: Harcourt, Brace & World, 1965); and Robert McAlmon, Being Geniuses Together, with supplementary chapters by Kay Boyle (New York: Doubleday, 1968).

Aaron, Daniel, J16, O14
"About Seven O'Clock,"
   M41
"Abyssinia and Spain,"
   F267
Academy, G330
The Achievement of
   Sherwood Anderson, D17
"Adam & Eve & Pinch Me,"
   F28
Adamic, Louis, F173,
   F279
"Adamic Omnibus," F279
Adams, James Truslow,
   F134
Adler, Mortimer J.,
   F419
"The Adventurer," M15
"Adventures of a Book
   Reviewer," A10
Adventures of an African
   Slaver, B1, B1a
"Aesthete: Model 1924,"
   G24
Aesthete: 1925, p. ix; G24
After the Genteel Tradi-
   tion, A4, A4a
"Afterthoughts on Dos
   Passos," G112
"Afterthoughts on T.S.
   Eliot," F231
"Afterthoughts on
   William Faulkner,"
   G321
"Afterword," B5, B5a

"An Afterword on the
   Modern Mind," B2
"Against Nightingales,"
   F13
Agassiz, Louis, G3
"Agassiz and Agony," G3
"Aidgarpo," F439
Aiken, Conrad, F26, F37,
   F50, F62, F95, F497,
   G48, G94, G109, G234
"Alastor," F111
"Albumblatt," F133
Aldanov, Mark, F393, G161
Aldington, Hilda
   Doolittle, F55
Aldington, Richard, F121,
   F341
Aldridge, John W., D10,
   D12, F487, O9
"Alfred Hayes," D3a
Alger, Horatio, F107,
   F437, G188, G328
"The Alger Story," F437
Algren, Nelson, B11, F352
Allen, Frederick Lewis,
   F303
Allen, Gay Wilson, F440,
   F505
Allen, Hervey, F93, F269
Allen, James S., F230
Allen, Colonel Robert S.,
   F457
"Ambulance Service," A3a,
   B15, G85
"America the So Beauti-

ful," F362
American Academy of Arts
  and Letters and the
  National Institute of
  Arts and Letters, Pro-
  ceedings, G258, G264,
  G273, G276, G281,
  G290, G296, G297,
  G309-13, G325, G329,
  G330a-b
"American and English
  Journals of Opinion,"
  G133
"American Books Abroad,"
  D9
"American Books Over-
  seas," G196
American Caravan, M91
American Critical Es-
  says, Twentieth
  Century, D14
"American Fables," F530
"American Fiction: The
  Postwar Years, 1945-
  1965," J15
American Heritage, A7,
  B15, G275, G291, G318
American Literature: A
  Critical Survey, B5
"American Literature in
  Wartime," G168
American Literature Sur-
  vey: The Twentieth
  Century, C12
American Literature: The
  Makers and the Making,
  A3a
"American Myths, Old and
  New," G294
"American Novels since
  the War," G240
"An American Patriot by
  Remote Control," F443
"American Scholar," F399
American Scholar, J5,
  J16
"American Scholar Forum:
  The New Criticism,"
  J5

"American Social Revolt
  as Mirrored in the Work
  of Five Novelists,"
  F502
"American Tragedy," F293
"American Writers and the
  First World War," G325
"American Writers and
  Where They Come From,
  F248
American Writers' Con-
  gress, D4, D5, G102
American Writers' Con-
  gress, F309, G100,
  G103, G137, J16
"American Writing Today:
  Its Independence and
  Vigour," F504
Amiel, Henri-Frédéric,
  F143
"Ancestors," F338
"And I Worked at the
  Writer's Trade,"
  pp. xi-xxxii
Anderson, Margaret, M30
Anderson, Sherwood, B13,
  D17, F461, F485, G282,
  J3
"Anderson's Lost Days of
  Innocence," D17, G282
"André Gide in Wartime,"
  G176
"André Gide's Retreat
  from Moscow," F250
"André Salmon and His
  Generation," G11
Andrews, Roy Chapman,
  F455
"Angelica," M72
"Angry Author's Com-
  plaint," F175
"Angry Professors," G63
Anna Karenina, C10
Ansley, Charles F., F216
"Ante Mortem," M9
"Apocalypse," F268
Apollinaire, Guillaume,
  F45, N1
"Après la guerre finie,"

G324
"The Apron-Strings of
    Vice," F105
Aptheker, Herbert, F417
Aragon, Louis, p. xxi;
    B4, B4a, E10, F240,
    F286, F349, G160,
    G187, G189, G190,
    G193, I2, I7, N2-13
"Aragon: A Little An-
    thology," G189
Aragon, Poet of Resur-
    gent France, B4a
Aragon, Poet of the
    French Resistance,
    B4, E10
Arendt, Hannah, G311
Arnold, Thurman, G130
"The Art of Insurrec-
    tion," A3a
Art of the Essay, A3a
"The Art of Visible
    Things," F86
"Art Tomorrow," G95
Arthurian legend, G43
"Artists, Conscience,
    and Censors," G293
"The Arts in Russia,"
    F275
Arvin, Newton, F482,
    G96, G132
"As If Written by Star-
    light," F124
"As Told in a Bazaar,"
    F103
Asbury, Herbert, F110
"The Ascent of Man,"
    F272
Asch, Nathan, p. xxvii;
    G246, G247, M67
"Aspects of the American
    Scene," F100
"The Assassinated Poet,"
    F415
Atlantic. See Atlantic
    Monthly
Atlantic Brief Lives,
    D21
Atlantic Monthly, D14,

F535, G270, G319a, G332
Den Atlantiske slave
    handels historie, A7a
Auden, W.H., F180, F323,
    F371, F428, F432
"Auden in America," F323
"Auden's a Better Poet
    Than Editor in Collect-
    ing His Own Works,"
    F432
Auslander, Joseph, F130
"The Author of Bliss,"
    F35
"The Author of His
    Being," H4
"Authors Speak for Them-
    selves," J8
An Autobiography, C14
Ayscough, Florence, F31

"Babbilogues," F108
Babbitt, Irving, G63
"Backstairs," F120
"Bad Company," F354
Bader, A.L., G272
Baird, Peggy, pp. xi-
    xxxii; M91
Baker, Denys Val, B3
Baldwin, Hanson W., F328,
    F356, K14
Baldwin, James, G311
"Ballade of French Ser-
    vice," M19
Balmer, Edwin, F159
Bancroft, Frederic, F147
"The Banquet," F373
Bantea, Marcela, A73
Barber, Frederick A.,
    F152
Barbusse, Henri, pp. xix-
    xx; E4, F67, G9
Bárcena, Agustín, A12a
Barker, George, F346
"Barn Dance," M33
Barnhart, Clarence L.,
    F486
Baroja, Pio, F18
Barrès, Maurice, E7
Barrett, William, J5

Barton, William E., F53
Barzun, Jacques, F527
Basso, Hamilton, F516,
   G306, G313
Bates, Ralph, F238
"The Battle over Ezra
   Pound," G220
Baudelaire, Charles,
   F83, F105, F126,
   F140, F227, F495
"Baudelaire as Revolu-
   tionist," F227
"Bayonet Drill: Two
   Sonnets," M28
Beach, Sylvia, G300
"The Beach at Palavas,"
   M50
Beard, Charles R., F92
Beard, Mary R., F92
Beauvoir, Simone de,
   I16
Beaver, Harold, D14,
   G270
"Beavers, Builders and
   Lakes," G26
Beck, Emily Morison,
   D21
Becker, Carl, G130
Bedel, Maurice, F127
Beebe, Lucius, F452
Beebe, William, F80,
   F109, G37
Beecher, Henry Ward, F98
Beer, Thomas, F78
"Before Closing," M14
"The Beginning Writer in
   the University," D16,
   G272
Bell, Ed, F215
Benchley, Robert, F76
"Benefit Show," F172
Benn, Gottfried, J2
Bennett, Arnold, F25
Benton, Thomas Hart,
   F258
"Benton of Missouri,"
   F258
Bergler, Dr. Edmund,
   G251

Bessie, Alvah, F298
Best, Marshall A., F97
Best, Mary Agnes, F92
"The Best of Medicine,"
   F42
Between Worlds, M57
"Beyond Poetry," F396
Bibesco, Princess Marthe,
   E5, E6
Bierstadt, Edward Hale,
   F17
"The Big Change in Pub-
   lishing," G284
"Big Town High School,"
   A3a
"Bill George," M87
Billinger, Karl. See
   Massing, Paul W.
"Biography," M91
"Biography and Legend,"
   F118
"The Biography of a
   Strike," G82
"Biography with Letters,"
   G234
"The Birth of a World,"
   F330
Bishop, John Peale, F373
Bishop, Morris, F77
Bizzarri, Edoardo, B5b
Black, Jack, F84
"Black and White," F43
Black Cargoes, A7, G291
"Black Earth," F335
Blackmur, Richard P., O3
Blake, William, D19, F281
Blewitt, Phyllis, F361
Blewitt, Trevor, F361
Bliven, Bruce, D11, G199
Blodgett, Harold W., B12
Blossom, Frederick A., F1
"The Blown Door," M45
Blue Juniata, pp. xxvi-
   xxxii; A2, L2, O1
"Blue Juniata," M83
Blue Juniata: Collected
   Poems, A11, L4, O18
Blume, Peter, M80, M142
Bodenheim, Maxwell, F36

The Bodley Head Scott
  Fitzgerald, B8, B14
Bogan, Louise, F346,
  G148
Bolivar Rodríguez,
  Eduardo, A7d
Bomei-sha kaeru, A3c
"Bonded Translation,"
  F31
"Bones of a House,"
  M83
Bongartz, Roy, O20
"The Book of Martyrs,"
  F390
Book Week, F523, F525-28
Book World (Washington
  Post, Chicago Tri-
  bune), F531, F532,
  F537, F542, G336, J20
Bookman, p. xix-xx; G9,
  G11, G13, G14, G17,
  G20, G23, M69
"Books and People," G167
"Books and Things,"
  F451-60
"Books Are Too Long,"
  G156
"Books by the Millions,"
  G165
"Books for Your Christ-
  mas List," G29
"Books in Brief," F190
"Books of the Spring
  Season," F73
Books That Changed Our
  Minds, B2
"Books That Changed Our
  Minds," G130, G132,
  G138, G138a
"Books To Send to a
  Distant Planet," J17
Borgers, Wilhelm, B11a
Born, Wolfgang, F454
Borsodi, Ralph, F134,
  F164
Bosch, Hieronymus, F454
"The Boston Story," F319
Bottome, Phyllis, F6
Bourke-White, Margaret,
F260
Bousquet, Joe, J2
"A Bow to the Institute,"
  G312
"Boy in Sunlight," M127
Boyd, Ernest, G24, G77
Boyd, James, F92
Boyd, Madeleine, F85
Boyle, Kay, F529, O24
"The Boys," F249
Bradford, Gamaliel, F84
Bradley, Sculley, B12
Bradley, William Aspin-
  wall, F52
Brand, Millen, F253
Brande, Dorothea, F173
Branton, John E., M97
Branton, Sara, M97
"Bread and Butter Letter,"
  F207
"Breakdown," F167
Breasted, Charles, F399
Breasted, James H., F82,
  F272, F399
Brée, Germaine, F315
Breit, Harvey, J7
Brentano's Book Chat, G32,
  G33, G36-38, G40, G42,
  G45, G46, G48, G49, G52,
  G55
Breton, André, p. xxi
Breuer, Bessie, p. xxiv
Brian, Denis, J22
Bridges, Robert, F144
"A Brief History of
  Bohemia," G8
Briffault, Robert, F211
Brion, Marcel, J2
Britten, Clarence,
  pp. xiii, xvii
"A Broken Axle," H3
Bromfield, Louis, F66,
  F95
Brooks, Cleanth, A3a, O21
Brooks, Howard L., F351
Brooks, Van Wyck, A8, C4,
  C14, F100, F129, F143,
  F237, F327, F348, F348a,
  F422, F462, F493, F500,

F534, G232, G259,
G285, G298
"Brooks and the 'Usable
Past'," F462
"Brooks in Progress,"
F422
"Brooks' Mark Twain:
Thirty-Five Years
After," G259
<u>Broom</u>, p. xxx; G10, G18,
G76-77, H6-8, I1-4,
M44, M53, M55, M67,
M71
Broun, Heywood, F90
Brousson, Jean Jacques,
F56
Brown, Alec, F207
Brown, Cecil, F374
Brown, Francis, F484
Brown, Slater, pp. xxiii,
xxvii-xxviii; G18, G76,
M61
Brown, Susan Jenkins,
pp. xxvii-xxviii; D20,
F533, K18
Brown, W. Slater. <u>See</u>
Brown, Slater
Bruccoli, Matthew J.,
F167, K19
Bruller, Jean, F415, G170
Brunngraber, Rudolf,
F165
Bryer, Jackson R., F167
Buck, Pearl, F194,
F294
Buckler, William E.,
A3a, G87
Bulkin, Eleanor, O21
Burke, Kenneth, F48,
F150, F478, F501,
G27, G76, G130, J3,
J5, J16, M75, O18
Burlin, Helen, B4, N13
Burnett, Whit, D14,
G270
Burnahm, James, F325,
F394
"The Business of Being a
Poet," F136

"The Business of Book
Reviewing," G131
Bussy, Dorothy, F63, F94,
F133
"But Listen, Dorothy,"
F380
"Buy 300 Steel," M78
Byas, Hugh, F376, F379

"The Caged Osprey," F112
Cain, James M., F442
Caldwell, Erskine, F146,
F260, F423
Canby, Henry Seidel,
pp. xvii-xviii, xxiii;
D9, G307, J2
Canot, Theodore. <u>See</u>
Conneau, Théophile
Cantwell, Robert, G96
Canzoneri, Robert, J18
Capote, Truman, B11
"Career of a Great
Teacher and Liberal
Editor," F466
Cargill, Oscar, G267
<u>Carico nero</u>, A7c
<u>Carleton Miscellany</u>, G314
"Carnaval in Provence,"
M68
"Carnaval in the Midi,"
M68
Carr, Edward Hallett,
F369
Carter, John, K3
Carter, Nick, novels, G46
Cary, Joyce, B11
"The Case against Mr.
Frost," G179
<u>The Case against the
Saturday Review of
Literature</u>, G220
"The Case of Bigger
Thomas," F304
"Cassandra's Children,"
F417
Cassidy, Henry C., F397
Casson, Stanley, F255
"The Cast-Iron Panthers,"
M58

Cather, Willa, F66,
   F521, G32
Catherine-Paris, E5
Cecil, David, M69, M88
Cendrars, Blaise, F85
A Century of Whitman
   Criticism, B12
Cervantes, Miguel de,
   B16
Chafee, Zechariah, Jr.,
   F113
Chamberlain, John, G94,
   G130
Chamberlain, Samuel,
   F362
Chamberlin, William
   Henry, F206
Chamson, André, F129
"The Chaos of English
   Grammar," F115
Chapbook, M65
Charles, Enid, F177
"Charles Vildrac," G14
Charm, p. xxiv; F53,
   F54, F56, F66, F73,
   F76, F78, F80, F81,
   F82, F84, F85, F88,
   F90, F92, F95, F98,
   F100, G19, G21, G22,
   G25-31, G34, G35,
   G41, G47, G50, G51,
   G53, G54
Chase, Richard, F482
Chase, Stuart, F239
"Château de Soupir:
   1917," M44
"Cheaper and Better
   Books," G66
Chekhov, Anton, F1
Chesterton, G.K.,
   F408, F409
"Chesterton's Later
   Years," F408, F409
"Chestnut Ridge," M84
"The Chestnut Trees
   Are Dead," M57
"The Chestnut Woods,"
   M57
Chevalier, Haakon M.,

F170, F234, F240, F286,
   F382
Chevalley, Abel, F190
Chevalley, Marguerite,
   F190
Chicago, G250
Chicago Daily News, Pano-
   rama, F536, J21
"Chicago Poem," F352
"The Chinless Age," F23
"Christmas Roses," B4,
   N13
"Churches Which Remember
   the Revolution," G28
Churchill, Sir Winston S.,
   F324, G148
"Circus in Town," M91
"The City of Anger," G76,
   G77, L2, L4
"Civil War Movie," F269
Clark, Walter Van Tilburg,
   J4
"Class Enemy," F210
"Classics and Best Sel-
   lers," F465
Clemens, Samuel L., C4,
   F389, F445, G259
"Clinic," M38
Clissold, William, F84
"Coal Town," M51
Coates, Robert M., F166,
   G76, G96, M76
Cocteau, Jean, F60, F87
"Cocteau's First Novel,"
   F60
Cohen, Morris R., G130
"The Coin of Greatness,"
   F94
"Colas Breugnon," F12
Cole, G.D.H., F163
Cole, Margaret, F163
"Collective Novel," F291
College English, D13,
   G169, G268
Collett, Anna, F458
"Colloquial French," F33
"Colloquy with Himself,"
   M36
"Colonizing Manhattan's

Lower West Side," G4
Colum, Mary M., G96
"Commemorative Bronze--
    1928," M93
"Commencing with the
    Simplest Things," C13
Compass, M111
The Complete Poetry and
    Prose of Walt Whitman,
    B7, G194
"Comrade Trotsky," F226
Comstock, Anthony, F90
"Concerning 'A Throw of
    the Dice'," E11
"Concerning the Preva-
    lence of Witches,"
    G224
Condor, Alan, G232
Congdon, Don, G83
"Congress in Madrid,"
    G118
Congress of Writers. See
    American Writers'
    Congress, and Inter-
    national Congress of
    Writers
Conklin, Groff, F193,
    G83, G106
Conneau, Théophile, B1
"Connecticut Valley,"
    G68
Conquest, Robert, F531
"Conrad Aiken: A Man of
    Letters," G48
"Conrad Aiken's Auto-
    biography," F497
"Conscience Fund," G105
Contat, Michel, I12a
Contempo, K4
"Continental Highway,"
    G70
Copeland, Charles
    Townsend, pp. xvi,
    xxii
Coppard, A.E., F28
Corăbiile negre: O
    istorie a Negotului cu
    sclavi din Atlantic,
    1518-1865, A7e

"Correspondence," K10
The Count's Ball, E8
Cournos, John, F69
Covici, Pascal, D15a
Coward, Noël, G31
Cowley, Peggy Baird. See
    Baird, Peggy
Cowley, Robert, A3a, B15,
    G318
"Cowley Finds Cain's New
    Novel Smothered in
    Celluloid," F442
"Cowley on Sholokhov: One
    Great Book," G319
Cox, Betty, O12
Cox, James M., G178
Cozzens, James Gould,
    F511, G290
Craigie, Sir William,
    F434
Crane, Hart, pp. ix,
    xxiii, xxvi-xxxii; A3a,
    D20, F141, F256, F533,
    G76, G144, G154, G267,
    G274, G280a, K18, M77
"Creating an Audience,"
    D9
"Creative Writing Sympo-
    sium," J11
Critic, B5, B5a, G321
"Critic Malcolm Cowley
    Appraises America's
    Literary Situation,"
    J14
"Criticism: A Many-Win-
    dowed House," G288
"A Critic's First Princi-
    ple," F501
"Critics of Two Genera-
    tions: Malcolm Cowley
    and Theodore Solo-
    taroff," J21
The Critique of Humanism
    A Symposium, D2, G63
Critiques and Essays on
    Modern Fiction, D10,
    D12
Croce, Benedetto, F495
Crockett, David, G186

Crosby, Harry, p. xxxi
Crout, C.H., F247, F248
Culler, Jonathan D.,
    M22, M25, M31
"The Cultural Heritage,"
    I6
Cummings, E.E., F149,
    F174, G295, G335
"Cummings: One Man
    Alone," G335
Current Opinion, M43
"The Curse of Beauty,"
    F128
Curtis, Charles P.,
    Jr., F178

D., H. See Aldington,
    Hilda Doolittle
"Dahomey," F292
Dalhousie Review, J13
Dali, Salvador, F382
Damon, S. Foster, D19,
    F217, G326, L1, M28
"Dan George," M87
Daniel, Howard, F454
"Danny," M34
"The Dark City," F50
Darwin, Charles, F84
Daudet, Léon, F70
Daughter of Earth, C1
Daumier, Honoré, F454
Davidoff, Paul, G337
Davis, Forrest, F367
Davis, H.L., F209
Davis, Robert Gorham,
    J5
Dawson, Dr. W.J., F54
Day, Dorothy, F46
Day Lewis, C., F197
"Day Coach," M46
"The Dead of the Next
    War," K6
"Dear Scottie, Zelda &
    Max," F522
"Death," M55
"Death of a Hero,"
    F314
"Death of a Nobody,"
    F102

"The Death of a Religion,"
    G92
"The Death of Crowds,"
    M80
"The Death of Debunking,"
    F365
"Deathbed," M100
"A Debate Continued: The
    Dead of the Next War,"
    K6
"Decadent Spring," G45
Decision, F334
"Decline and Fall,"
    F154, F349
"Defense of the Hemis-
    phere," K14
Delafield, E.M., F88
Delisle, Françoise, F124
Dell, Floyd, F142
Delteil, Joseph, E2,
    F118
"Democrats All," F343
"Desert, Jungle and
    Prairie," F98
"Desk-Size Dictionaires,"
    G209
Detzer, Karl, F337
Deutsch, Babette, F39
"The Devil a Monk Was
    He," F421
Devoto, Bernard, F420,
    F445, G173, G174, O5
"Devoto, with Chipless
    Shoulders, Edits Por-
    table Mark Twain,"
    F445
Dewey, John, F378, G233
"Dewey in an Age of Un-
    reason," G233
Dial, pp. xi-xiii,
    xv-xvi, xxiii; F9,
    F12, F13, F23, F26,
    F28-31, F34-39, F41,
    F48, F49, F62, F77,
    F86, F91, F93, F99,
    F111, G12, G18, M43,
    M63, M64, M74, M90
Dickens, Charles, F282,
    G30

"Dickens and the Revo-
  lution," F282
Dickes, E.W., F289
Dies Committee, K15
Diller, George E., F363
Dillon, George, F227,
  J3
"Directions for Making a
  Genius," G106
"A Discourse over the
  Grave of Dada," G91
Discovery of Europe, A3a
"Disillusionment," F296
"The Dispossessed," F357
"Do Artists Make Good
  Husbands?" p. xxiv;
  G21
"Dr. Canby and His Team,"
  G307
Doesburg, Theo van,
  p. xxi; M73
"The Dog Fox," M102
Doi, Kochi, F20
"Doing Your Play-Going
  at Home," G31
Doolin, Paul Rice, F96
Doolittle, Hilda. See
  Aldington, Hilda Doo-
  little
"Donkey Town," F182
Dorei shônin bôkenki, B1b
Dorgelès, Roland, F24
Dos Passos, John, A4,
  F151, F236, F246,
  F265, F296, F338,
  F448, F472, F512,
  G94, G112, G215,
  G330a, G334
"Dos Passos," G334
"Dos Passos and His
  Critics," G215
"Dos Passos and His
  Predecessors," F448
"Dos Passos: Poet against
  the World," A4, G112
Dostoyevsky, Anna, F125
Dostoyevsky, Fyodor, F125
Double Dealer, M56
"A Double Life, Half

Told," F535
Doyle, Sir A. Conan, G25
Drake, William A., F102,
  F120
"The Dream of a Slave
  Empire," A7
"The Dream of the Great
  Bird," F289
Dreiser, Theodore, F43,
  F464, F523, G203, G204
"Drought," G70
The Dry Season, A5, L3,
  M76, M103, M105
"The Dry Season," M108
"Duce, Duce!" F401
Duclaux, Mary, F16
Duhamel, Georges, G13
"Duhamel, M.D.," G13
Dumarchey, Pierre,
  p. xxv; E1, G23, I1
"Dumbwaiter Song," M91
Duncan, Thomas W., F453
Dunlop, Geoffrey, F139,
  F165
Durant, Will, F80, F82
Durtain, Luc, J2
Dušanović, Klara, A3b
"Dynamic Liberalism,"
  F113
"The Dynamics of Peace,"
  F369

"E.M. Forster's Answer,"
  F407
"Eagle Orator," F176
"Eastern Front: 1918,"
  F278
Eastman, Max, F160
"The Eater of Darkness,"
  M76
Eaton, Richard, F79
"Echoes of a Crime," G10
"Echoes of a Suicide,"
  A3a
Eckstein, Friedrich, F12
Edel, Leon, G311
"The Edgar Allan Poe Tra
  dition," G56
"Edge of the Sword, I8

"Editing Eliot," F537
"Editor's Notes," B14
"Edmund Wilson in
    Russia," F232
"Edmund Wilson's Speci-
    men Days," F498
"Edwin Arlington Robin-
    son," A4a, F471, G42
"Eight Melons," M106
Eight More Harvard
    Poets, D1, L1
"Eighteenth-Century Son-
    net," M37
"The Eighth Volume," F301
Eisenhower, Dwight, I10
"Eisenhower Africanus,"
    I10
"Election Night in
    Sheridan," G182
Eliot, T.S.,
    p. xxxii; F231, F308,
    F327, F396, F537,
    G90, G216, J3
Eliot, Valerie, F537
Ellison, Ralph, G311
"Elsa, I Love You," B4,
    N7
Emerson, Ralph Waldo,
    F475
"Emperor Hughes," G67
"Empty Barn, Dead Farm,"
    M86
"The Enchanted Castle,"
    F153
The Encyclopaedia Bri-
    tannica, G173
"The End of a Trilogy,"
    F236
"The End of the New
    Deal," G159
"The End of the Rea-
    soning Man," G138-38a
"The End of the World,"
    M113
"Ending Dreiser's
    'Trilogy of Desire',"
    F464
"The Enemy Within," M130
Engels, Friedrich, F247

"England under Glass,"
    F344
Engle, Paul, F176, F225
"English Eyes upon Us,"
    F504
"Entertaining Plays," F21
"Epilogue: New Year's
    Eve," A3a, B15
"Episodes in a Poet's
    Life," F295
"Epitaph," M99
"Epitaph for Scribner's,"
    G135
"The Era of Disillusion,"
    F18
"Ernest," M103
"Ernest Hemingway: A Fare-
    well to Spain," F155
"Errors and Asterisks,"
    F79
"The Escape from America,"
    G62
"Escape from the Galleys,"
    F403
Escholier, Raymond, F71
Esquire, G274, G284, G299,
    G303, G304, G323, J23
"Essay in Ideas," F299
Essays in Modern Literary
    Criticism, D7
The Essential Faulkner,
    B5c
Ethical Problems for the
    Sixties, D15
"Ethics in the Arts," D15
"Eugene O'Neill, Writer
    of Synthetic Drama,"
    G36
"Euphues," F36
"Europe: Death and Re-
    birth," F383
"Europe in Exile," F411
"Europe Was a Success,"
    F192
"The European Travel
    Diary of a Humanist,"
    F467
Evans, Rosalie, G69
"Everyday Life in Hell,"

F200

Evolutionary Thought in
   America, D10

"Exact Fancy," F59

"An Excellent Manual,"
   F52

"Execution," M3

"Exiles of the Arts,"
   G136

Exile's Return, p. xii;
   A3, B15, G73, O5, O6,
   O8, O9, O13

"Exile's Return: Coffee
   and Pistols for Two,"
   G76

"Exile's Return: Signi-
   ficant Gesture," G74

"Exile's Return: Women
   Have One Breast," G77

"The Existence of Sym-
   bolism," E11, I13

"Exploring a World of
   Nightmares," F520

"The External Emerson,"
   F475

"The Extra," I2

"Ezra Pound at the Hôtel
   Jacob," M52

"F. Scott Fitzgerald:
   The Romance of Money,"
   G237

"Fable for Russian Child-
   ren," F244

"Fable in Slang," F281

Facetas de la Crítica,
   A12a

Fadiman, Clifton, F102,
   F342, F525, G96, G132

"Fadiman, the I.P. Man,
   Sums Up His Reading,"
   F342

Fagin, N. Bryllion, G267

"Faith and the Future,"
   D6

"A Faith for Writing,"
   F500

"Fall Catalogue," F260

"Family Adventures," F40

"A Farewell to Spain,"
   F155

"A Farewell to the Last
   Harvard 'Dandy'," G295

"A Farewell to the
   1930's," G139

"The Farm Died," M45

Farr, Finis, F542

Farrell, James T., F243,
   F499, O6

"Farrell's Time Obliter-
   ated," F499

Fassett, Jacob S., Jr.,
   F19

Fast, Howard, F365

Faulkner, William,
   p. ix; A9, A9a-c, B5,
   B5a-c, B11, D7, D12,
   F201, F242, F290, F305,
   F358, F469, F477, F488,
   F489, F503, F506, F519,
   G181, G184, G185, G319a
   G320, G321, J12, K19

Faulkner: A Collection of
   Critical Essays, B5

"Faulkner by Daylight,"
   F305

The Faulkner-Cowley File
   Letters and Memories,
   1944-1962, A9, A9a

"The Faulkner Pattern,"
   F489

"Faulkner Stories, in
   Amiable Mood," F477

"Faulkner: The Yokna-
   patawpha Story," B5a

Faulkner to watashi:
   shokan to tsuioku,
   1944-1962, A9b

"Faulkner: Voodoo Dance,"
   F201

Faulkner's Powerful New
   Novel: Biblical Over-
   tones, Daring Symbols,"
   F503

Fay, Bernard, F96

Fay, Eliza, F56

"Federal Writers' Project
   F539

"Fellow Traveler," F203
Ferber, Edna, F81
Ferguson, Otis, G166
Ferrero, Guglielmo, G155
"Ferrero in Washington,"
  G155
"Festoons of Fishes," F49
Feuchtwanger, Lion, F85
"A Few Books Well Worth
  Keeping," F53
"A Few Novels Worth Keep-
  ing," G27
"A Few Translations and
  Reprints," F85
"Fiction, Philosophy and
  Bandits," F80
Fiedler, Leslie A., A3a,
  F520
"Fifteen Minutes," M40
"Figures in a Crowd," F166
"A Final View," J10
Fine, Ronald E., B5
"Finger Exercise," F331
"First Blood," F377
The First World War, K6
"The Firstborn," M110
Fischer, Eric, F417
Fischer, Louis, F326
Fisher, William J., G267
"Fisherman's Luck on
  Barnegat Bay," G47
"The Fishes," M63
Fitzgerald, Edward, F221
Fitzgerald, F. Scott,
  A3a, B8-10, B15, B76,
  F167, F174, F433, F513,
  F522, G94, G143, G225,
  G226, G229, G237, G302
Fitzgerald and the Jazz
  Age, A3a, B15
"Fitzgerald: The Double
  Man," G226
"Fitzgerald's Goodbye to
  His Generation," F167
"Fitzgerald's 'Tender'--
  The Story of a Novel,"
  G229
"Five Acts of The Scarlet
  Letter," D13, G268

"Five Tributes," G327
Flanagan, Hallie, F313
Flaubert, Gustave, C7
"Flem Snopes Gets His
  Come-Uppance," F519
Fleming, Peter, F181
Fletcher, John Gould,
  F26, F138
"Flight from the Masses,"
  F232
"The Flight of the Bonus
  Army," G83
"The Flower and the Leaf,"
  M133
"The Flower in the Sea," M77
Flynn, John T., F414
Foley, Richard Nicholas,
  F426, F427
Follett, Wilson, F527
Fontamara, C11
"A Footnote on French
  Prosody," G175
"Footnotes to a Life of
  Marx," F221
"For a Georgian An-
  thology," M32
"For a New Hymnal," M54
"For Otis," G166
"For St. Bartholomew's
  Eve," M95
"For the Postwar Writers,"
  G191
Forbes-Robertson, Sir
  Johnston, F56
Ford, Corey, F76
Ford, Ford Madox, F536
Ford, Henry, F138
"Ford or Lenin," F138
"A Foreword on the
  Books That Changed Our
  Minds," B2
"Foreword: The Revolt
  against Gentility," A4
"Former Fugleman," G97
Forster, E.M., B11, F407
Fort, Paul, G17
"The Forty Days of Thomas
  Wolfe," F192
'48, M119

Forum and Century, G66
"The Foundations of a
    Library," G30
"Four Biographies and
    a Novel," F84
"Four Books about Our-
    selves," F78
"Four Horological Poems,"
    M40
Four Quarters, J10, J11
Fournier, Alain, F124
"A Fourth Bronte," F97
"Fox in Flight," G227
France, Anatole, F56
Franco, Francisco, F388
Frank, Waldo, F183, F307,
    G76, J3, K8
Frankel, Charles, D15
"Frankenstein; or, the
    Poetical Faculty,"
    F57
Frankfurter, Felix, G130
Franklin, Benjamin, F84,
    F284
Franklin, William, G53
"Fraulein Ophelia," F64
"Free Clinic," M38
Freeman, John, F34
Freeman, Joseph, F241,
    F390
Freeman, Al, F32, G8,
    G15, G16
Frenaye, Frances, F366
French, Joseph Lewis,
    F99
"The French and Our New
    Poetry," G7
"French Poetry and the
    New Spirit," G44
"French Verse in
    English," F72
"A Fresh Look at Faulk-
    ner," G320
Freud, Sigmund, F253
"Freud in Fiction,"
    F253
Fréville, Jean, F247
"From A to Zymurgy,"
    F486

"From a Young Wife," M39
"From 'Flowers of Evil'
    to the Super-Realists,"
    F83
"From Hegel to Hitler,"
    F378
"From the Diary of a
    Restoration Gentleman,"
    M12
"From the Finland Sta-
    tion," F312
Frost, Robert, G178, G179
"Frost: A Dissenting
    Opinion," G178
"The Führer's Followers,"
    F412
Fülöp-Miller, René, F125
Fugitive poets, G315
"The Function of an Aca-
    demy," G258
Furioso, G227

G., R. See Goldschmidt,
    Rosie
Galantière, Lewis, F60,
    F101
Gallicus (pseud.). See
    Soupault, Pierre
Galsworthy, John, F156,
    G31
"A Game of Chess," F229
"Gammon for Dinner,"
    G256
Gannett, Lewis, G96
"Garcong! Garcong!" G33
Gargoyle, H5, M50
Garnett, Constance, F1
Garry, Stephen, F335
"Gaucho Drama," F17
Gautier, Théophile, F86
Geismar, Maxwell, F359,
    F463, F502
"The Generation That
    Wasn't Lost," G169
"Genius in the Raw," F523
"Genji, Aging, Disports
    Himself Sedately in
    This Third Volume,"
    F89

Genne, V.M., F397
"The Geographer of
  Love," F101
"Geopolitik," F350
"George F. Babbitt's
  Revenge," F264
"Georgians and Post-
  Georgians," F15
"Gertrude Stein for the
  Plain Reader," F429
"Gertrude Stein, Writer
  or Word Scientist?"
  F446
Ghiselin, Brewster, G144
"A Ghost Story of the
  Jazz Age," G302
Gide, André, E9, F63,
  F94, F133, F171, F250,
  F451, F526, G176, I11,
  I12
"Gide as Friend and
  Colleague," F526
Gilbert, Stuart, F320
Glaser, Alice, J20
Glasgow, Ellen, F8,
  G192
Glassco, John, F538
"Go Down to Faulkner's
  Land," F358
"Going with the Wind,"
  G113
Gold, Michael, F334,
  G75
"The Golden House,"
  F99
"The Golden Legend,"
  F270
"The Golden Legend of
  Li Ning," F179
Goldschmidt, Rosie, F188
Goldstein, Alfred, F247,
  F248
"Gongorism," F122
"Good Books for
  Christmas Giving,"
  F82
"Good Books That Almost
  Nobody Has Read," G94
"The Good Earthling,"

F194
"Good Reading," F174
Goodman, Henry, C2
"Gorham B. Munson," M71
Gosse, Philip, F157
Gould, Gerald, F58
Gould, Jean, F532
Gourmont, Rémy de, F121
Graebner, Walter, F397
Graelle, L.L., J13
"Graham Greene," F395
"The Grammar of Facts,"
  F400
Grammont, Maurice, F33
Grattan, C. Hartley, D2,
  G63
The Great Gatsby, B10
Great Scenes from Great
  Novels, C6
Great Tales of the Deep
  South, C3
Green, Julien, F97, F112
The Green Parrot, E6
Greene, Graham, F395 G336
"The Greene-ing of the
  Portables," G336
Gregory, Horace, G94
Grew, Joseph C., F379
Griggs, Arthur Kingsland,
  F70
Gross, Chaim, G311
Gross, Seymour L., C12
"Grosse Margot's Lover,"
  F114
Grosz, George, F246
Grubbs, Verna Elizabeth,
  D3a
Guedalla, Philip, F90
Guérard, Albert J., B3,
  F351, F417
Guerard, Maclin B., B3
Guest, Stephen Haden, F67
"Gulliver," F48
Gunther, John, F220, F418
"The Guru, the Beatnik
  and the Good Gray Poet,"
  G279
Guterman, Norbert, F340,
  F349

Guthrie, Ramon, F363,
    F518, G76

"H.G. Wells in the
    Kremlin," F202
Haas, Joseph, J21
Habe, Hans, F340
Hacker, Louis M., F259
Hackett, Francis,
    p. xiii; F333
Haffmans, Gerd, B5a
Hall, Donald, M4, M11,
    M22
"Haloes for the Damned,"
    F74
Hamilton, Thomas J., F388
"Hamilton Basso, 1904-
    1964," G313
Hammerstein, Mrs. Oscar,
    G64
"A Handbook for Dema-
    gogues," F178
Hankel, Walter S.
    (pseud.), p. x; D3,
    G24, G65, M80
Hansen, Harry, G96
"The Happiness Boys,"
    K16
"Happiness Made Easy,"
    F142
"The Harbor at Night,"
    M8
"Hard-Boiled and Roman-
    tic," F135
Hardy, Daphne, F329,
    F361
Harper's, G57, G236,
    G251, M132
Harper's Bazaar, I12a
Harry, Myriam, F10
Hart, Henry, D4, G102
"Hart Crane," M77
"Hart Crane: The Evi-
    dence in the Case,"
    F533
Harvard Advocate, p. xiii;
    F1-4, F7, H1-3, M1-6,
    M9-12, M15, M16, M19-
    26, M28, M31, M37

"The Haunted Castle,"
    F123
"The Haunted House," G157
"Haven't You Read These
    Novels?" G235
Hawkes, John, B3
Hawthorne, Nathaniel, B6,
    B6a, D13, F470, F474,
    G2, G3, G177, G212,
    G213, G223, G268, G275
"Hawthorne as Tragic Art-
    ist: A Fine Study,"
    F474
"Hawthorne in Solitude,"
    G212
"Hawthorne in the Looking
    Glass," G213
"The Hawthornes in Para-
    dise," G275
Haycraft, Howard, D6a,
    F386, O7
Haydn, Hiram, J5
Hayes, Alfred, D3a, F473
"He Wrote Honestly and
    Well," F541
Hearn, Lafcadio, C2, G217
Hearst, William R., F214
"Hearts of Whipped
    Cream," F127
"Heathen Days: 1890-
    1936," F389
"Heavenly City," F276
Hegel, Georg Wilhelm
    Friedrich, F378
Heiden, Konrad, F195,
    F412
Held, John, Jr., F540
Hélion, Jean, F403
"Hell under England," F20
Hemingway, Ernest,
    p. xxii; B3, B16, C13,
    F132, F155, F174, F214,
    F257, F285, F314, F481,
    F496, F535, G55, G177,
    G180, G183, G186, G214,
    G287, G323, G330, G333,
    J12, J22, K19
Hemingway: A Collection
    of Critical Essays, B3

"Hemingway: A Farewell
    to Spain," F155
"Hemingway and the Hero,"
    G183
"Hemingway at Midnight,"
    G177
"Hemingway: Image and
    Shadow," G333
"Hemingway in Madrid,"
    F285
"Hemingway in Paris,"
    C13
"The Hemingway Legend,"
    G55
"Hemingway Mixed with
    Hearst," F214
"Hemingway: Work in Pro-
    gress," F257
"Hemingway's 'Neverthe-
    less'," F314
"Hemingway's Novel Has
    the Rich Simplicity
    of a Classic," F496
"Hemingway's Portrait of
    an Old Soldier Pre-
    paring To Die," F481
Henderson, Sir Nevile,
    F306
"Henri Barbusse,"
    p. xix; G9
Henriot, Emile, F71
Henschke, Alfred, F61
"Her Name Was a Singing
    Line of Verse," F532
"Here with the Long Grass
    Ripling," M131
Hersey, John, F413
Herskovits, Frances,
    F169
Herskovits, Melville J.,
    F169, F292
Heym, Stefan, F468
Hibben, Paxton, F98
"Hickory Cove," M43
Hicks, Granville, F162,
    F176, F228, F447,
    F524, G130, J16, Q24
"Hicksborough," F449
"Hicks's Life of John

Reed," F228
Hieronymus Bosch, F454
Hill, Frank Ernest, F130
"The Hill above the Mine,"
    M92
Hilléret, René, A9c
Hills, L. Rust, F530
Hills, Penney Chapin, F530
Hillyer, Robert Silliman,
    L1
Hindus, Maurice, F397, G75
Historia de la trata de
    negros, A7d
"History," M56
"The History of a Push,"
    G2
Hitler, Adolf, F195
    F306, F316, F333, F339,
    F378, F412
Hoffman, Frederick J., B5
"Holding the Fort on Au-
    dubon Terrace," G329
Holman, Clarence Hugh,
    G270
Holmes, E.K., D2, G63
"Holocaust," F168
Holthusen, Hans Egon,
    F495
"Holy Horatio," G188
"Homage to Ancestors,"
    F222
"Homage to Marianne Moore
    on Her Seventy-Fifth
    Birthday," G297
Homans, George C., F178
"The Homeless Generation:
    Mansions in the Air,"
    G84
"Homesteads, Inc.," F164
Hone, Joseph, F384
Hook, Sidney, G161
"A Hope for Poetry," F197
Hopkins, Gerard, F212,
    F301, F317
Hopkins, Gerard Manley,
    F144
Hopwood Lectures, D16
"Horatio Alger: Failure,"
    G328

Horizon, G324, G328,
  G333
Horton, Philip, F256
"The Hosting of the
  Shee," F384
Hound & Horn, F173, M35,
  M82, M98
House, Col. Edward M.,
  F78
"How Do We Talk
  American?" F434
"How Do You Do Your
  Reading?" G22
"How Far Back to the
  Land," G88
"How Has the Most Famous
  Third-Rate Burglary
  Affected Your Life?"
  J23
"How the Writer Lives,"
  G199
"How To Interview Ring
  Lardner," G38
"How Writers Earn Their
  Livings," G249
"How Writers Live," D11
"How Writers Lived," D9
"How Writers Write,"
  G269
Howard, Alexander L.,
  F19
Howe, Irving, F485
Hughes, Howard, G67
Hugo, Howard E., B16
Hulbert, James R.,
  F434
"Humanizing Society,"
  D2, G63
"Humbert Wolfe," F104
Humphries, Rolfe, B4,
  N2, N5-9, N11, N12
"Hunter," M103
Hurst, Fannie, F73
Hurwitz, Lise, A7a
Hutchens, John K., J6
Huxley, Aldous, F23,
  F169, F263, F302,
  F345, G281
"Hymn of Hate," F246

"'I Am the Prison'," F119
"I Sometimes Said to
  Stéphane Mallarmé . . .
  I15
"I Wait for Her Letter at
  Sunset," B4, N8
"I Would Sometimes Say to
  Stéphane Mallarmé . . .
  E11
"Icy Fire," F55
"The Ideas of an Artist,"
  F521
"If You Want To Write . .
  D8
"An Ikon," F61
An Illustrated History of
  the United States, D18
Imaginary Interviews, E9
"The Imp of the Perverse,
  F382
"Impersonal History," F32
"Importance of Knowing
  Ernest," J22
"In Congress Here As-
  sembled," G103
"In Defense of Sherlock
  Holmes," G25
"In Defense of the
  1920's," F420
"In Love with Germany," F
"In Memoriam," F309
"In Memory of Florence
  Mills," M96
"In Praise of the Re-
  jected," G247
"In Vindication of Mr.
  Horner," F32
"In Which Mr. Faulkner
  Translates Past into
  Present," F488
"An Indispensable Guide
  to a Fuller Under-
  standing of Herman
  Melville," F490
"Inquiry about the
  Malady of Language,"
  J2
"Inquiry into the Spirit
  and Language of Night,"

"Inside Germany," F368
Interim, G256
"Interment," M59
International Congress
   of Writers, G103,
   G107, G118, K9
"The Interrupted Poem,"
   B4, N5
"An Interview with
   Malcolm Cowley," J13,
   J18
"Into That Rarer
   Ether . . .," M70
"Introduction to the
   Method of Leonardo da
   Vinci," E11
"Introduction to William
   Faulkner," D7, D12,
   G185
"Invitation to Innova-
   tors," G45
Irving, Washington, F422
"Is the Small Farmer
   Dying?" G75
"Israfel," F93
Istrati, Panaït, F103
"It Could Happen There,"
   F219
"It's the Telling That
   Counts," F510
"Ivory Towers To Let,"
   G93
Izgubljena generacija,
   A3b

Jackson, T.A., F282
James, Henry, F426
"James Joyce," G20
"James Thurber's Dream
   Book," F430
Jameson, Storm, F219
"Japan after the War,"
   F379
"Jargon and Its Dis-
   contents," F527
Jarrell, Randall, F377
"Jean-Paul Sartre at
   Walgreen's," G250
"Jean Paul Sartre:

Strictly Personal," I12a
Jefferson, Thomas, F53
"Jeremiad," F316
"Jesse Stuart: Man with a
   Hoe," F184
Jesus, E4, F54
Jesus, E4
"Joan Miró," I5
Joan of Arc, E2
"A Job To Do," G289
"John Dos Passos," G330a
"John Fenstermaker," M89
Johnson, Thomas H., D8,
   D9
Jones, P. Mansell, F495
Josephson, Clifford, B3
Josephson, Hannah, B4,
   B4a, F349
Josephson, Matthew,
   p. xxiii; F45, F174,
   G76, K4, M78, O24
"Journey in the Slave
   States," F372
"The Journey to Paris,"
   H5
Joyce, James, G20, G90
"Junketing for Science,"
   F109
"Justice for Federal
   Workers," K15

Kane, Elisha K., F122
Kataev, Valentine, F165
Kauffman, Reginald
   Wright, pp. xii;
   F5
Kaye-Smith, Sheila,
   p. xvii; F9
Kayser, Rudolf, F139
Kazin, Alfred, p. vii;
   F433, O15
Kearney, Patrick, G31
"Keats and Hearst," F34
Kelly, George, G31
"Kelly's Barroom," M35
Kempton, Murray, O10
Kennedy, Margaret, C9,
   F517
"Kenneth Burke," M75

"Kenneth Burke: Unwilling
  Novelist," F150
"Kentucky Coal Town," G81
Kenyon Review, D10, G205,
  G316, I13, I15
Kessel, Joseph, F116
Kesten, Hermann, F411
King-Hall, Magdelen, F73
"King Mob and John Law,"
  G86
Kiplinger, W.M., F355
Kirstein, Lincoln, F454
Kitchin, George, F210
Klabund. See Henschke,
  Alfred
Knopf, Alfred, F525
Knox, Cleone. See King-
  Hall, Magdelen
Koestler, Arthru, F329,
  F349, F361, F406
Koestler: The Disen-
  chanted," F361
Krasnowolska, Ewa, A6c
Kreymborg, Alfred, F21,
  F49, F100, F135, F136
Kriegel, Leonard, O16
Krivitsky, W.G., F300
"Krivitsky," F300
Kroneberg, Eckart, A6a-b
Kronenberger, Louis, D21
Krutch, Joseph Wood,
  F192, F470, G60
Kunitz, Stanley J., D6a,
  D12a, F386, O7
Kyôichi, Harakawa, A9b

"The Lady from Harlem,"
  M96
Lafayette, Marquis de,
  F118
"Lafcadio Herun-san," C2,
  G217
LaFollette, Suzanne, G94
Laforgue, Jules, G301, M30
"Laforgue in America:
  A Testimony," G301
Lahey, G.F., F144
"A Lake Is Backdrop for
  Debate," G337

Lalou, Renê, F52
"A Lamb among Wolves," F4
Lania, Leo, F357
Lardner, Ring, F76, G38
Laski, Harold J., F398, G
Lassaigne, Jacques, F454
"The Last Days of
  Pompeii," F211
"The Last Flight from Mai
  Street," F484
"The Last Great European,
  F235
"The Last International,"
  M104
"Last Man around the
  World," F392
"Last Night We Held Great
  Argument," M21
"The Last of Lyric Poets,
  F149
"The Last of the Lost
  Generation," G299
"Last Veterans of the
  Revolution," G54
"Last Visit to Mallarmé,"
  E11
"The Last Years of Ernest
  Hemingway," G330
Laughlin, James, F318
"Laurel Mountain," M85
"Laureate of the Maquis'
  Campfires," G190
"Laval's Republic," F351
Lawler, James R., E11
Lawrence, T.E., F90, F213
"Leading His Flock of Lor
Legged, Flat-Chested
  Flappers," F540
"Leander," M90
Leaves of Grass, A Nortor
  Critical Edition, B12
Leaves of Grass: The Firs
  1855, Edition, B12a
Lebeck, Michael, F526
Le Clercq, Jacques, F118
Leech, Margaret, F90, G1₄
Legman, G., F476
Leiris, Michel, I5
Leitner, Paul S., F247

F248
Lenin, Vladimir, F138,
  F206
"Leon Trotsky: Martyr or
  Renegade," K10
"Leonardo da Vinci," I14
"Leonardo and the Philo-
  sophers," E11
Leonardo, Poe, Mallarmé,
  E11, E11a, I16
"Leonora," M91
"The Leopard in Hart
  Crane's Brow," G273
Lerner, Max, F287, F299
The Lessons of the Mas-
  ters, B16
"Let's Build a Railroad,"
  G80
"Letter about Mallarmé,"
  E11
"Letter from the States,"
  G99
"Letter: John Carter," K3
"Letter to England," G99
"A Letter to Jim," M6
Levine, Lawrence W.,
  A6
Levinson, Ronald, M42
Lewis, D.B. Wyndham,
  F117
Lewis, Ethelreda, F98
Lewis, R.W.B., A3a, O21
Lewis, Sinclair, F108,
  F158, F264, F484, G33,
  G94, G111, M52
Lewis Wyndham, F106
Lewisohn, Ludwig, F253
Leyda, Jay, F490
"A Liberal Policy," F27
Librescot, Solon, E4
Life, D9, G197, G214, I7
"The Life and Death of a
  Fire Eater," F516
"The Life and Death of
  Thomas Wolfe," F508
"Life of the Hunter,"
  F506
Lightning in a Mist,"
  F87

Lillard, Richard G.,
  F460
"Limbo-by-the-Sea," F441
"The Limits of the Novel,"
  C6, G261
"Limousines on Grub
  Street," G199
Lincoln, Abraham, F53,
  F73, F82
Lincoln, Victoria, F187
Lindley, Ernest K., F367
"Lions and Lemmings,
  Toads and Tigers," F509
"The Literary Atmosphere
  of Two Eras," G218
"The Literary Business,"
  G61
"The Literary Business in
  1943," G164
"A Literary Calendar:
  1911-1930," A4, G116
Literary Digest, M97
Literary History of the
  United States, D9,
  G196
Literary Review of the
  New York Evening Post,
  pp. xvii-xviii; F16-22,
  F24, F25, F27, F33,
  F40, F42-46, F83, F89,
  G5, G7, G43, M41, M42,
  M52, M54
The Literary Situation,
  A6, O9
"The Literary Situation:
  1953," G239
"The Literary Situation,
  1965," G317
Literary Times, J14
Literatur in Amerika,
  A6a
"Literature and Politics,"
  F191
Littell, Philip, G167
"The Little Magazines
  Growing Up," G206
Little Review, p. xiii;
  I5, M30, M38, M40,
  M71, M75-81

"Little Suite for Loud-
    speaker, II," B4, N9
Litz, A. Walton, A6
"A Lively and Deadly
    Wit," F387
"Lives and Times," F386
"The Living Dead - IX:
    Sherwood Anderson's
    Epiphanies," G282
"The Living Water," M120
"Local Color," F148
Loeb, Harold, F59, K17,
    M97, O11
London, Kurt, F275
London Magazine, D17,
    G282
Long, Haniel, F22
"Long Black Song," F274
"The Long View," F196
"The Long Voyage," M111
"The Longest Book Re-
    view," F333
Loos, Anita, F76
"Lord of These Elements,"
    F288
"Lost! A Lady. Found!
    An Artist," G32
"Lost Battalion," F298
"The Lost People," M114
"Lost Worlds," F375
"Louis Aragon," F240
"Louis Aragon: Poet of the
    French Resistance," G193
"Louisburg Square," M23
"Love and Death," M66
Loveman, Amy, p. xvii
Lovett, Robert Morss,
    F466
"Low Bridge and Lock
    Ahead," G34
Lowe-Porter, H.T., F235,
    F331
Lowell, Amy, F29, F31,
    F217
Lucas, Barbara, F458
"The Lucky Generation,"
    G332
Ludwig, Emil, F85
Luhan, Mabel Dodge, F244

"Luke Lea's Empire," F402
"Lycidas and Thanatopsis,"
    F130
Lynd, Helen Merrell, F252
Lynd, Robert S., F252,
    G132
Lyon, F.H., F64
Lytton, Antony, F224
Lytton, Earl of, F224

McAlmon, Robert, F529,
    O24
McCaffery, John K.M., G21
McCarthy, Mary, F216,
    F354, G231
MacCurdy, Edward, F288
McFee, William, F3
McGreevy, Thomas, F218
"Machine-Made America,"
    F134
McKenney, Ruth, F291
Maclean, M.S., D2, G63
MacLeish, Archibald, F91,
    F199, F225, F254, G89,
    G146, K6
"MacLeish vs. Cowley:
    Lines for an Interment,"
    G89
"MacLeish's Poetic Drama,"
    F199
MacOrlan, Pierre. See
    Dumarchey, Pierre
Macy, John, F66
"Mad about Poetry: And
    Other Things Too,"
    F483
Madame Bovary, C7
"Mme. Duclaux on France,"
    F16
"Madrigals," pp. xxii-
    xxiv; M73
"Magazine Business: 1910-
    46," G198
Mailer, Norman, F507
"Making It: Gossip of the
    Literary Marketplace
    Reported by Alice
    Blaser," J20
"The Making of a Writer,"

F228
"The Making of an
    Englishman," F224
Malamuth, Charles, F165
Malcolm, David (pseud. of
    MC), G4
"Malcolm Cowley," M79
Maline, Julian L., G294
Mallarmé, Stéphane, E11,
    I12, I15, I16
Mallet, Robert, F526
Malraux, André, F170,
    F234, F268, I6
"Malraux on Man's Soli-
    tude," F170
"Malthus Was Wrong,"
    F177
The Man Christ Jesus, F54
"Man of Good Will,"
    F315
"A Man of Letters," F63
"The Man of Promise,"
    M119
"The Man Who Abolished
    Time," G263
"The Man Who Lived Twice,"
    F366
"The Man Who Would Be
    King," F185
"Man with a Hoe," F184
Mangione, Jerre, F539
"Manhattan Melody,"
    G78
"Manifesto to the Trade,"
    G79
Mann, Heinrich, I8
Mann, Klaus, F411
Mann, Thomas, F235,
    F270, F271, F331
Mannix, Daniel P., A7,
    G291
A Man's Reach: Some
    Choices Facing Youth
    Today, D8
"Man's Solitude," F170
Mansfield, Katherine,
    F30, F35
A Many-Windowed House,
    A12, B7, B13, C2,

C14, D10
"Marcel Proust's Un-
    finished Symphony,"
    F189
"The March on Berlin,"
    F195
"Marginalia," F327, G147-
    49, G154, G161, G170,
    G173, G231
"The Margins of Infinity,"
    F91
Maritain, Jacques, F330
"Marizibill," N1
Markand, David, K8
Marquand, John P., F319,
    F514
Marshall, Margaret, F216
Martin du Gard, Roger,
    F85, F261, F320
"The Martyrs, by Their
    Witness," B4, I7
Marx, Karl, F221, F247,
    F248, G100, K8
"Marx and David Markand,"
    K8
"Marx and Plekhanov,"
    F247, F248
Masafumi, Ôba, B1b
Massing, Paul W., F200
Masters, Edgar Lee, F40
"Matthew Josephson," M78
Matthews, Herbert L.,
    F267
Matthews, T.S., G94
Matthiessen, F.O., F426,
    F427, F467
Maude, Aylmer, F353
Maude, Louise, F353
Maugham, W. Somerset, F2,
    F175, F273, F421
"The Maugham Enigma," F273
Mauriac, Claude, F526
Mauriac, Francois, B11,
    F128
Maurois, André, D18
May, J. Lewis, F71
Mayer, Brantz, B1
Mayes, Herbert R., F107
Mead, Margaret, F205

Mécano, pp. xx-xii;
   M73
"Mediterranean Beach,"
   M50
Mehring, Franz, F221
Melville, Herman, F462,
   F482, F490, G177
"Memoranda of a Decade,"
   G318
"Memphis Johnny," M67
Men and Books, D2
"Men and Ghosts," F199
"Men of Good Intentions,"
   F212
"Men of Good Will," F381
"The Men of the Road,"
   F129
Mencken, H.L., F389,
   F436, G40, G96
"Mencken Adds a 789-Page
   Rider to His American
   Language," F436
"Mencken and Mark Twain,"
   F389
Mercure de France, G300
"The Meriwether Connec-
   tion," G315
"A Messiah of the Skep-
   tics," F121
"The Michael Golden
   Legend," F334
Michigan Alumnus Quar-
   terly Review, D16, G272
"The Mid-Victoria Cross,"
   G104
"The Middle American
   Style: D. Crockett to
   E. Hemingway," G186
"The Middle Passage,"
   A7, G291
Middlekauff, Robert, A6
Middleton, George, F14
"Midsummer Fiction and
   Biography," F95
"Midsummer Medley," F173
The Military Novel, A6
"Mill Shadows," G82
Millay, Edna St. Vincent,
   F227, F295, F532

Miller, Edwin H., B12
Miller, Katherine, F12
Millin, Sarah G., F90
"Million Dollar Baby,"
   F223
Mills, Florence, M96
"Mine No. 6," M51
Minnegerode, Meade, F54
Miró, Joan, I5
"The Mirror of Innocence,
   F77
Mirsky, Dmitri, F207
"A Miscellany of Winter
   Books," F66
"The Miserly Millionaire
   of Words," G265
"Miss Glasgow's Purga-
   torio," F322
Miss Lonelyhearts, C8
"Mr. Brooks Dissenting,"
   F348, F348a
"Mr. Cholerton's Beard,"
   G162
"Mr. Churchill Speaks,"
   F324
"Mr. Eliot's Tract for
   the Times," F308
"Mr. Huxley's New Jeru-
   salem," F263
"Mr. Mailer Tells a Tale
   of Love, Art, Corrup-
   tion," F507
"Mr. Moore's Golden
   Treasury," p. xxiv; F51
"Mr. Warren's New Novel
   Is His Longest and
   Richest," F479
Mitchell, Joseph, F400
Mitchell, Margaret, G113
Mizener, Arthur, F433,
   F513, F536, O13
"Mizener on Ford Madox
   Ford," F536
Modern American Fiction:
   Essays in Criticism, A6
Modern Quarterly, J1
Modern S4N Review, M82
Modley, Rudolf, F259
Monat, G214

Moncrieff, C.K. Scott,
    F75, F189
"Monsieur de Monther-
    lant," F218
Montagu, Ashley, F480
Montherlant, Henry de,
    F218
"A Monument to Proust,"
    G12
"Moonrise," M32
Moore, George, p. xxiv;
    F51
Moore, Marianne, F346,
    G297
Morand, Paul, F101
Moravia, Alberto, B11
More, Paul Elmer, G63
"More about Neglected
    Books," G96
"More about Romains,"
    G98
"More Fighting Words,"
    K12
"More Marginalia," G232
Morgan, Charles, F153
Morris, Lawrence S., F127
Morris, Lloyd, 08
Morris Canal, G34
Morrow, Felix, 04
"Mortality," M55
"Mortuary," M55
"Moscow Trial: 1938,"
    F277, G126
"The Mother," M109
"Motley Verse," F22
Mott, Frank Luter, F465
"Mountain Farm," M45
"Mountain Slum," G88
"Mountain Valley," M43
"Much Stranger Than
    Fiction," F90
"Muddletown," F204
Muir, Edwin, F85
Muir, Willa, F85
Mumford, Lewis, F100,
    F135, F276, F311,
    F491, F534, G132
Munson, Gorham B.,
    pp. xxix-xxx;

F131, G76, K4, M71, O2
"Munsoniana," K4
Murasaki, Lady, F89
"Murder, Piracy and Jus-
    tice," F68
Murray, Gilbert, F27
"Muse at the Microphone,"
    F254
"My Countryside, Then and
    Now," G57
"My Dear Jean," I4
Myers, Rollo H., F87
Myrer, Anton, F492
"Mythology and Melville,"
    F482

"Nantasket," M31
Napoleon, F85
"The Narrow House," M75
Nathaniel Hawthorne: The
    Selected Works, B66
Nation, M95, M97, M129,
    M130
National Institute of
    Arts and Letters. See
    American Academy of
    Arts and Letters
The National Temper:
    Readings in American
    History, A6
"A Natural History of
    American Naturalism,"
    D10, G202, G205
"Naturalism in American
    Literature," D10, G202
"Naturalism's Terrible
    McTeague," G202
"Necromancy," F7
Neff, Emery, F471
"A New American War
    Novel That May Stand
    the Test of Time," F473
"New America's Primer,"
    F310
"The New Critics and the
    New Fiction," G238
New Masses, D4, G58, G102,
    G118, K16
"New Novels: Hardbacks or

Paperbacks," G241
"New Novels in Soft
  Covers," G242
"The New Primitives,"
  G60
The New Republic,
  pp. xii-xiv, xvi; A3,
  B3, B4, B6-9, B13,
  C2, C4, C6, C9,
  D2-3, D9-11, D17, E3,
  E9, F5-6, F8, F10-11,
  F14-15, F68, F104-10,
  F112-13, F115, F118-19,
  F122-23, F130, F135,
  F137, F141-42, F146-70,
  F172-73, F175-333,
  F335-36, F338-41, F343-
  46, F348-86, F388-423,
  F426-27, F430-31, F434-
  35, F437, F439, F441,
  F444, F447, F462, F465,
  F468-72, F475-76, F478,
  F482, F486, F489, F491-
  92, F494, F497-501,
  F508, F515, F517, F538-
  39, G39, G61, G63-65,
  G67-86, G88-98, G100-
  01, G103-17, G119-26,
  G128-30, G132-44, G146-
  68, G170, G173, G177-
  79, G182-83, G187,
  G191-92, G194-96, G198,
  G201-4, G207-10, G212,
  G215, G217, G220-22,
  G224-25, G229-33, G235,
  G240-44, G247, G252-
  54, G259-61, G266,
  G271, G279, G282, G331,
  I6, I8-10, K5-9, K11-
  16, M103-7, N2
The New Republic Antho-
  logy, G83, G103
The New Statesman, G133
"New Tendencies in the
  Novel: Pure Fiction,"
  G221
"New Times, New Values,"
  G244
New World Writing, G255

New York, J24
New York Evening Post, G4
New York Herald Tribune,
  F451-60, G319
New York Herald Tribune
  Book Review, D13, F474,
  F477, F479, F480, F481,
  F483, F485, F487, F488,
  F490, F493, F495, F496,
  F502, F503, F507, F513,
  F518, G277, J6, J8, J15
New York Herald Tribune
  Books, pp. xxiv-xxv;
  F51, F55, F57-59, F61,
  F63-65, F67, F69-72,
  F74-76, F79, F87, F94,
  F96-97, F101-3, F114,
  F116-17, F120-21, F124-
  29, F131-34, F136, F138,
  F139-40, F143-45, F171,
  F443, F461, F463, F466-
  67, F483, G59-60, G62,
  G287, G295
New York Herald Tribune
  Weekly Book Review,
  F446, G216, G218, G219,
  G223
New York Sunday Tribune,
  M33, M34
New York Times, G337
New York Times Book
  Review, C8, F429, F438,
  F440, F449, F450, F464,
  F473, F484, F505-6,
  F510-12, F514, F516,
  F519-22, F524, F529-30,
  F534, F540-41, G181,
  G186, G206, G211, G278,
  G308, J7, J12, J17, J19
New York Tribune, G6
New Yorker, F433, G171,
  G172, M112, M113, M118,
  M122
The Newberry Library,
  pp. ix, xi
"The Newest Machiavelli,"
  F394
"News from New Guinea,"
  F205

"The Next-to-Longest
Novel," F320
"Nick Carter," G46
Nicolson, J.U., F114
"'Nigger Fever'," F147
"Nights," B4, N11
Niles, Blair, F119
"1919," F317
"The 1930's Were an Age
of Faith," G308
Nixon, Richard M., J23
"No Defense," F328
"No More Damned Non-
sense," F364
"No Prophet," F163
"No Rules for What
Sherwood Anderson
Tried To Do," F485
Nobel Prize, G319
"Nobel Prize Novel,"
F261
"Nobel Prize Oration,"
G111
"Nobel Prizeman," F156
"Nocturnal Landscape,"
M58
"Nocturne," M82
Norris, Frank, G202
North American Review,
M51
"Not All Our Poetry,"
F341
"Not Evil Enough," F492
"'Not Men': A Natural
History of American
Naturalism," G205
"Not Stendhal," F139
"Not without Bias,"
F206
"Not Yet Demobilized,"
F132
"Note and Digression,"
E11
"A Note by Malcolm
Cowley," D20
"A Note on Marxian Cri-
ticism," G100
"A Note on Publishing,"
G200

"Notes for a Hemingway
Omnibus," G180
"Notes on a Writers'
Congress," G137
"Notes on the Enemy,"
F376
"Notes on the Literary
Stock Exchange,"
G230
"Novelists, Pioneers of
the New Generation,"
F463
"Novelized Biography,"
G51
"Novels after the War,"
F413
"Now the Age of Cuckoo
Humor," F76
Nowell, Elizabeth, F508

Oakes, Rev. Roland D., A8
O'Brien, Edward J., F69,
F134
O'Brien, Justin, F451
O'Connor, Frank, B11
O'Connor, William Van,
G262
Oddera, Bruno, A3e
"Ode in a Time of Crisis,"
M129
Oechsner, Frederick, F376
"Oedipus; or, The
Future of Love," D3
"Oedipus: The Future of
Love," G65
"Of Clocks and Calendars,"
G143
O'Faolain, Sean, G134
"Off Campus," M132
O'Flaherty, Liam, F88
O'Hara, John, F214, F541
Ôhashi, Kenzaburô, A3c,
A9b
"An Old Fellow to His
Friends," M11
"The Old House in Chel-
sea," G314
"The Oldest Inhabitant,"
M13

"The Oldest Quaker
    Colony," G50
O'Malley, Ernie, F249
Omori, Annie Shepley,
    F20
On Board the Morning
    Star, p. xxv; E1
"On Board the Morning
    Star," I1
"On Giving Books," G52
"On Issue 25," K2
"On Literature and
    Revolution," G114
"On Poe's Eureka," E11
"On Rereading Words-
    worth," M2
"On the Books, On an
    Author," J6
"On Visiting the Revere,"
    M16
"On Writing as a Pro-
    fession," G222
"100 Years Ago: Hawthorne
    Sets a Great New Pat-
    tern," G223
"One Man's Hemingway,"
    G287
"One O'Clock at
    O'Connors," M35
"One Poet and the War,"
    G187
O'Neill, Eugene, G31,
    G36, G267
O'Neill, Joseph, F208
Opffer, Ivan, p. xx;
    G23
"The Orange Moth," F62
The Ordeal of Mark Twain,
    C4
"Oregon Trail," F209
"The Other England,"
    F306
"The Other Side of the
    Tracks," A3a
"The Other War," G324
"Our Last Royal Gover-
    nor," G53
"Our Own Generation,"
    G59

The Outlaws on Parnassus,
    C9
"Outline of Wells' His-
    tory," F186
Outlook, G56
"Overbeck's Barn," M86
"The Owl and the Nightin-
    gale," F38

P.M., F337, F342, F347,
    F424, F425, F432, F436,
    F442, F445, F449
Packard, Eleanor, F376
Packard, Reynolds, F376
Pagan, M35, M36, M39
"Page Dr. Blum!" F30
Paige, D.D., F483
Paine, Thomas, F92
Palache, John Garber,
    F74, F86
Palmerston, Lord, F90
"Panorama," F165
Panorama (Chicago Daily
    News), F536, J21
"Papa and the Parricides,"
    G323
"The Paperback Title
    Fight," G283
Pareto, Vilfredo, F178
"The Paris Congress of
    Writers," K9
"Paris Express," A3a
Paris Review, G246
'Paris Review.' Writers
    at Work, B11a
Parish, Anne, F88
Parker, Dorothy, B11
Parker, Ralph, F397
"Parnassus-on-the-Seine,"
    M19
"Parting--Gare du Nord,"
    M29
Partisan Review, G129,
    K11, K12, I12
"Partisan Review," G129
"Partisan Review Finale,"
    K12
Pascal Covici, 1888-1964,
    D15a

Pascin, Jules, G10
"Pascin's America,"
G10
"Passport Blues," M121
"Patriot and Expa-
triate," F125
Paul, Cedar, F85, F165
Paul, Eden, F85, F165
Paul, Elliot, F351
"Paul Fort," G17
"Paul Valéry," D21
Peabody, Sophia, G275
"Peace and the Pundits,"
F419
"The Peasants of New
York," F110
Peck, Walter Edwin, F111
"A Pedagogue's Love
Affair," F143
"A Pedlar of the King,"
F70
Peffer, Nathaniel, F379
Pelitti, Elsa, A7c
Pember, Timothy, F458
Pemberton, Madge, F125
"The People's Theatre,"
F313
"The Peppermint Gardens,"
M62
Perkins, Maxwell, G171,
G172
Perromat, Charles, F32
Per/Se, J18
"The Personal Element,"
F220
"Personal Histories,"
F340
"Personal History," F391
The Personal Voice: A
Contemporary Prose
Reader, B3
"Personalism: A New
School of Fiction,"
G253
Persons, Stow, D10, G202
"Perspectives," F255
Perspectives U.S.A., G239
Peter, Czar of Russia,
F61

Peterson, R. Stanley, M88
"Phantasus," F39
Phillips, Frances L., F19
Phillips, M. Ogden, F310
Phillips, William, J16
Phillpotts, Eden, F8
"Pictures Tell the Story,"
F259
"Pierre MacOrlan," G23
Pierre-Quint, Léon, F171
"Pilgrim's Progress,"
F183
"Piney Woods," M122
Piper, Henry Dan, A10,
A12
Pitkin, Walter B., G66
Pittsburgh Gazette Times,
G1
"Play It for Me Again:
The Theme Repeated,"
M47
"Played Straight," G72
Plekhanov, George V.,
F247
Plivier, Theodor, F165
Poe, Edgar Allan, F93,
F439, G56, G177
"Poe in Mississippi,"
F242
"Poem for Amy Lowell,"
F217
"Poem for Two Voices,"
M57
"Poem" ("Meanwhile I
observed him from a
gable"), M49
"Poem" ("One morning
during carnival"), M48
"The Poet and the World,"
F151
"Poet in Politics,"
F283
"Poet of This War," G160,
G187
"Poetic Love," M20
Poetry, F387, F428, G127,
M32-34, M57-62, M76, M83-
89, M108-11, M114-17,
M120, M121, M127, M128

"Poetry Project," G127
"Poetry Tomorrow," F280
"Poets and Prophets,"
    G146
"A Poet's Anthology,"
    F245
"Poets as Reviewers,"
    G142
"Poets March in the
    Van," F96
"Poet's Privacy," G109
"Poison," I3
Pollock, John, F56
Pooley, Robert C., M111
Porché, François, F126
"Port of Refuge," F406
The Portable Faulkner,
    B5, K19
The Portable Hawthorne,
    B6, B6a, B6b
The Portable Hemingway,
    B3, K19
"Portrait of a Genius,"
    F44
"Portrait of a
    Publisher," G58
"A Portrait of James T.
    Farrell as a Young
    Man," F243
"A Portrait of Mister
    Papa," G214
"Portrait of the Artist,"
    F243
Postgate, Raymond, F68
"Postscript," D18
"Postscript to a
    Paragraph," F233
"Postscript: Twenty
    Years of American
    Literature," A4
Pound, Ezra, A3a, F483,
    G167, G220, G227,
    G286, M52
"Pound Reweighed,"
    G286
"Poverty Hollow," M43
Pozner, Vladimir, I8
"Praise for the S4N,"
    K1

"A Preface to Hart Crane,"
    F141
A Preface to Our Times,
    A3a
"Presentation of Arts and
    Letters Grants," G264
"Presentation of Awards,"
    G273
"Presentation of Grants
    and Awards," G276,
    G296, G309, G310
"Presentation to Aldous
    Huxley of the Award of
    Merit Medal for the
    Novel," G281
"Presentation to James
    Gould Cozzens of the
    Howells Medal for
    Fiction," G290
"A Primer of Fascism,"
    F161
"Primitive Peoples," F169
"The Problems of André
    Gide," F171
"Processional of the Third
    Season," M65
"Programme Music," F29
Prokosch, Frederic, F383
"Prolegomena to Kenneth
    Burke," F478
"A Promise Paid," G192
"Properties," F41
"Prophetic," M61
"Prophets without Honour?
    The Public Status of
    American Writers," G257
Proust, Marcel, F189, G12,
    G90
Provincetown Players,
    p. xviii
Pryce-Jones, Alan, F504
"Psychoanalysis and
    Writers," G251
"Public Speakers," F225
Publishers' Weekly, G131,
    J23
"Punishment and Crime,"
    F329
"The Puritan Legacy," F23

Putnam, Samuel, O24
"The Pyre," M128

Der Querschnitt,
   p. xxii
"A Question of Commit-
   ment," J19
Quiz (pseud.), F58

"Rabbit by Day," M126
Rabelais, Francois, G6
"Rabelais Returns to His
   Own Home Town," G6
"Race between a Subway
   Local and a Subway
   Express," H9
Racine, Jean, pp. xxii-
   xxiii; A1, G15, G16,
   G268
Racine, pp. xxii-xxiii; A1
"Racine," G15, G16
Rader, A.L., D16
Radiguet, Raymond, E8
"Ragtime," M10
Rahv, Philip, A3a,
   F426, F427
Railo, Eino, F123
"Rain in the Cumber-
   lands," F215
Ramsey, Warren, G301
Randall, John H., F521
"Random Reflections," F25
Rascoe, Burton, F193, G99
"Rattling around the War,"
   F418
Rauschning, Hermann, F336
"Reading America First,"
   F92
Reading for Rhetoric, B3
"Reading in Wartime," G152
"The Real Horatio Alger
   Story," F437, G188, G328
"The Real Jungle King,"
   G37
"The Real Tragedy of the
   Farmer," F145
"The Real World," F286
"Rebecca West Has Found
   Clue to Europe's Sick-

ness," F347
"The Rebirth of French
   Poetry: An Imaginary
   Interview," I11
"The Rebirth of Tragedy,"
   F234
"The Reconquest of Europe,"
   F321
"The Record of a Trial,"
   F251
Rector, George, F92
"The Red and the Black,"
   F363
"The Red Branch," M118
"Red China," F262
"Red Day in Washington,"
   G86
"Red Ivory Tower," K11
Redding, J. Saunders,
   F372
Reed, John, F228
"A Regional Poet," O1
Reisenberg, Felix, F88
"The Religion of Art,"
   G90, G91, G92
"The Religion of Humanity,"
   F491
"Remembering Hart Crane,"
   G144
"A Remembrance of the Red
   Romance," G303-4
"A Reminiscence: Edmund
   Wilson on The New
   Republic," G331
Reporter, F509, G248, G262,
   G265, G267, G283, G286
"A Resentment of Rabbits,"
   M126
"Restaurateur with Music,"
   M116
Reston, James B., F364
"Resurrection of a Poet,"
   F144
"Retreat from Moscow,"
   F250
"The Return of Henry
   James," F426
"The Reviewer Cleans
   House," G41

"Reviewers on Parade,"
    F265
"Revolution by Consent,"
    F398
Ricci, Corrado, F77
Rice, John Andrew, F375
"Richard II Forty," B4,
    N6
"Richard Wright: The
    Case of Bigger Thomas,"
    F304
Richardson, Dorothy M.,
    F171
Richman, Robert, G240
Rilke, Rainer Maria,
    F495
Rimbaud, Arthur, F267,
    G232
Il ritorno degli esuli,
    A3e
"The Road of Excess,"
    F67
"The Road to Damascus,"
    F213
Road to Life, G80
Roanoke Review, M64, M126
"The Roaring Boy," F256
Robber Rocks: Letters and
    Memories of Hart Crane,
    D20
"Robert Frost: A Dissent-
    ing Opinion," G178,
    G179
"Robert M. Coates," M76
Roberts, Elizabeth Madox,
    F148, F174
Robinson, Edwin Arlington,
    A4a, F471, G42
"The Rocking Chairs,"
    M41
Rodman, Selden, F280,
    M92, M95, M111
Rodríguez, Eduardo Bolivar.
    See Bolivar Rodríguez,
    Eduardo
Rölvaag, O.E., F95
"Roger Martin du Gard:
    The Next-to-Longest
    Novelist," F320

"The Role of the Hero in
    Hair-Pants Romances,"
    G43
Rolland, Romain, F12, K7
Rolo, Charles J., F418
Romains, Jules, F185,
    F212, F301, F315,
    F317, G98
"Romance in a Major Key,"
    M82
"Rosalie Evans' Ranch,"
    G69
Rosenfeld, Alvin H., D19,
    G326
Rosenfeld, Paul, F100,
    F135, F461
Rosenfield, Claire, B3
Ross, Alan, F510
Roszak, Theodore, G311
Roth, Joseph, F165
Roussy de Sales, Raoul
    de, F339
"Roxane," M115
"The Rubber Plant," M98
Rukeyser, Muriel, G128
"Runaway," M26
Rusk, Ralph L., F475
Russell, Phillips, F84
"Russian and American
    Fiction: Two Ideals,"
    G243
"Russian Turnabout,"
    F397
"A Russo-Chinese Docu-
    mentary," F168
Rybalka, Michel, I12a

"S. Foster Damon: The New
    England Voice," D19,
    G326
S4N, K1-3, M68, M82
Sacco, Niccola, G108
The Sacred Hill, E7
Sagan, Francoise, B11
"St. Apollinaire," F45
"The Saint in Politics,"
    F345
"St. Mallarmé the Eso-
    teric," I12

Salmon, Andre, G11

Salute, G193

Salzman, Jack, G129, K12

"Samson," F307

"Sanctuary," F290

Sandburg, Carl, F37, F73, F82, F337, G49

"Sandburg's Ties, Speech, Forelocks, etc.," F337

Sansculotte, H4, M7, M13, M14, M17

Santayana, George, F4, F378, F410, F431

"Santayana at Harvard," F410

"Santayana in Society," F431

Saroyan, William, F424

Sartre, Jean-Paul, G250, I12a

Sassoon, Siegfried, F13

Saturday Review of Literature, B3, B4, B8, B11-12, C5, C14-15, F47, F50, F52, F60, F504, G44, G145, G180, G184, G190, G220, G226, G228, G238, G245, G249, G263, G269, G280, G285, G288-89, G292-94, G298, G302, G305-7, G320, G322, G329, I11, M124-25, M131

Saturday Review Reader, G226

Scarfe, Francis, F371

The Scarlet Letter, D13

Scheffauer, Herman George, F61

"Schlaraffenland," F187

Schmalhausen, Samuel D., F137

Schneider, Helen, p. xxviii

Schneider, Isidor, p. xxviii; F57, G76, G94

Schnitzler, Arthur, F64, F120

Schrieke, B., F230

Schuman, Frederick L.,

F316, K10

"The Scott Fitzgerald Story," G225

Scribner's Magazine, G87, G135

"The Sea Jacobins," F157

Seabrook, W.B., F98

Secession, p. xxx: M49, M66, M67, M70

A Second Flowering: Works and Days of the Lost Generation, A13 A13a, O19

"Second Thoughts on 'Joseph'," F271

Sedgwick, Henry Dwight, F118

Seghers, Anna, F370

664 Pagine di William Faulkner, B5b

The Selected Writings of Lafcadio Hearn, C2

"The Self-Obliterated Author: S. Foster Damon," G326

"The Sense of Guilt," G316

"Sentimental," M24

"Sermon against War," F152

"Seven," M117

"Seven O'Clock," M41

"The Seven Years of Crisis," D5

"Several," M81

Sewanee Review, D7, D20, F533, G185, G189, G213, G280a, G301, M123, N3-7

Sewell, Elizabeth, F495

"The Sex Boys in a Balloon," F137

"Sex, Censorship and Superman," F476

"Sex Murder Incorporated," F494

Seymour, Charles, F78

Shanks, Lewis Piaget, F140

Shapiro, Charles, D13, G223

Shapiro, Karl Jay, F387
Shayon, Robert Lewis,
    D15
Sheean, Vincent, F196,
    F391
Shelley, Percy Bysshe,
    F111
Shenandoah, G327
Sherman, Stuart Pratt,
    p. xxv
Sherrod, Robert, F418
"Sherwood Anderson,
    Still Fresh and New,"
    F461
"Sherwood Anderson's
    Book of Moments," B13,
    D17, G282
Shipley, Joseph T., F72,
    F83
"Shipwreck," F311
Shirakawa, Yoshio, A3c
Shirer, William L., F332,
    F456
Sholokhov, Mikhail, F335,
    G319
Shoolman, Regina, F454
Shrodes, Caroline,
    B3
Siegfried, André, F98
Silone, Ignazio, C11,
    F182, F366, I9
"Silone's Villagers,"
    F182
"The Silvery Fishes,"
    M63
Simenon, Georges, B11
Simonson, H.P., G266
Sinclair, Upton, F381
"The Singapore Story,"
    F374
"Sir, I Have the Honor,"
    G330b
"Sister Carrie's Brother,"
    G203, G204
Sitwell, Dame Edith, F15
Sitwell, Sacheverell, F41
"Sixteen Propositions,"
    G140
Slate, M8, M18

Slatkin, Charles E., F454
"The Slow Triumph of Sis-
    ter Carrie," G204
"The Smart Set Legend,
    F193
"Smash Your Guitar," G49
Smedley, Agnes, C1, F179,
    F404
"Smiles," M7
Smith, Bernard, B2, F343,
    F440
Smith, Chard Powers, F444
Smith, Edith, F361
Smith, Harrison, pp. xxiv,
    xxx
Smith, Howard K., F368
Smith, J. Russell, F310
Smith, John, D15
Smith, Lillian, F416
Smith, Margaret Binney,
    O17
Smith, William Gardner,
    F468
Smits, Lee J., G96
"A Smoke of Birds," M64
"Snapshot of a Young
    Lady," H8
Snow, Edgar, F262
"So Perish Time," M40
"Socialists and Sym-
    bolists," G128
"Sociological Habit Pat-
    terns in Linguistic
    Transmogrification,"
    G262
"The Soldier and the
    Saint," F370
"A Solemn Music," M47
"The Solitude of William
    Faulkner," G319a
Solotaroff, Theodore, J21
"Some Books for Fall
    Reading," F56
"Some Dangers to American
    Writing," G254
"Some Interesting Biog-
    raphies," F54
"The Sorrows of Elmer
    Davis," G158

Soupault, Philippe, I4
Soupault, Pierre, I10
"The Source," M120
Southern Review, D19,
    G315, G326, G330b,
    G334, K10, M133
A Southern Vanguard, D7
"Southways," F416
"The Soviet Socialist
    Republic of the Dead,"
    F531
"Spain in Revolt," F238
"Spanish War Posters,"
    G121
"Speaking of Books,"
    G278
Spender, Stephen, F180,
    F197, F222, F371,
    G128
"Spender and Auden,"
    F180
"Spender, Auden and
    After," F371
Spengler, Oswald, G60
Spillane, Mickey, F494,
    G231
Spiller, Robert E.,
    D9, F534
Spriggs, Cecil, F495
Spykman, Nicholas John,
    F350
Squire, Sir John C.,
    F7, F34
Squires, Radcliffe,
    G280a
Stalin, Joseph, F202,
    F300, F531, G115
"Stalin or Satan?" G115
Stallings, Laurence,
    G89, K6
Starkie, Enid, F267
"The Starlings," M64
"The State Department,"
    F367
Stearns, Harold, H7,
    M52
Stefansson, Vilhjalmur,
    F53
Stegner, Page, J18

Stegner, Wallace, J4
Stein, Gertrude, F429,
    F443, F446, G186
Steinbeck, John, F293,
    F425, F449
"Steinbeck Brings 'em
    Back under Glass," F449
"Steinbeck Delivers a
    Mixture of Farce and
    Freud," F425
Steinbrinker, Günther,
    B11b
Stendhal, F75, F139
"Stendhal Complete,"
    F75
"Stéphane Mallarmé," E11
"Stepmother Congress,"
    F385
Stern, J.P., F495
Stern, James, F450
Stern, Milton R., C12
Stern, Philip Van Doren,
    F439
Stewart, Donald Ogden,
    F309
Stewart, Randall, F470
"Still Life," M101
"Still Middletown?" F252
Stillman, Clara G., G94
Stone, I.F., G132
"Stone Horse Shoals,"
    M112
The Stories of F. Scott
    Fitzgerald, B8, G226
"The Story Tellers'
    Story," G271
"Storyteller Strikes
    Back," F517
Strachey, John, F161,
    F191
"The Strange Companion,"
    M69
Stratford, Philip, G336
"The Streets of Air,"
    M89
"The Streets of Palermo,"
    G163
"Strictly Private," G101
Strong, Anna Louise, F203

Stuart, Henry Longan,
    F71, F77, F85, F112
Stuart, Jesse, F184
"Stuart Little; or,
    New York through
    the Eyes of a Mouse,"
    F438
"Style and Fashion," F107
Styron, William, B11,
    F489, O19
"Success Story: 1930-39,"
    F359
"Success That Somehow Led
    to Failure," F512
"Sudden Encounter," M60
Sullivan, Mark, F78
"Sunday Afternoon (After
    Jules Laforgue)," M30
Sunrise, B12, G280
"Sunrise over the
    Heiterwand," M70
"Survival by Co-opera-
    tion," F480
Sutton, Eric, F128, F278
"Swan into Swami," F302
Swanberg, W.A., F523
Sweet's Architectural
    Catalogue, pp. xviii,
    xxiii
Symons, Arthur, F65, F83,
    F105
O sytuacji w literaturze,
    A6c

"T.S. Eliot's Ardent
    Critics--and Mr. Eliot,"
    G216
"Tablet," M93
"A Tabular History of the
    Literary Life, 1924-
    1949," G219
"A Talented Subaltern,"
    F116
"Talk with Malcolm
    Cowley," J7
Talmadge, Irving Dewitt,
    D6
Tambimuttu, Thurairajah,
    G297

Tan Shih-hua, F168
"Tapestry of the Great
    Fear," B4, N10
"Tar Babies," M94
Tarkington, Booth, F88
Tate, Allen, p. xxiii;
    D7, F229, F259, F373,
    G185, G280a, J4, J5,
    M74, O1
Taussig, Lucie, p. xxiv
Taylor, George R., F259
Tchelitchew, Pavel, F454
"The Teaching and Study
    of Writing," J4
"Tears Are Alike," B4,
    N12
"Tell Your Countrymen,"
    F404
"A Ten-Dollar Shelf: 20th
    Century American Liter-
    ature," G277
"Ten Good Farms," M61
"Ten Little Magazines,"
    G201
Tender Is the Night, B9
Tennenbaum, Joseph, F137
"Tennessee Blues," C6
Terrall, Robert, C6, G261
"That Excellent Black-
    guard," F117
Thayer, Scofield, p. xv
"A Theme with Variations,"
    M25
"Then Fear Crept in at
    the Window," H1
"A Theologian of Letters,"
    F131
"There Have To Be Censors,"
    G125
"There Is a Moment," M66
"There's Always a Point
    of No Return," F514
"These Things Are Banal .
    . .," F26
"They Carry Him Off in a
    One-Horse Hack . . .,"
    M67
"They Cheered One Another
    On," F534

"They Die for France,"
   I7
"The Things I Stand For,"
   I9
Think Back on Us, A3a, A10,
   D2, D4, O16
"Third Act and Epilogue,"
   F433
"Thirty Years Later:
   Memories of the First
   American Writers' Con-
   gress," J16
This Is My Best, D14
"This Man's Army," G141
"This Morning Robins,"
   M105
"This War and Peace,"
   F353
"This Youngest Genera-
   tion," G5
"Thomas Mann's Joseph
   Legend," F270-71
"Thomas Wolfe: The Pro-
   fessional Deformation,"
   D14, G270
"Thomas Wolfe's Legacy,"
   F297
Thomason, John W., F78
Thompson, Dorothy, F380
Thoreau, Henry David,
   F470
A Thornton Wilder Trio,
   C5
Thorp, Willard, D9
"Those of Lucifer," M74
"Those Paris Years,"
   F529
"Three Americans in
   Paris," M52
"Three Cycles of Myth in
   American Writing," B10
Three Great American
   Novels, B10
"Three Hils," M62
Three Novels (of Ernest
   Hemingway), C13
Three Novels of F. Scott
   Fitzgerald, B10
"Three Poets," F346

"Three Songs for Leonora
   (And for Peggy Baird),"
   M91
"Through Yellow Glasses,"
   F5
"Thunder over Aldanov,"
   F393
Thurber James, B11, F430,
   F509, G289
"A Tidy Room in Bedlam,"
   G236
Time, G188
"Time," M40
Time and Tide, G99
"The Time of Crossword
   Puzzles," B4, N4
"The Time of the Rhetori-
   cians," G255
Times Literary Supplement,
   G257, F504
Tippett, Tom, G82
"Tired Feminist," F158
"To a Chance Acquaintance,"
   M5
"To a Dilettante Killed
   at Vimy," M22
"To a Girl I Dislike," M4
"To a Revolutionary
   Critic," F162
"To Certain Imagist Poets,"
   M1
"To Greet New Members,"
   G311
"To Madrid," G119-20,
   G122-24
"To Save Ernst Torgler's
   Life," K7
"To the Editors of the
   Dial," G18
To the Young Writer, D16
"To Whom It May Concern,"
   G24
"Today's Young Writers:
   Are They Doomed to
   Failure?" F487
Tolstoy, Leo, C10, F353
"Tomorrow Morning," M107
Torrès, Henry, F349
"Toward a Universal

Mind," G39
"Towards a More Passionate
    Apprehension of Life,"
    M71
"Towers of Song," M74
"Town Report: 1942,"
    G153
"Tract for Our Times,"
    F287
"Tract for the Times,"
    F308
"Transatlantic Review,"
    A3a
"Transatlantic View,"
    G133
Transition, H9, J2, J3,
    M41, M57, M92-94,
    M96
"Transluscent Fingers,"
    M72
"Travellers' Cheque,"
    A3a
"Travels with a Mirror,"
    F181
Tretiakov, Sergei, F168
"Triangle, Pentagon,
    Square," F515
"Tribute to Ben Franklin,"
    F284
"Tribute to Mary Vorse,"
    F360
Trilling, Lionel, J4
"The Triumphant Lie,"
    F339
Trotsky, Leon, F160,
    F226, F251, K10
"Trotsky and the Art of
    Insurrection," F160
True, J9
"Tumbling Mustard," M97
Turnbull, Andrew, F522
Turner, Addie, pp. xxvi-
    xxvii
"The Turning of the
    Year," M102
Twain, Mark. See Clemens,
    Samuel L.
Twelve Original Essays
    on Great American

Novels, D13, G223
"The Twenties in Mont-
    parnasse," G322
Twentieth Century Authors,
    D6a, D12a, O6
Twentieth Century Un-
    limited, D11, G199
"Twenty by Scott Fitz-
    gerald," F513
"Twenty-Five Years After:
    The Lost Generation
    Today," G228
"Twenty-Four Youngsters,"
    G71
"Twenty Lessons in How To
    Write Like Saroyan, Who
    Says It's Easy," F424
"Twenty Years After," B4,
    N3
"Twenty Years of American
    Letters," G117
"Two American Poets," F37
"Two Anthologies," F69
"Two Books about the
    Negro," F230
"The Two Erskine Caldwells"
    F423
"Two French Towns," M27
"The Two Henry Jameses,"
    F426, F427
"Two Items for Reference,"
    F216
"Two Judgments of American
    Earth," F146
"Two Kinds of Travel
    Books," G35
"Two Men of Letters,"
    F470
"Two Novels from the
    French," F71
"Two Sides of the Barri-
    cades," G110
"Two Swans," M48
"Two Wars--And Two Genera
    tions," G211
"Two Winters with Allen
    Tate and Hart Crane,"
    G280a
"Two Winters with Hart

Crane," G280a

Tzara, Tristan, p. xxi

"U.S. Books Abroad,"
  G197
"U.S. Volunteer Tells
  of French Battle
  Front Visit-- No
  Union Hours," G1
Über William Faulkner,
  B5a
Ullman, James Ramsey,
  F459
Underwood, Edna Worthley,
  F11
"Unfinished Symphony,"
  F241
Unger, Leonard, G90
"The Unholy Alliance,"
  F336
"A Unique Case," F528
United Press Berlin
  Staff, F376
University of Mississippi
  Studies in English,
  G317
"The Unsettled Literary
  Future of the U.S.,"
  G292
"Unshaken Friend,"
  G171-72
Unterecker, John,
  p. xxxi; F533
"Untranslatable Genius,"
  F65
"Unwilling Novelist,"
  F150
Updike, John, G311
Updike, Mary, pp. xiii-xiv
"Urbanites," F58
"The Urn," M88

Valéry, Paul, D21,
  E3, E11, F495,
  F526, G39, G90, I13-
  16
Vallentin, Antonina,
  F289
"Valuta," A3a, B15, M53

"Valuta Girl," F188
Van Doren, Carl, F172
Van Doren, Irita,
  pp. xxiv-xxv; F132
Van Doren, Mark, F145,
  F172, F284, F474
"The Vanguard of Spring
  Novels," F88
Van Orden, Bianca, F515
Vansittart, Baron, F405
"Vansittartism," F405
Van Vechten, Carl, F81,
  F446
Van Wyck Brooks, A8
"Van Wyck Brooks: A
  Career in Retrospect,"
  G298
"Van Wyck Brooks and the
  New England Legacy,"
  F237
"Van Wyck Brooks at 75,"
  G285
"Van Wyck Brooks' Great
  Evocation of Our
  Literary Past," F493
"Van Wyck Brooks's
  'Usable Past'," C14,
  G284, G298
Vanzetti, Bartolomeo,
  G108
Varian, Wiley, p. xxvii
"Variations on a Cos-
  mical Air," M123
Variety, E3
Veblen, Thorstein, F378
Vercors. See Bruller,
  Jean
Verdi, Giuseppe, F73
"The Veteran," M17
"The Vice Squad Carries
  On," G64, G64a
Vickers, O.W., B5
"The Victim of a Mask,"
  F140
"Victory When?" F356
Vildrac, Charles, G14
"The Village Smell,"
  F46
Villeneuve, Jacques, G6

Villiers de L'Isle Adam,
    Comte de, F65
Villon, Francois, F114,
    F117
Vinci, Leonardo da,
    E11, F288, F289, I14
"Virginia Woolf: England
    under Glass," F344
"Virtue and Virtuosity:
    Notes on W.H. Auden,"
    F428
Vitrac, Roger, I3
"Voices from Home: 1923,"
    M125
"Voices from the Nazi
    Rubble Pile," F450
"Voodoo Dance," F201
Vorse, Mary Heaton, F360
"The Voyager of Dreams,"
    F126
Voyetekhov, Boris, F397

"The Wages of Death,"
    H2
Wagner, Charles A.,
    M83-89
Wake, G234
Waley, Arthur, F89
"Walt Whitman, Champion
    of America," F505
"Walt Whitman: Poet of
    America?" F440
"Walt Whitman: The
    Miracle," G194
"Walt Whitman: The
    Philosopher," G207
"Walt Whitman: The
    Secret," G195
"Walt Whitman's Buried
    Masterpieces," G280
Walt Whitman's Leaves of
    Grass: The First (1855)
    Edition, B12
Walter, Erich Albert, F284
"Walter S. Hankel,"
    M80
"The Waltz of the Twenty-
    Year-Olds," B4, N2
"Wang Lung's Children,"
F294
"The War against Writers,"
    G174
"War and the Poets,"
    F435
"War in Bohemia," G87
"The War Is Only the
    Beginning," I8
"War Novels: After Two
    Wars," A6
"A War-Time Squad," F24
Ward, Maisie, F408, F409
Ware, Caroline F., F204
Warren, Robert Penn, A3a,
    B5, B11, F402, F479,
    O21
Washington, George, F84
"Washington Is Like Hell,"
    F355
"Washington Wasn't Like
    That," F472
"The Waste Land," F239
Watson, E.H. Lacon, F58
Watson, Sibley, p. xv
Waugh, Evelyn, F154
"We Had Such Good Times,"
    F538
Wechsler, James A., O24
"A Weekend with Eugene
    O'Neill," G267
Weeks, Robert P., B3
Weinhardt, Carl J., F540
Weiss, M. Jerry, G268
Weiss, Paul, G132
"The Well-Bred Borzoi,"
    F525
Wells, H.G., F84, F186,
    F202, M42
Wells, W.B., F185
"Wells in the Kremlin,"
    F202
"Wells' Springs of
    History," M42
Welty, Eudora, G327, J4
Werfel Franz, F73, F102
Werner, M.R., F54, F110
Weseen, Maurice H., F115
West, Nathanael, C8, F510
West, Ray Benedict, D7,

G185

West, Dame Rebecca, F223, F347

Western Review, G237, J4

Weston, Christine, F407

Wharf, Michael, F182

"What Are the Qualities That Make an Author Modern?" F495

"What Is a Show Boat, Anyway?" F81

"What New Directions?" F318

"What Poets Are Saying," G145

"What Poets Are Saying: 1941," G145

"What the Revolutionary Movement Can Do for a Writer," D4, G102

"What Writers Are and Why," G252

Wheen, A.W., F165

"When a Young American," G300

"Where the World Is Going," F325

"While They Waited for Lefty," G305

Whitaker, John T., F401

White, E.B. F438

White, Maude Valerie, F103

White, Ray Lewis, D17, G282

"Whither the American Writer," J1

Whither, Whither; or, After Sex What? D3

Whitman, Walt, B7, B12, F440, F462, F505, G194, G195, G207, G208, G260, G279, G280

"Whitman: A Little Anthology," G260

"Whitman: The Poet," G208

"Whitman: The Poet and the Mask," B7, G194, G195, G207, G208

"Who Are the Intellectuals?" G266

"Who the Hell is Hemingway?" J9

"Who Was Right about Spain?" F388

"Who's Fascist Now?" F414

"Who's To Take the Place of Hemingway and Faulkner?" J12

"Whose Housatonic?" F444

Whose Revolution? D6

Wie sie schreiben, B11b

"The Wild Body," F106

Wilder, Thornton, B11, C5, F81, F528, F542, G94, G263

"The Wilder Side of Life," F542

"Wilder: Time Abolished," C5

William Blake: Essays for S. Foster Damon, D19, G326

William Faulkner, correspondence et souvenirs de 1944 à 1962, A9c

"William Faulkner Revisited," G184

William Faulkner: Three Decades of Criticism, B5

"William Faulkner's Human Comedy," G181

"William Faulkner's Legend of the South," D7, G185

"William Faulkner's Nation," F469

"William L. Shirer Speaking," F332

"William Wilson," M69

Williams, Francis, F321

Williams, Oscar, F435

Willkie, Wendell L., F392

"The Willow Branch," M63

Wilson, Angus, B11

Wilson, Edmund, B10, F174, F232, F233, F312, F433,

F441, F498, G94, O16
Wilson, Harry Leon, F42,
  F47
Wilson, James R., B3
Wilson, Romer, F44
Wilstach, Paul, F53
Winesburg, Ohio, B13
Winslow, Ann. See Grubbs,
  Verna Elizabeth
"Winter Tenement," M124
"Winter: Two Sonnets,"
  M102
"Wistfulness," M18
Wittels, Fritz, F137
Wolfe, Humbert, F104
Wolfe, Thomas, D14,
  F198, F297, G150,
  G265, G270
"Wolfe and the Lost
  People," G150
"The Woman of Thornden,"
  F9
"Woman of Japan," F20
Woodward, W.E., F84
Woolf, Virginia, F344
Wordsworth, William,
  M2
The Works of Walt Whit-
  man, B7a
"World Congress against
  War," K5
"The World of Arthur
  Winner, Jr.," F511
"World's End Tomorrow,"
  F159
"The World's Timber," F19
"Wowsers on the Run,"
  G40
Wreden, Nicholas, F393
Wright, Richard,
  F274, F304
Writer, D11, G199
"The Writer as Crafts-
  man," G306
The Writer in a Changing
  World, D5
Writers at Work: The Paris
  Review Interviews, B11
Writers' Congress. See

American Writers'
  Congress, and Inter-
  national Congress of
  Writers
Writers of Today, B3
"The Writers' Inter-
  national," G107
"Writing in Wartime," G15
Wycherley, George, F107
Wycherley, William, F32
Wylie, Elinor, F38
Wylie, Philip, F159, G156

Yakovlev, Y.A., G75
Yale Review, G335
"Yankee Crusader on the
  Left," F524
"The Yankee Slavers," A7
Yarmolinsky, Avrahm, F39
"Years of Protest," K12
Yeats, William Butler,
  F245, F283, F384, G128,
  G134
"Yeats and O'Faolain," G
"Yeats and the 'Baptism
  of the Gutter'," F283
"Yeats as Anthologist,"
  F245
"Yesterbook," F303
"Yesterday Snow," M105
Young, Brigham, F54
Young, Philip, O22
Young, Roland, F385
Young, Thomas D., B5
"The Young Conquerors,"
  G210
"Young Kuppenheimer Gods
  M31
"Young Man with Spec-
  tacles," H6
"Young Mr. Elkins," H7
Youth: Poetry of Today,
  M27, M29

Zabel, Morton Dauwen, F1
  F155
Ziegfeld, Florenz, G72
Zola, Emile, F174
Zweig, Arnold, F278